AN ANTHOLOGY OF MEDIEVAL HEBREW LITERATURE

At Prayer

(From *Orpheus* by Solomon Reinach, Liveright Publishing Corp., New York, 193

AN ANTHOLOGY OF MEDIEVAL HEBREW LITERATURE

Edited by
ABRAHAM E. MILLGRAM

ABELARD-SCHUMAN
London New York Toronto

To the Memory of

My Father

ISRAEL M. MILLGRAM

Library of Congress Catalogue
Card Number: 61-15321

Printed in the United States of America

EDITOR'S PREFACE

THE editor of this anthology has set for himself the task of providing a collection which, through its organization, scope and choice of material, will make it possible for Jewish and non-Jewish readers alike to come into contact with an important field of Hebrew literature through English translations. He earnestly hopes that this anthology will allow both students and general readers to get, if not an insight, at least a glimpse of the spiritual glory that was Jewish literary creativity during the medieval period.

In presenting this work to the public, the editor feels it necessary to explain certain inconsistencies and what may superficially be termed inaccuracies. In the first place, the term "medieval" when applied to Jewish history does not have the connotation it has in general European history. As a result of the physical barriers of the ghetto walls and the social and economic barriers of medieval discriminations, the Jewish Middle Ages extended far beyond the Renaissance and did not end until the French Revolution. Hence this anthology of "medieval" Hebrew literature samples the Hebrew literature created approximately between the eighth and the eighteenth centuries.

It must also be noted that the title of this work "An Anthology of Medieval *Hebrew* Literature," is not altogether accurately descriptive. A few of the excerpts are not translations from the Hebrew but from the German, the Judaeo-German, and the Arabic. But the reader can easily accept this inconsistency, not through indulgence but for the contributions these excerpts are to the appreciation of the values of Jewish life as they expressed themselves through the medium of medieval Jewish literature.

There are other faults which the critical reader may find. But it should be borne in mind that many a lovely vision cannot be fully realized. Thus the original plan of this anthology called for excerpts from the famous *Letter of Sherira Gaon* for the chapter on medieval chronicles, for excerpts from the *Book of Creation* for the chapter on the Kabbalah, and for many other selections. But many logical plans had to be abandoned for practical considerations. One of the most important of these considerations was that the anthology was edited not for the Hebrew scholar, but for students and general readers who are practically strangers in this field and must be led into it slowly and gently. The road had to be cleared of all such obstacles as are created by obscure and irrelevant matter, however important it may be to the scholar.

The critic may also miss a chapter on medieval commentaries and one on the apologetic literature. The former field simply failed to yield any useful selections, and the latter is adequately represented by the chapter on medieval Jewish philosophy which is characteristically apologetic. Particularly so are the excerpts from Joseph Albo's *The Book of Principles* which, by their undisguised attacks on Christianity, fully reflect the medieval religious disputations.

In acknowledging his gratitude to the many publishers for their kind permission to reprint from their publications, the editor wishes to single out The Jewish Publication Society of America for special praise because its works proved most indispensable in his present task. In his many necessary adventures in "Hebraic bookland," the editor has become firmly convinced that no organization has tapped the resources of Jewish literature for the benefit of the English speaking Jew in any way comparable to or even approaching the achievements of this distinguished institution.

ABRAHAM E. MILLGRAM

CONTENTS

Chapter I

THE POETRY OF THE "GOLDEN ERA" OF SPAIN

Chapter II

PRAYERS, HYMNS, AND DIRGES

Chapter III

PHILOSOPHIC LITERATURE

Chapter IV

ETHICAL LITERATURE

Chapter V

THE *ZOHAR*—THE "BIBLE" OF THE MEDIEVAL JEWISH MYSTICS

Chapter VI

LEGAL LITERATURE

Chapter VII

MEDIEVAL JEWISH CHRONICLES

Chapter VIII

TRAVELERS' ACCOUNTS

Chapter IX

FOLK-TALES

AN ANTHOLOGY OF MEDIEVAL HEBREW LITERATURE

Chapter I

THE POETRY OF THE "GOLDEN ERA" OF SPAIN

THE last decade of the seventh century witnessed the climax of the cruel persecutions of the Spanish Jews at the hands of the Visigoths. Their property was confiscated and their religion proscribed; they were enslaved and distributed as gifts among the Christians of the Peninsula, while their children were placed in the custody of good Christians for the eradication of all traces of Judaism. But the miraculous delivery which quickly followed substantiated the psalmist's faith in God

"Who raiseth the poor out of the dust
And lifteth up the needy out of the dunghill,
That he may set him with princes,
Even with the princes of his people" (Ps. CXIII, 7-8).

Only a decade and a half after the inauguration of this campaign of extermination, the impoverished and degraded Jewish slaves rose to the rank of trusted and respected allies of their deliverers, the Arabs. It was in the year 711 that the Mohammedan conquerors crossed the Straits of Gibraltar and began their successful invasion of the Spanish Peninsula which they were destined to rule in whole or in part for almost eight centuries. The Jews received their deliverers with joy and acclamation, and the conquerors on their part were quick to perceive the sincerity of their Jewish friends. They therefore armed the Jewish population and entrusted it with the care of the captured cities. After the war, the conquerors acknowledged their indebtedness to their loyal Jewish allies and rewarded them with the removal of all their social and political disabilities. Except for the poll tax which was levied on all non-Mohammedans, the Jews were accorded complete civic equality and religious liberty. Thus the erstwhile slaves were almost literally "lifted up out of the dunghill" and "set with the princes."

With the arrival of the Arabs in Spain a new era dawned for the Jews. The Mohammedans brought to Spain not only a liberal government but also an enlightened spirit which encouraged science, philosophy, and literature. The Jews were quick to avail themselves of all the opportunities such a government offered them. Unlike the Mozarabs of the Spanish Peninsula, who forgot their Gothic Latin and were ashamed of their Christianity, the Jews returned to Judaism and evinced great love for the sacred tongue. Academies were founded and scholarship flourished. Those Jews who rose to high positions in the service of the state used their wealth and prestige to encourage scholarship. Like their Arab masters, they surrounded themselves with scientists, philosophers, and poets, whom they amply rewarded. Thus was brought about an ideal adjustment wherein the Jew retained his own culture and assimilated what he considered best in the culture about him. It is not surprising, therefore, to find the Spanish Jews once more singing "the Lord's song in a strange land" (Ps. CXXXVII, 4). Like the psalmists of old, these Hebrew poets of the "golden era" of Jewish history created a poetic literature sublime in thought and elevated in diction. And like their predecessors in Judaea, they did not consecrate their Muse to the glorification of the battlefield or the idolization of love, but devoted their songs primarily to God and to Israel.

One of the first great singers of that era was Solomon Ibn Gabirol, whom Heinrich Heine described as "a nightingale singing in the darkness of the Gothic mediaeval night." He was one of those unfortunates whose lives are filled with suffering, and his songs are the outpourings of an anguished heart. The emotional depth and piety of these poems have won for them a permanent and honorable place among the classics of the world.

Even greater and more famous than Ibn Gabirol is Judah Halevi, whose poetry breathes fervor, piety, and love of God and man. His songs reach their highest beauty when they express his longing for Zion. There is such joyful ecstasy in them, such deep yearning for the Land of Israel, such passionate aspiration for Israel's redemption that they still stir the heart of the Jew, awakening his pride in Israel's great past and his concern for its precarious future. Judah Halevi undoubtedly stands out as the greatest Hebrew poet since the days of the psalmists.

Two other poets, Moses Ibn Ezra and Abraham Ibn Ezra, have been chosen for this anthology to illustrate the poetry of that "golden era." Moses Ibn Ezra is famous for his many fervent penitential hymns, his tender love songs, and other secular poems; the restless and versatile Abraham Ibn Ezra is known for his mastery of the epigram as well as for his devotional poems.

Almost one thousand years have passed since that "golden era" when these and many other poets sang their songs in cultured Spain. This lapse of almost a millenium has only served to intensify our admiration for those poets and to deepen our appreciation of their achievements. Their songs still express the aspirations and longings of the Jewish people and are still a potent force in strengthening and inspiring the Jew in the many vicissitudes of diaspora life.

I. THE POETRY OF SOLOMON IBN GABIROL

RELIGIOUS POEMS

At the Dawn

At the dawn I seek Thee,
  Rock and refuge tried,
In due service speak Thee
  Morn and eventide.

'Neath Thy greatness shrinking,
  Stand I sore afraid,
All my secret thinking
  Bare before Thee laid.

Little to Thy glory
  Heart or tongue can do;
Small remains the story,
  Add we spirit too.

Yet since man's praise ringing
  May seem good to Thee,
I will praise Thee singing
  While Thy breath's in me.

(Translated by Israel Zangwill)

From Thee to Thee

When all within is dark,
  And former friends misprise;
From them I turn to Thee,
  And find Love in Thine eyes.

When all within is dark,
  And I my soul despise;
From me I turn to Thee,
  And find Love in Thine eyes.

When all Thy face is dark,
  And Thy just angers rise;
From Thee I turn to Thee,
  And find Love in Thine eyes.

(Translated by Israel Abrahams)

My Refuge

I have made Thee my refuge, my terror and trembling,
  And when straitly besieged I have made Thee my tower,
When to left and to right I have sought for a helper,
  I could look for dear life to no aid but Thy power.

More than all earthly treasure I have made Thee my portion,
  Through all cares the delight and desire of my days,
In the flood of Thy love I have rapture eternal
  And prayer is but an occasion for praise.

(Translated by Israel Zangwill)

I Have Sought Thee Daily

I have sought Thee daily at dawn and twilight,
  I have stretched my hands to Thee, turned my face,
Now the cry of a heart athirst I will utter,
  Like the beggar who cries at my door for grace.

The infinite heights are too small to contain Thee,
  Yet perchance Thou canst niche in the clefts of me.
Shall my heart not treasure the hope to gain Thee,
  Or my yearning fail till my tongue's last plea?
  Nay, surely Thy name I will worship, while breath in
        my nostrils be.

(Translated by Israel Zangwill)

Six Years Were Decreed

Six years were decreed for a slave to wait [1]
  When his freedom he sought at his master's hand,
But the years of my bondage lack term or date,
  It is hard, O my Master, to understand.

Why, Sirs, should a hand-maid's son [2] bear sway,
  And me with affliction and anguish task?
There cometh no answer, howe'er I pray,
  In despite that each day for reply I ask.

What word at the last wilt Thou say, my King?
  An Thou findest no ransom, O Lord, take me!
Take me for Thy people as offering,
  I will serve Thee for ever and ne'er go free.

(Translated by Israel Zangwill)

[1] The Biblical law (Ex. XXI, 1-6) limits the bondage of a Hebrew slave to six years, but if the Hebrew slave refuses to be liberated, the law prescribes that the slave's ear shall be bored with an awl to the door-post and that he shall serve his master for ever.

[2] Ishmael, Hagar's son, is traditionally believed to be the ancestor of the Arabs.

A Song of Redemption

Captive of sorrow on a foreign shore,
A handmaid as 'neath Egypt's slavery;
Through the dark day of her bereavement sore
She looketh unto Thee.
Restore her sons, O Mighty One of old!
Her remnant tenth shall cause man's strife to cease.
O speed the message; swiftly be she told
Good tidings, which Elijah shall unfold:[1]
Daughter of Zion, sing aloud! behold
The Prince of Peace!

Wherefore wilt Thou forget us, Lord, for aye?
Mercy we crave!
O Lord, we hope in Thee alway,
Our King will save!

Surely a limit boundeth every woe,
But mine enduring anguish hath no end;
My grievous years are spent in ceaseless flow,
My wound hath no amend.
O'erwhelmed, my helm doth fail, no hand is strong
To steer the bark to port, her longed for aim.
How long, O Lord, wilt Thou my doom prolong?
When shall be heard the dove's[2] sweet voice of song?
O leave us not to perish for our wrong,
Who bear Thy Name!

Wherefore wilt Thou forget us, Lord, for aye?
Mercy we crave!

[1] It is traditionally believed that Elijah will be the forerunner of the Messiah. See Mal. III, 23-24.
[2] Israel's.

O Lord, we hope in Thee alway,
Our King will save!

Wounded and crushed, beneath my load I sigh,
Despised and abject, outcast, trampled low;
How long, O Lord, shall I of violence cry,
My heart dissolve with woe?
How many years, without a gleam of light,
Has thraldom been our lot, our portion pain!
With Ishmael as a lion in his might,
And Persia as an owl of darksome night,
Beset on either side, behold our plight
Betwixt the twain.

Wherefore wilt Thou forget us, Lord, for aye?
Mercy we crave!
O Lord, we hope in Thee alway,
Our King will save!

Is this thy voice?
The voice of captive Ariel's woe unhealed?
Virgin of Israel, arise, rejoice!
In Daniel's vision, lo, the end is sealed:

When Michael on the height
Shall stand aloft in strength
And shout aloud in might,
And a Redeemer come to Zion at length.
Amen, amen, behold
The Lord's decree foretold.
E'en as Thou hast our souls afflicted sore,
So wilt Thou make us glad for evermore!

Wherefore wilt Thou forget us, Lord, for aye?
Mercy we crave!
O Lord, we hope in Thee alway,
Our King will save!

(Translated by Nina Davis)

God and Israel

God:
Though bereaved and in mourning, why sit thus in tears?
Shall thy spirit surrender its hopes to its fears?
Though the end has been long and no light yet appears,
Hope on, hapless one, a while longer.

I will send thee an angel My path to prepare,
On the brow of Mount Zion thy King to declare,
The Lord ever regnant shall reign again there,
Thy King, O proclaim, comes to Zion.

Israel:
How long, O my God, shall I wait Thee in vain?
How long shall Thy people in exile remain?
Shall the sheep ever shorn never utter their pain
But dumbly through all go on waiting?

God:
Have faith, hapless one, I will pardon and free,
Not always shalt thou be abhorrent to Me,
But be Mine e'en as I shall return unto thee,
'Tis yet but a little space longer.

Israel:
How long till the turn of my fate shall draw near,
How long ere the sealed and the closed be made clear,
And the palace of strangers a roof shall appear? [1]

God:
Hope on for a shelter and refuge.
With healing shall yet thy entreaties be graced,
As when Caphtor was crushed shalt thou triumph re-taste,
And the flowers cast off shall re-bloom in the waste,
Hope on but a little space longer.

Israel:
My people of yore 'neath one people was drowned,
But from Egypt or Babel deliverance found,
But now we are hopelessly compassed around
By four birds of prey grim and speckled. [2]
They have eaten my flesh, yet to leave me are loath.

God:
The Rock you must trust to remember His oath,
Your lover that went shall return to His troth,
Hope on, hapless one, a whit longer.

(Translated by Israel Zangwill)

Establish Peace
(Abridged)

Establish peace, for us, O Lord,
In everlasting grace,
Nor let us be of Thee abhorred,
Who art our dwelling-place.

[1] In the Hebrew, this line reads: *Armon zarim mathai tistor.*
[2] This line refers to the four beasts of Daniel's dream. See Daniel VII,17.

We wander ever to and fro,
  Or sit in chains in exile drear,
Yet still proclaim where'er we go,
  The splendour of Our Lord is here.

Sore-tried, involved in heathen mesh,
  Deep-sunk as though in midmost sea,
Each morn the thought is roused afresh
  Who will arise to set us free?

All realms behold our driven seed,
  Like wounded doves we fly their hate.
All nations hunt us and impede
  And in the desert lie in wait.

How many periods are past,
  And we in exile lingering,
By enemies encompassed fast,
  Who jeer that now we have no King!

Shine forth, great God, in splendid flame
  Bare Thy great arm of ancient days,
Be jealous for Thy glorious name,
  Not unto us, O Lord, the praise.

Our heritage they have possessed,
  Exiled, devoured us at their will,
Consumed and wasted and oppressed
  And machinate against us still.

So low our nation hath been brought,
  So many masters override,
A little more and it were naught,
  Had not the Lord been on its side.

O glorious sovran of the height,
  Abase, destroy their topmost tower,
The final marvel bring to light,
  Arise and save us, show Thy power.

Uplift the lowly from the mire,
  And make our meditation sweet,
The lily gather from the brier,
  And our salvation, Lord, complete.

O break the yoke, the slave release,
  Rebuke the arrogant again,
And send Thy messenger of peace,
  Whose feet are welcome as the rain.

Rejoice, my dear despised, the King
  In all His beauty thou shalt see,
And this the song that men shall sing
  In Judah's land, our own and free.

The prayer of the meek finds grace,
  And God will hearken and forgive,
Tread down corruption, sin erase,
  And in His light will let us live.

Delight and peace from Thee we hail,
  Thy hand Thy people's sin outscored,
Drew o'er iniquity a veil
  Nor gave wrongdoing its reward.

Perpetual ascent to Thee
  Thy people's and Thy servants' cries,
O let us Thy compassion see,
  And Thy salvation greet our eyes.

(Translated by Israel Zangwill)

SELECTIONS FROM "THE ROYAL CROWN"

Wonderful are thy works, as my soul overwhelmingly knoweth,
Thine, O Lord, are the greatness and the might, the beauty, the triumph, and the splendour.
Thine, O Lord, is the Kingdom, and Thou art exalted as head over all.
Thine are all riches and honour: Thine the creatures of the heights and depths.
They bear witness that they perish, while Thou endurest.
Thine is the might in whose mystery our thoughts can find no stay, so far art Thou beyond us.
In Thee is the veiled retreat of power, the secret and the foundation.
Thine is the name concealed from the sages,
The force that sustaineth the world on naught,
And that can bring to light every hidden thing.
Thine is the loving-kindness that ruleth over all Thy creatures,
And the good treasured up for those who fear Thee.
Thine are the mysteries that transcend understanding and thought.
Thine is the life over which extinction holdeth no sway,
And Thy throne is exalted above every sovereignty,
And Thy habitation hidden in the shrouded height.
Thine is the existence from the shadow of whose light every being was created,
Of which we say, in His shadow we live.
Thine are the two worlds between which Thou hast set a boundary,
The first for deeds and the second for reward.
Thine is the reward which Thou for the righteous hast stored up and hidden,
Yea, Thou sawest it was goodly and didst hide it.

Thou existest, but hearing of ear cannot reach Thee, or
vision of eye,
Nor shall the How have sway over Thee, nor the Wherefore
and Whence.
Thou existest, but for Thyself and for none other with Thee.
Thou existest, and before Time began Thou wast,
And without place Thou didst abide.
Thou existest, and Thy secret is hidden and who shall
attain to it?
"So deep, so deep, who can discover it?"

Thou art great, and compared with Thy greatness all
greatness is humbled and all excess diminished.
Incalculably great is Thy being,
Superber than the starry heaven,
Beyond and above all grandeur,
"And exalted beyond all blessing and praise."

Thou art the God of Gods, and the Lord of Lords,
Ruler of beings celestial and terrestrial,
For all creatures are Thy witnesses
And by the glory of this Thy name, every creature is bound
to Thy service.
Thou art God, and all things formed are Thy servants
and worshippers.
Yet is not Thy glory diminished by reason of those that
worship aught beside Thee,
For the yearning of them all is to draw nigh Thee,
But they are like the blind,

Setting their faces forward on the King's highway,
Yet still wandering from the path.
One sinketh into the well of a pit
And another falleth into a snare,
But all imagine they have reached their desire,

Albeit they have suffered in vain.
But Thy servants are as those walking cleareyed in the straight path,
Turning neither to the right nor the left
Till they come to the court of the King's palace.
Thou art God, by Thy Godhead sustaining all that hath been formed,
And upholding in Thy Unity all creatures.
Thou art God, and there is no distinction 'twixt Thy Godhead and Thy Unity, Thy pre-existence and Thy existence,
For 'tis all one mystery.
And although the name of each be different,
"Yet they are all proceeding to one place."

. . . .

May it please Thee, O Lord my God,
To subdue my fierce desire.
O hide Thy face from my sins and trespasses,
Do not carry me off in the midst of my days,
Until I shall have prepared what is needful for my way
And provender for the day of my journeying,
For if I go out of my world as I came,
And return to my place, naked as I came forth,
Wherefore was I created
And called to see sorrow?
From the day of his birth man is hard-pressed and harrowed,
"Stricken, smitten of God and afflicted."
His youth is chaff driven in the wind,
And his latter end is flying straw,
And his life withereth like a herb,
And God joineth in hunting him.
From the day he cometh forth from his mother's womb
His night is sorrow and his day is sighing.
If to-day he is exalted,

To-morrow he shall crawl with worms.
A grain of chaff putteth him to flight,
And a thorn woundeth him.
If he is sated, he waxeth wicked,
And if he is hungry, he sinneth for a loaf of bread.
His steps are swift to pursue riches,
But he forgetteth Death, who is after him.
Man entereth the world,
And knoweth not why,
And rejoiceth,
And knoweth not wherefore,
And liveth,
And knoweth not how long.
In his childhood he walketh in his own stubbornness,
And when the spirit of lust beginneth in its season
To stir him up to gather power and wealth,
Then he journeyeth from his place
To ride in ships
And to tread the deserts,
And to carry his life to dens of lions,
Adventuring it among wild beasts;
And when he imagineth that great is his glory
And that mighty is the spoil of his hand,
Quietly stealeth the spoiler upon him,
And his eyes are opened and there is naught.
And when his hour hath come, he passeth from the courts
 of his house to the court of Death,
And from the shadow of his chambers to the shadow of
 Death.
And he shall strip off his broidery and his scarlet
And shall put on corruption and the worm,
And lie down in the dust
And return to the foundation from which he came.
And man, whom these things befall,

When shall he find a time for repentance
To scour away the rust of his perversion?
For the day is short and the work manifold,
And the task-masters irate,
Hurrying and scurrying,
And Time laughs at him
And the Master of the House presses.
Therefore I beesech Thee, O my God,
Remember the distresses that come upon man,
And if I have done evil
Do Thou me good at my latter end,
Nor requite measure for measure
To man whose sins are measureless,
And whose death is a joyless departure.

May it please Thee, O Lord my God,
To return to me in mercy,
And to bring me back to Thee in perfect repentance.
O dispose my heart and turn Thine ear to supplication,
And open my heart to Thy law,
And plant in my thoughts the fear of Thee,
And decree for me good decrees,
And annul the evil decrees against me,
And lead me not into the power of temptation,
Nor into the power of contempt,
And from all evil chances deliver me,
And hide me in Thy shadow until the havoc pass by,
And be with my mouth in my meditation,
And keep my ways from sin through my tongue,
And remember me when Thou rememberest and favourest
    Thy people,
And when Thou rebuildest Thy Temple,
That I may behold the bliss of Thy chosen ones,
And purify me to seek diligently Thy Sanctuary devastated
    and ruined,

And to cherish its stones and its dust,
And the clods of its desolation,
And rebuild Thou its wastes!

(Translated by Israel Zangwill)

MISCELLANEOUS POEMS

Water Song

The Feast's begun
  And the Wine is done,
So my sad tears run
  Like streams of Water, streams of Water.

Three score and ten were Wine's bold braves.
But a full score more were Water's knaves, [1]
And silent are our watery graves.
  For—whence tuneful note?
  When the minstrel's throat
Tastes naught but Water, Water, Water!

Around the board you see no smile;
Untasted dishes rest in file,
How can I touch these dainties while
    There stands my cup
    To the brim filled up
With hated Water, Water, Water!

Old Moses chid the Red Sea tide,
  And Egypt's dusky streams he dried,
  Till Pharaoh's fools for Water cried!

[1] The numerical value of the Hebrew word for "wine" is 70, while the value of the Hebrew word for "water" is 90.

But Moses dear,
Why dost thou here
Turn all to Water, Hated Water?

Can I myself to aught compare?
To the frog who damp in watery lair,
With dismal croakings fills the air.
So frog and I
Will sing or cry,
The song of Water, the dirge of Water.

The man whom Water can delight
For aught I care may turn Nazarite;
Total abstention shall be his plight!
And all his days
To his lips shall raise
Cups of Water, always Water!

The Feast is done,
And Wine there's none;
So my sad tears run
Like streams of Water, streams of Water.

(Translated by Israel Abrahams)

A Degenerate Age

(A Poem in Defiance of His Critics)

Where is the man who has been tried and found strong and sound?
Where is the friend of reason and of knowledge?
I see only sceptics and weaklings.

I see only prisoners in the durance of the senses.
And every fool and every spendthrift
Thinks himself as great a master as Aristotle.
Thinks't thou that they have written poems?
Call'st thou that a Song?
I call it the cackling of ravens.
The zeal of the prophet must free poesy
From the embrace of wanton youths.
My song I have inscribed on the forehead of Time,
They know and hate it—for it is lofty.

(Translated by Emma Lazurus)

II. THE POETRY OF JUDAH HALEVI

POEMS DEALING WITH HIS JOURNEY TO ZION

My Heart Is in the East

My heart is in the east, and I in the uttermost west—
How can I find savour in food? How shall it be sweet to me?
How shall I render my vows and my bonds, while yet
Zion lieth beneath the fetter of Edom, and I in Arab chains?
A light thing would it seem to me to leave all the good
things of Spain—
Seeing how precious in mine eyes it is to behold the dust
of the desolate sanctuary.

(Translated by Nina Salaman)

Beautiful of Elevation

Beautiful of elevation! Joy of the world! City of the
Great King!
For thee my soul is longing from limits of the west.

The tumult of my tenderness is stirred when I remember
Thy glory of old that is departed—thine habitation which
is desolate.

O that I might fly on eagles' wings,
That I might water thy dust with my tears until they
mingle together.

I have sought thee, even though thy King be not in thee
and though, in place
Of thy Gilead's balm, are now the fiery serpent and the
scorpion.

Shall I not be tender to thy stones and kiss them,
And the taste of thy soil be sweeter than honey unto me?

(Translated by Nina Salaman)

Ode To Zion

(Abridged)

Art thou not, Zion, fain
To send forth greetings from thy sacred rock
Unto thy captive train,
Who greet thee as the remnants of thy flock?
Take Thou on every side,
East, west and south and north, their greetings multiplied.
Sadly he greets thee still,
The prisoner of hope who, day and night,
Sheds ceaseless tears, like dew on Hermon's hill.
Would that they fell upon thy mountain's height!

Harsh is my voice when I bewail thy woes,
But when in fancy's dreams
I see thy freedom, forth its cadence flows,
Sweet as the harps that hung by Babel's streams.
The glory of the Lord will ever be
Thy sole and perfect light;
No need hast thou then, to illumine thee
Of sun by day, or moon and stars by night.
I would that, where God's spirit was of yore
Poured out unto thy holy ones, I might
There too my soul outpour.

Oh, who will lead me on
To seek the spots where, in far distant years,
The angels in their glory dawned upon
Thy messengers and seers!
Oh, who will give me wings
That I may fly away,
And there, at rest from all my wanderings,
The ruins of my heart among thy ruins lay?
I'll bend my face unto thy soil, and hold
Thy stones as special gold.
And when in Hebron I have stood beside
My fathers' tombs,[1] then will I pass in turn
Thy plains and forest wide,
Until I stand on Gilead and discern
Mount Hor and Mount Abarim, 'neath whose crest
Thy luminaries twain,[2] thy guides and beacons rest.
Thy air is life unto my soul, thy grains
Of dust are myrrh, thy streams with honey flow

[1] The Patriarchs are buried at Hebron.
[2] Moses and Aaron.

Naked and barefoot to thy ruined fanes
How gladly would I go!
To where the ark was treasured, and in dim
Recesses dwelt the holy cherubim.

Perfect in beauty, Zion, how in thee
Do love and grace unite!
The souls of thy companions tenderly
Turn unto thee; thy joy was their delight,
And weeping they lament thy ruin now.
In distant exile, for thy sacred height
They long, and towards thy gates in prayer they bow.
Shinar and Pathros! come they near to thee?
Naught are they by thy light and right divine.

To what can be compared the majesty
Of thy anointed line?
To what the singers, seers, and Levites thine?
The rule of idols fails and is cast down;
Thy power eternal is, from age to age thy crown.

The Lord desires thee for His dwelling place
Eternally, and bless'd
Is he whom God has chosen for the grace
Within thy courts to rest.
Happy is he that watches, drawing near,
Until he sees thy glorious lights arise,
And over whom thy dawn breaks full and clear,
Set in the orient skies.
But happiest he, who, with exultant eyes,
The bliss of thy redeemed ones shall behold,
And see thy youth renewed as in the days of old.

(Translated by Alice Lucas)

To Mount Abarim

Peace be to thee, Mount Abarim![1]
Peace be to thee on every side!
Within thee is gathered the chosen of mankind,
In thee is the chosen of all sepulchres.
If thou knowest him not, ask thou
Of the Red Sea which was rent apart;
And ask of the bush and ask of the mount—
Ask of Sinai—they shall return answer unto thee:
He that faithfully bore the message of God,
Even though no man of words![2]
God helping,
I have vowed an early pilgrimage to thee.

(Translated by Nina Salaman)

On The Sea

My God, break not the breakers of the sea,
Nor say Thou to the deep, "Be dry,"
Until I thank Thy mercies, and I thank
The waves of the sea and the wind of the west;
Let them waft me to the place of the yoke of Thy love,
And bear far from me the Arab yoke.
And how shall my desires not find fulfillment,
Seeing I trust in Thee, and Thou art pledged to me?

(Translated by Nina Salaman)

[1] Moses' burial place.

[2] See Exodus IV, 10—"And Moses said unto the Lord: 'Oh Lord, I am not a man of words . . . for I am slow of speech, and of a slow tongue'."

The Storm

The waters roar
As their wheels roll o'er,
Becoming less and more
    On the face of the sea.

The waters grow black
Grim lowers the rack,
The breakers rear back
    Till the depths you can see.

The cauldron boils o'er
With a hiss and a roar,
And none can restore
    Its tranquillity.

And brave men must fear
As the waves disappear,
And a mountain is here,
    And there a valley.

The ship turns like a vane,
Bows and rises again;
And the eye asks in vain,
    Where, pilots, are ye?

And my heart then stands still,
But bows down to His will
Who to Moses gave skill
    To divide the Red Sea.

To the Lord I would call,
But to sin I've been thrall,
And I fear to recall
    The punishment due.

(Translated by Joseph Jacobs)

The Pride of the Jew

With all my heart, in truth, and passion strong,
I love Thee; both in solitude and throng
Thy name's with me, alone I shall not bide:
My friend art Thou, though others from me glide.
My lamp art too: my light shall never fade,
Nor shall my foot e'er slip, by Thee upstayed.
They little knew who have despised me so,
That shaming me doth cause my pride to glow.
O Fountain of my life, I'll bless Thee aye,
And sing Thy praises, O my song, alway!

(Translated by Israel Cohen)

Servant of God

(Hymn for the Day of Atonement)
(Abridged)

O would that I might be
A servant unto Thee,
Thou God, by all adored!
Then, though by friends out-cast,
Thy hand would hold me fast
And draw me near to Thee, my King and Lord!

Spirit and flesh are Thine,
O Heavenly Shepherd mine,
My hopes, my thoughts, my fears, thou seest all,
Thou measurest my path, my steps dost know.
When thou upholdest, who can make me fall?
When Thou restrainest, who can bid me go?

O would that I might be
A servant unto Thee,
Thou God, by all adored!
Then, though by friends out-cast,
Thy hand would hold me fast,
And draw me near to Thee, my King and Lord!

So lead me that I may
Thy sovereign will obey.
Make pure my heart to seek Thy truth divine,
When burns my wound, be Thou with healing near!
Answer me, Lord! for sore distress is mine,
And say unto Thy servant, I am here!
O would that I might be
A servant unto Thee,
Thou God, by all adored!
Then, though by friends out-cast,
Thy hand would hold me fast,
And draw me near to Thee, my King and Lord!

(Translated by Alice Lucas)

Vision of God

To meet the fountain of the life of truth I run,
For I weary of a life of vanity and emptiness.
To see the face of my King is mine only aim;
I will fear none but Him, nor set up any other to be feared.
Would that it were mine to see Him in a dream!
I would sleep an everlasting sleep and never wake.
Would I might behold His face within my heart!
Mine eyes would never ask to look beyond.

(Translated by Nina Salaman)

The Lord Is My Portion

Servants of time, lo! these be slaves of slaves;
But the Lord's servant hath his freedom whole,
Therefore, when every man his portion craves,
"The Lord God is my portion," saith my soul.

(Translated by Nina Davis)

Before Thee Is My Whole Desire
(Abridged)

O Lord, before Thee is my whole desire—
Yea though I cannot bring it to my lips.

Thy favour I would ask a moment and then die—
Ah, would that mine entreaty might be granted!

That I might render up the remnant of my spirit to Thine hand,
Then should I sleep, and sweet my sleep would be.

When far from Thee, I die while yet in life;
But if I cling to Thee I live, though I should die.

Only I know not how to come before Thee,
Nor what should be my service nor my law.
Show me, O Lord, Thy ways!
And turn me back from bondage of my folly;

And teach me, while there yet is power in me
To bear affliction; scorn not mine abasement

Ere yet the day I grow a burden on myself,
The day my limbs weigh heavy each on each;

When I am bowed despite me, and the moth
Eateth my bones aweary of sustaining me;

And I fare forth whither my fathers fared,
And where they rested find my camping place.

And how then shall I serve my Maker, while
A captive to my lust, a slave to my desire?

And how upon a day of gladness shall my heart be glad?—
I know not if it shall be well with my tomorrow;

And what hath fate for me if not Thy favour?
If thou art not my lot, what is my lot?

I am despoiled and naked of good works,
Thy righteousness alone my covering—

But why make longer speech, why question more?
O Lord, before Thee is my whole desire.

(Translated by Nina Salaman)

The Ways of God

Fair in mine eyes are all Thy ways,
And sweet it is to walk therein,
For there man stumbles not, nor strays,
There is no pitfall, snare, or sin.
There do I move
With gladness, drawn to Thee by bonds of love.

Fountain of life, my soul's desire,
My hope and refuge, Thou Most High,
To see Thy glory I aspire,
Too great a bliss for such as I;
Thus when I yearn
For Thee, unto Thy house my steps I turn.

O be Thy love my shield and stay!
Strengthen my heart to serve Thee still,
Then shall Thine anger pass away,

For I have not transgressed Thy will.
My chief delight
Is in Thy law, my study day and night.

The favour of Thy countenance
Strengthened my arm in days of yore,
Thy service mine inheritance
Has been, and shall be evermore.
Thou leadest me,
Yea, though Thou slay me, I will trust in Thee.

(Translated by Alice Lucas)

Wonderful Is Thy Love

May my sweet song be pleasing in Thy sight, and the goodness of my praise,
O Belovéd, who art flown afar from me, at the evil of my deeds!
But I have held fast unto the corner of the garment of love of Him who is tremendous and wonderful.
Enough for me is the glory of Thy name; that is my portion alone from all my labour.
Increase the sorrow, I shall love but more, for wonderful is Thy love to me.

(Translated by Nina Salaman)

The Physician's Prayer

My God, heal me and I shall be healed;
Let not Thine anger be kindled against me so that I be consumed.
My medicines are of Thee, whether good
Or evil, whether strong or weak.

It is Thou who shalt choose, not I;
Of Thy knowledge is the evil and the fair.
Not upon my power of healing I rely;
Only for Thine healing do I watch.

(Translated by Nina Salaman)

Sabbath, My Love

I greet my love with wine and gladsome lay;
Welcome, thrice welcome, joyous Seventh Day!

Six slaves the week days are; I share
With them a round of toil and care,
Yet light the burdens seem, I bear
For thy sweet sake, Sabbath, my love!

On First-day to the accustomed task
I go content, nor guerdon ask,
Save in thy smile, at length, to bask—
Day blest of God, Sabbath, my love!

Is Second-day dull, Third-day unbright?
Hide sun and stars from Fourth-day's sight?
What need I care, who have thy light,
Orb of my life, Sabbath, my love!

The Fifth-day, joyful tidings ring;
"The morrow shall thy freedom bring!"
At dawn a slave, at eve a king—
God's table waits, Sabbath, my love!

On Sixth-day doth my cup o'erflow,
What blissful rest the night shall know,
When, in thine arms, my toil and woe
Are all forgot, Sabbath, my love!

'Tis dusk. With sudden light distilled
From one sweet face, the world is filled;
The tumult of my heart is stilled—
 For thou art come, Sabbath, my love!

Bring fruits and wine, and sing a gladsome lay,
Chant: "Come in peace, O blissful Seventh Day!"

(Translated by S. Solis-Cohen)

The Sun and Moon Forever Shine

The sun and moon for ever shine. By day
And night they mark the Eternal's high design,
Changeless and tireless, speeding on their way,
 The sun and moon for ever shine.

Symbols are they of Israel's chosen line,
A nation still, though all around decay,
A nation still, though countless foes combine,
 Smitten by God and healed by God are they.

They shall not fear, safe 'neath the Rock divine
Nor cease to be, until men cease to say,
 The sun and moon for ever shine.

(Translated by Alice Lucas)

LOVE, BRIDAL, AND OTHER POEMS

Unto the Stars to Reach Thee

Would that morning might pursue me with the wind
That kisseth her mouth and swayeth her body;
And would the clouds might bear to her my greeting—

Then like her frame, so would the hardness of her heart
be moved.
Thou gazelle, that choosest to rest upon the stars,
Have pity upon him who must fly unto the stars to reach
thee.

(Translated by Nina Salaman)

Separation

And so we twain must part! Oh linger yet,
And let me still feed my glance upon thine eyes.
Forget not, love, the days of our delight,
And I our nights of bliss shall ever prize.
In dreams thy shadowy image I shall see,
Oh, even in my dream be kind to me!

Though I were dead, I none the less would hear
Thy step, thy garment rustling on the sand.
And if thou waft me greetings from the grave,
I shall drink deep the breath of that cold land.
Take thou my days, command this life of mine,
If it can lengthen out the space of thine.

No voice I hear from lips death-pale and chill,
Yet within my heart it echoes still,
My frame remains—my soul to thee yearns forth.
A shadow I must tarry still on earth.
Back to the body dwelling here in pain,
Return, my soul, make haste and come again!

(Translated by Emma Lazarus)

Dove Beside the Water Brooks

(Abridged)

Dove beside the water brooks—
A delight is she to the eyes.

Lo, there is a mine for silver,
But one like my dove, who can find?
Beautiful is my love like Tirzah,
  Comely as Jerusalem.

Why turneth she hither and thither
To dwell in tents,
Since in my heart is a camp for her dwelling,
  Great and wide?

Her bosom hath taken spoil of my heart
And wrought upon me
Enchantments, which the magicians
  Of Egypt could not do.

A graceful doe, like gold of Ophir,
With her light she shameth the light of day;
Like the moon, like paved work of sapphire,
  As it were the very heaven.

There is no darkness before her radiance,
Her lamp is not quenched at night;
To the light of day her light is joined,
  Till it be sevenfold.

The times of love draw nigh to thee,
The season cometh to make us one;
So shall draw near the time of times
  To the dancing of two camps.

(Translated by Nina Salaman)

To the Bridegroom

Rejoice, O young man in thy youth,
And gather the fruit of thy joy,
Thou and the wife of thy youth
Who cometh to thine house.

Precious blessings of the only God
Shall come upon thine head together,
And thine house shall be at peace from dread,
And all who rise against thee shall be cut off.
And when thou liest down thou shalt not be afraid;
    Thou shalt lay thee down and thy sleep be sweet.

In thine honour, my bridegroom, ride on and prosper,
Raise up and put forth thy beauty;
And the heart of thine enemies God shall pierce,
And the sins of thy youth He will forgive,
And will bless thee in all the doings
    Of thine hand and in all thine increase.

And remember thy Rock and thy Creator
When the good cometh which He shall bring thee;
For children, in course of the days, shall come to thee,
And as thy days, so shall thy strength be.
Blessed be thou in thy coming in
    And blessed be thou in thy going out.

Thy word shall be with men of perfection,
So thou be discreet wherever thou turn;
And thine house shall be firmly builded,
And "Peace," thou shalt call and God shall reply,
And peace shall be thine habitation, and with the stones
    Of the field thy covenant.

Thine honour shall ascend, and tarry not,
And thee shall He call, yea, shall choose,
And thy light in the night and the gloom
Then shall break through like the dawn;
And for thee, from the womb of the morning,
    The dew of thy youth!

(Translated by Nina Salaman)

Amid the Myrtles

The bridal pair stand amid the myrtles,
Sending forth pure myrrh on every side.
The myrtle desireth the sweetness of their fragrance,
And spreadeth his wings like a cherub above them.
The myrtle thinketh to cover their fragrance,
But the sweetness of their spices overwhelmeth his scent.

(Translated by Nina Salaman)

Wake, My Darling, From Thy Slumbers

Wake, my darling, from thy slumbers,
Wake and fill my day with bliss:
Didst thou dream some daring lover
Ravished from thy lips a kiss?
I am skilled in dreams and omens,
And thy vision, love, means—this.

(Translated by S. Solis-Cohen)

The Rogue

Once I nursed Love on my knee.
He saw his likeness in my eye,
He kissed the lids so tenderly,
'Twas his image he kissed, the rogue, not me.

(Translated by Joseph Jacobs)

The First White Hair

I spied a white hair lurking in my beard,
And straightway plucked it thence. "Thou'rt brave," it
sneered,
"'Gainst a lone scout—quite brave. But wilt thou be
As plucky, when my troop comes, seeking me?"

(Translated by S. Solis-Cohen)

III. THE POETRY OF MOSES IBN EZRA

PENITENTIAL AND OTHER RELIGIOUS POEMS

Dawn

I rose at dawn to praise Thy name,
My sins o'erwhelmed my soul with shame,
But comfort after penance came,
For all my hopes are set in Thee.

Thou, O almighty, knowest all
The passions that my heart enthrall,
Thy many mercies I recall,
And to Thy throne for refuge flee.

No profit unto Thee it were
That I Thy chastening rod should bear,
Turn then, O Lord, and hear my prayer
And pardon mine iniquity.

To Thee my hopes, my longings, rise,
To Thee my soul for succour flies,
And I bewail my sins with sighs,
Like to the moaning of the sea.

Thy name puts all my cares to flight,
And radiates through my darkest night.
The thought of Thee is my delight,
And sweet as honey-comb to me.

(Translated by Alice Lucas)

O Thou That Graciously Attendest
(Abridged)

O Thou, that graciously attendest
To the voice of suppliants,
And to the sweet words of psalmody,
Bethink Thee of the trustful one
Who knocks at the gates of prayer,
And in the darkness at the dead of night
Whilst the world sleeps,
Cries: "I stand upon my ward
All the night."

Of old, Thou madest Israel like a vineyard—
Wherein Thou didst plant tender vines.
Alas! Thou didst break down his fences,
All they that pass by, hiss at him.
Thou hast strengthened the hands of his foes
And destroyed him utterly.
They have stript off his branches
And heaped them up in the road.

Oh, hear the cry of Thy people
And incline unto their plea—
In their misery,
Hide not Thine eyes from their grief!
Oh, hasten their deliverance—
For Thou art their Redeemer—
And cast all their sins
Like a stone, into the depths.

(Translated by S. Solis-Cohen)

Penitential Prayer
(Abridged)

Sleepless, upon my bed the hours I number,
And, rising, seek the house of God, while slumber
Lies heavy on men's eyes, and dreams encumber
Their souls in visions of the night.

In sin and folly passed my early years,
Wherefore I am ashamed, and life's arrears
Now strive to pay, the while my bitter tears
Have been my food by day and night.

Short is man's life, and full of care and sorrow,
This way and that he turns some ease to borrow,
Like to a flower he blooms, and on the morrow
Is gone—a vision of the night.

My youth wanes like a shadow that is cast,
Swifter than eagle's wings my years fly past,
And I remember not my gladness past,
Either by day or yet by night.

Proclaim we then a fast, a holy day,
Make pure our hearts from sin, God's will obey,
And unto Him, with humbled spirit, pray
Unceasingly, by day and night.

May we yet hear His words: "Thou art my own,
My grace is thine, the shelter of My throne,
For I am thy Redeemer, I alone;
Endure but patiently this night!"

(Translated by Alice Lucas)

To Dwell with All-Soul Doth My Soul Desire

(Abridged)

"*With my soul have I desired Thee, in the night*" (Is. XXVI, 9).

To dwell with All-Soul doth my soul desire,
Unto the Fountainhead of life aspire;
With longing keen as a consuming fire,
She seeks the holy courts by day and night!

The banner of Thy grace is o'er me ever,
And from mine heart Thine awe is absent never;
O Lord, Thou knowest my thought and mine endeavor,
Hast searched me, proved me, watched me in the night!

Pure soul, imprisoned in a form of clay,
Reflect! this world is but a transient way,
Awake! Awake in the still watch, and pray;
Rise! call upon thy Maker in the night!

Born, without choice, into a world of care,
Mankind scheme evil, suffer sorrow there;
They are like to flowers that blossom and fall bare—
They vanish as the visions of the night!

Heavy, the yoke of grief upon me weighs,
That still my feet incline to froward ways;
I faint with moaning, as days follow days
And flood my couch with tears, night after night!

Vanished like shadows, youth's bright days are done;
Swifter than eagles fly, my years have flown.
A time of joy, my life indeed has known,
But I remember naught—no day, no night!

Observe the fast, cleanse ye and sanctify;
Purge dross of sin from hearts—stand steadfastly.
Remembrancers of God, cease not to cry
On Him for pardon, all the day and night!

(*God speaks*)
Hear, daughter: thine is the heritage of My grace,
And gently will I lead thee to the place
Of Mine abode, to give thee rest therein.
Than I, is none more near to thee of kin—
I will redeem thee; bide in trust, the night.

(Translated by S. Solis-Cohen)

God That Doest Wondrously

(El Nora 'Alilah)

God, that doest wondrously,
God, that doest wondrously,
Pardon at Thy people's cry,
As the closing hour draws nigh!

Few are Israel's sons, and weak;
Thee, in penitence, they seek.
O, regard their anguished cry,
As the closing hour draws nigh!

Souls in grief before Thee poured,
Agonize for deed and word;
"We have sinned; Forgive!" they cry,
As the closing hour draws nigh!

Heal them! Let their trust in Thee
Turn aside Wrath's dread decree;
Doom them not, but heed their cry,
As the closing hour draws nigh!

Mercy, grace, for these low-bowed!
But upon the oppressor proud,
Judgment for his victims' cry,
As the closing hour draws nigh!

For our fathers' righteousness,
Save us now in our distress;
Make us glad with freedom's cry,
As the closing hour draws nigh!

Join, O Shepherd, as of old,
Zion's with Samaria's fold;
Call Thy flock with tend'rest cry,
As the closing hour draws nigh!

Elihah, Michael, Gabriel,
Come! the hoped-for tidings tell;
Let "Redemption!" be your cry,
As the closing hour draws nigh.

God, that doest wondrously,
God, that doest wondrously,
Pardon at Thy people's cry,
As the closing hour draws nigh.

(Translated by S. Solis-Cohen)

SECULAR POEMS

An Excerpt from the Book of "Tarshish"

By friendship's waters, with a chosen few,
Noble of soul, of jocund heart and true,
Drink, to the sound of laughter, lute and song,
And joy in precious talk of old and new.

Come friends, within—the cheerful cup to drain;
The world is bleak, without—November's rain
Beats on chill fields, of their green mantles stript,
And boughs are bare, and furrows void of grain.

Drink with me, till the magic of the wine
Makes this a palace-court, where we recline;
Yon sound of water is the fountain's plash—
And hark! The nightingale in song divine!

Drink! Whilst the rain-drenched earth for summer yearns,
And shivering forests dream that spring returns,
The ruby wine glows in its crystal cup
Like flame of God, within the hail that burns.

Mark how the lightnings of the cup leap forth
To smite my serried sorrows; floods of mirth
Beat down my troubles, as the floods of heaven
Level the ridges of the furrowed earth.

O spirit, ransomed of the bowl, burn bright
For these, my friends! Shine through the starless night,
A beacon to guide hitherward their joys
And put the shadows of their cares to flight!

Come, *Ophrah,*[1] fill my cup—but not with wine.
The splendor of thine eyes therein let shine;
So shall the draught thou pour'st this night in Spain,
Bear to far lands and days, thy fame—and mine!

Drink, friends, the days of wintry chill are done;
Earth thrills to the embraces of the sun
And drops the mask of age. O'er hill and dale,
The green-clad hosts of youth march swiftly on.

(Translated by S. Solis-Cohen)

[1] Beautiful cupbearer; literally, gazelle.

How Long at Fate's Behest
(Abridged)

How long yet must my feet, at Fate's behest,
The path of exile tread, and find no rest?

The sword of Separation hath he drawn
To harry me over the earth;
And with the battle-ax of Wandering,
From each new refuge doth he drive me forth.

Upon me he hath loosed his brood of ills;
I totter, yea I fall, before their might—
Whilst like a fading shadow, day by day,
    My life takes flight.

If in mine exile, I might meet but one,
    With whom to hold sweet converse of the mind,
Then would I willingly forgive Fate's spite,
    That sent me forth, so dear a friend to find.
From town to town I haste,
    But everywhere

It is to Folly's tents that men repair;
To Learning's gate they cannot find the way—
Yet never do I bar it, night or day,
And none need weary to gain entrance there.

Yet may not Fate, that hath been harsh so long
    Relent at last;
And grant my heart's desire—and lead me back
To that fair city where my youth was passed?
There wait the roofs of friends, and there might I
Sit by a loved one's threshold, and exchange
Greetings of friendship with the passers-by.

But who can say if those dear, distant ones
Cherish or scorn the love I treasure yet?—
If I forget them, may my hand forget
Its cunning—if, from them apart,
One thought of joy can enter in my heart.

Oh, if indeed, the Lord would me restore
To beautiful Granada-land, my paths
Would be the paths of pleasantness once more;
For in that land my life was very sweet—
A kindly Fate laid homage at my feet,
And deep I quaffed at Friendship's fount; as now
I fain would quaff the waters of Senir,
Whose snowfed current bears the swimmer high
When Eden's streams run scant and sluggishly.

Though hope be long deferred, though heart be faint,
On God I wait,
Unto whose mercy there is no restraint—
And whose decree
Can break the shackles and unbar the gate,
And set the prisoner of exile free.

(Translated by S. Solis-Cohen)

The Garden Dons a Coat of Many Hues

The garden dons a coat of many hues;
The mead a broidered carpet hath unrolled;
The woods are brave in chequered mantles—Now
A wondrous scene may every eye behold:

The newborn flowers acclaim the newborn Spring,
And forth to meet his coming, gaily throng;
High, at their head, on sovereign throne is borne
The rose—the flowrets' queen—queen of my song.

From prisoning leaves she bursts, and casts aside
Her captive garb, in royal robes to shine.
I drink to her! Nor heaven forgive the wretch—
If such there be—who spares his choicest wine!

(Translated by S. Solis-Cohen)

Hopeless Love

With hopeless love my heart is sick,
    Confession bursts my lips' restraint.
That thou, my love, dost cast me off,
    Hath touched me with a death-like taint.

I view the land both near and far,
    To me it seems a prison vast.
Throughout its breadth, where'er I look,
    My eyes are met by doors locked fast.

And though the world stood open wide,
    Though angel hosts filled ev'ry space,
To me 'twere destitute of charm
    Didst thou withdraw thy face.

(Translated by G. Karpeles)

IV. THE POETRY OF ABRAHAM IBN EZRA

DEVOTIONAL POEMS

Resignation

I hope for the salvation of the Lord,
    In Him I trust, when fears my being thrill,
Come life, come death, according to His word,
    He is my portion still.

Hence doubting heart! I will the Lord extol
    With gladness, for in Him is my desire,
Who, as with fatness, satisfies my soul,
    That doth to heaven aspire.

All that is hidden, shall mine eyes behold,
    And the great Lord of all be known to me,
Him will I serve, His am I as of old;
    I ask not to be free.

Sweet is ev'n sorrow coming in His name,
    Nor will I seek its purpose to explore,
His praise will I continually proclaim,
    And bless Him evermore.

(Translated by Alice Lucas)

Prayer for Help

Lord, I pray with hands uplifted
And my tears flow fast,
For my manifold transgressions
And my sinful past.
Heal mine inward wound and straighten

All my ways at last.
Merciful, O Father, be,
Even when Thou judgest me,
Answer when I call on Thee,
God of my salvation!

Glad yet fearful, I am seeking
Pardon, 'midst the throng
Of Thy chosen congregation
With sweet sound of song,
Hymns and praise and patient striving
To amend the wrong.
Lord, Thy power I will proclaim,
And exalt Thy glorious name,
Yea, my love for Thee like flame
Burns, Thou my salvation!

Thou o'er heavenly heights who ridest
Know'st the inmost parts,
And Thy love accepts repentance
When it sorest smarts,
Counting it as off'rings ever,
Strengthening feeble hearts.
Thou wilt lead Thy flock aright
To the land of my delight,
Thou my refuge, rock, and might,
Heritage and portion.

Well-spring Thou of strength and gladness,
Lord, I hope in Thee,
And declare the power eternal
Of Thy sovereignty.
O! command Thou Thy salvation

To abide with me.
Let it guide me on my way,
Evermore my help and stay,
Bringing me from day to day
Still my daily portion.

Thou wilt save me, Thou wilt guard me,
Mine exalted King.
Have regard to my entreaty
And good tidings bring.
Unto us Thy needy people
Let Thine answer ring:
Fear thou not, for I behold thee,
I will strengthen and enfold thee,
Yea, my right hand shall uphold thee!
I am thy salvation!

(Translated by Alice Lucas)

God Everywhere

Wheresoe'er I turn mine eyes
Around on earth or toward the skies,
I see Thee in the starry field,
I see Thee in the harvest's yield,
In every breath, in every sound,
An echo of Thy name is found.
The blade of grass, the simple flower,
Bear witness to Thy matchless pow'r.
My every thought, Eternal God of Heaven,
Ascends to Thee, to whom all praise be given.

(Translated by D. E. de L.)

When I Hunger to Praise Thee

When I hunger to praise Thee, I'm sated;
When to worship I thirst, I am drunk.
Then my heart is secure, when I fear Thee
When in terror and awe I am sunk.
When I bow to Thee low, I am lifted;
When I fall in Thy presence, I rise.
I am free when I serve, for Thy name's sake,
My oppressors who Thy name despise.
All suffering is sweet to my heart,
When I know that My God Thou art.

(Translated by Meyer Waxman)

EPIGRAMMATICAL POEMS.

Out of Luck

'Twas sure a luckless planet
That ruled when I was born—
I hoped for fame and fortune,
I have but loss and scorn.

An evil fate pursues me
With unrelenting spite;
If I sold lamps and candles,
The sun would shine all night.

I cannot, cannot, prosper
No matter what I try—
Were selling shrouds my business,
No man would ever die!

(Translated by S. Solis-Cohen)

To Whom Shall I Cry in My Anguish?

To whom shall I cry in my anguish?
  And where shall I flee from the flies?
No breathing-space do they allow me;
  They treat me as would enemies.
They buzz in my ears all their love-songs,
  And creep on my brow and my eyes.
  I try to partake of my breakfast—
  They swarm on the coveted prize.
They drink of my wine from the goblets,
  Considering me in no wise.

(Translated by Meyer Waxman)

Born Without a Star

I come in the morn
To the house of the nobly born.
They say he rode away.
I come again at the end of the day,
But he is not at his best, and needs rest.
He is either sleeping or riding afar—
Woe to the man who was born without a star.

(Translated by Meyer Waxman)

Chapter II

PRAYERS, HYMNS, AND DIRGES

A NATION in the course of its normal life has many occasions for singing. National victories and defeats, heroes of the battlefield and the playground, spring and harvest, love and beauty have always furnished the poet with inspiring themes. But the non-Spanish mediaeval Jew was not privileged to experience these normal joys and sorrows. His lot was that of the homeless and despised wanderer. He was always at the mercy of his persecutors, and like the hunted animal, could hope for nothing more than evasion of his pursuers. "What then could he do better than pray or cry? In his prayers he sought for strength and power of endurance to resist the temptations of persuasion and persecution," and in his lamentations he "gave vent to the feelings which he dared betray only to his God."[1]

This abnormal life of the mediaeval Jew furnished his poets with unusual themes. Like the psalmist of Biblical days he "knew of but one subject worthy of enthusiasm and adoration—God and His providence."[2] Whereas the poets of all nations continued to "sing of arms and the man," the mediaeval Hebrew poets continued to exclaim, like the ancient psalmist, "I will sing of mercy and justice; unto Thee, O Lord, will I sing praises." These hymns of praise, though in no way comparable to the psalms in respect to poetic beauty, depth, and charm nevertheless evince the same religious fervor and complete submission to God's will.

Next to his faith in God was the Jew's faith in Israel's

[1]Schechter, Solomon—"A Hebrew Elegy" in *Transactions of the Jewish Historical Society of England*, 1893-94, p. 10

[2]Graetz, H.—*History of the Jews*, Vol. III, p. 113, Jewish Publication Society of America, Philadelphia, 1894.

future. The long dark night of the exile could not dim the memory of the preceding bright day, nor did it quench the hope for a new dawn. True the Jew was oppressed, persecuted, hounded, but he found hope and courage in the knowledge that the same God who had redeemed Israel from tyranny in days past promised a redeemer in time to come, one who would dispel the clouds of oppression and cause light to shine forth abundantly. These memories and hopes furnished the Jewish poets with inspiring themes and gave rise to hymns of redemption describing in glowing terms the glory of the past and the bright vision of the future.

But the Jew was not content with mere waiting for the Messiah. By nature religious, he sought the cause of his affliction in his own conduct. He directed his attention to an examination of himself and characteristically found himself unworthy of those divine standards of perfection which he had been chosen to exemplify. This sense of unworthiness was expressed by the Jewish poets of the Middle Ages in penitential hymns which, in spite of their frequent awkwardness, abound in religious fervor, depth of feeling, and elevation of thought.

Finally, the burning memory of the innumerable martyrs who had died "for the sanctification of God's name" inspired the Jewish poet to sing their heroic deeds in many somber dirges and elegies. These too are often awkward, but they always contain religious depth and unbounded love for Israel, and reflect complete submission to God's will. On fast days the Jew read them and found in them a source of strength and courage, enabling him to bear his tribulations with greater resolution.

The following selections, gleaned from the prayer books and other sources, will no doubt explain why the Jewish poet's "only scene of action was the synagogue, his only audience the congregation assembled for prayer and instruction."[1]

[1]Ibid., p. 113.

I. HYMNS OF PRAISE

Lord of the Universe

Before the glorious orbs of light
Had shed one blissful ray,
In awful power, the Lord of might
Reign'd in eternal day.

At His creative, holy word
The voice of nature spoke,
Unnumber'd worlds with one accord
To living joys awoke.

Then was proclaim'd the mighty King
In majesty on high!
Then did the holy creatures sing
His praises through the sky.

All-merciful in strength He reigns
Immutable! Supreme!
His hand the universe sustains,
He only can redeem.

Almighty, powerful and just!
Thou art my God, my friend,
My rock, my refuge and my trust,
On Thee my hopes depend.

O! be my guardian whilst I sleep,
For Thou didst lend me breath:
And when I wake, my spirit keep,
And save my soul in death.

Author Unknown
(Translated by D. N. Carvalho)

The Lord Is King

Ere space exists, or earth or sky,
The Lord is King!
Ere sun or star shone forth on high,
The Lord was King!
When earth shall be a robe outworn,
And sky shall fade like mists of morn,
Still shall the Lord fore'er be King!
The Lord is King! The Lord was King! Forever
shall the Lord be King!

When earth He flings mid star-filled space,
The Lord is King!
When living creatures there found place,
The Lord was King!
When homeward from earth's corners four,
He calls the scattered folk once more,
Then shall the Lord fore'er be King!
The Lord is King! The Lord was King! Forever
shall the Lord be King!

Author Unknown
(Translated by S. Solis-Cohen)

The Lord Is King, the Lord Was King, the Lord Shall Be King for Ever and Ever

(Abridged)

The terrible sons of the mighty race
Shout in thunder the Lord is King,
The angels whose figure the lightnings trace
Flame to the world that the Lord was King,

And seraphs whose stature is one with space,
Proclaim that the Lord shall be King for ever.
The Lord is King, the Lord was King, the Lord shall be King for ever and ever.

The bards who remember the songs of yore
Sing aloud that the Lord is King,
The sages enshrouded in mystic lore
Find and proclaim that the Lord was King,
And rulers of spans of the heavenly floor
Cry that the Lord shall be King for ever.
The Lord is King, the Lord was King, the Lord shall be King for ever and ever.

The heirs of the Torah, Thy rich bequest,
Chant in joy that the Lord is King,
The lordly warriors with crown and crest
Crown Thee, declaring the Lord was King,
And angels in fiery garments drest
Repeat that the Lord shall be King for ever.
The Lord is King, the Lord was King, the Lord shall be King for ever and ever.

Thy people in passionate worship cry
One to another the Lord is King.
In awe of the marvels beneath the sky
Each explains that the Lord was King.
One sound from Thy pastures ascends on high:
One chant that the Lord shall be King for ever.
The Lord is King, the Lord was King, the Lord shall be King for ever and ever.

The universe throbs with Thy pauseless praise,
Chorus eternal, the Lord is King.
Thy glory is cried from the dawn of days,
Worshippers calling the Lord was King.
And ever the Saints who shall witness Thy ways
Shall cry that the Lord shall be King for ever.
The Lord is King, the Lord was King, the Lord shall be King for ever and ever.

Eleazar Kalir
(Translated by Israel Zangwill)

Palms and Myrtles

Thy praise, O Lord, will I proclaim
In hymns unto Thy glorious name.
O Thou Redeemer, Lord and King,
Redemption to Thy faithful bring!
Before thine altar they rejoice
With branch of palm, and myrtle-stem,
To Thee they raise the prayerful voice—
Have mercy, save and prosper them.

May'st Thou in mercy manifold,
Dear unto Thee Thy people hold,
When at Thy gate they bend the knee,
And worship and acknowledge Thee.
Do Thou their heart's desire fulfil,
Rejoice with them in love this day,
Forgive their sins, and thoughts of ill,
And their transgressions cast away.

They overflow with prayer and praise
To Him, who knows the future days.
Have mercy Thou, and hear the prayer
Of those who palms and myrtles bear.
Thee day and night they sanctify
And in perpetual song adore,
Like to the heavenly host, they cry
"Blessed art Thou for evermore."

Eleazar Kalir
(Translated by Alice Lucas)

Hymn of Unity for the Seven Days of the Week

I

Eternal King, the heavens and earth are thine,
Thine are the seas and every living thing.
Thy hand upholds creation's vast design,
Eternal King!

The mighty waters with Thy glory ring,
Unnumbered lands to chant Thy praise combine,
And kings of earth to Thee their worship bring.

Thy people Israel for Thy love benign
Blesses Thy name, and joys Thy praise to sing.
Thou art the God of truth, the one, divine,
Eternal King.

II

I worship Thee for all Thy boundless store
Of righteousness and mercy shown to me,
And for Thy holy book of sacred lore
I worship Thee.

To Thee alone our fathers bent the knee
And Thee alone do we this day adore,
Bearing our witness to Thy unity.

Thou art our God, Thy favour we implore,
Thou art our Shepherd and Thy flock are we,
Therefore I bless Thy name, and evermore
I worship Thee.

III

I know it well; Thou art all good, all wise.
Thou slayest, but Thy touch death's power can quell.
Thou woundest, but Thy hand the balm supplies:
I know it well.

Nor sin, nor grief can in Thy presence dwell,
Slumber and sleep come not unto Thine eyes,
Great God, eternal and unchangeable!

The soul of all mankind before Thee lies,
Thou searchest all their hearts, their thoughts canst tell,
Thou hearest graciously their prayerful cries:
I know it well.

IV

We will extol the Lord of lords, whose name
Is evermore and everywhere adored.
In songs and hymns our lips His praise shall frame:
We will extol the Lord!

He is the hope of Israel, His word
A lamp unto our feet, a guiding flame
To those who trust in Him with full accord.

He is through countless ages still the same,
The shield of our salvation and our sword,
And generations, each to each, proclaim:
We will extol the Lord!

V

Who shall narrate Thy wonders wrought of old?
The utterance of the lips Thou didst create,
But all Thy majesty and power untold
Who shall narrate?

Thy ways on earth in song we celebrate,
Though none may Thy similitude behold,
Yet know we by Thy works that Thou art great.

Thousands of angels, by Thy word controll'd,
To do Thy bidding Thy commands await:
Yet of them all, Thy wonders manifold
Who shall narrate?

VI

Alone didst Thou, O Lord, the heavens' wide tent
Uprear, and bid the earth beneath be shown!
Thy word the oceans in their boundaries pent
Alone.

No aid or counsel hadst Thou save Thine own,
When Thou with lights didst hang the firmament
And call the hosts celestial round Thy throne

Thy works, in universal cadence blent,
Give praise to Thee and make Thy glory known:
Thou madest all, great God beneficent,
Alone.

VII

Of old Thou didst the Sabbath bless and praise,
Because thereon Thou didst Thy work behold,
Completed in the sun's new-kindled rays
        Of old.

Bless Thou this day with mercies manifold
Thy people, that in love and awe obeys
Thy word, and chants Thy righteousness untold.

Lord, we desire to do Thy will always!
Make pure our hearts like thrice refinéd gold,
And these, our prayers, accept as in the days
        Of old.

Samuel ben Kalonymus
(Translated by Alice Lucas)

Loved of My Soul!

Loved of my soul! Father of grace!
    Lead on Thy servant to Thy favouring sight;
He, fleetly as the hart, shall speed his pace
    To bow him low before thy glorious might.
Sweet is Thy love to him beyond compare,
Sweeter than honey, fairer than things fair.

Splendour of worlds! honoured, adored!
    My soul is sick with pining love of Thee;
    My God! I pray Thee, heal her: be implored;
        And o'er her let Thy holy sweetness be
    A soothing strength to stay her yearning sore;
    And joy shall be for her for evermore.

Source of all good! pity Thou me!
And be Thou moved for thy belovéd son,
For lo, how oft my soul hath longed to see
The beauty of Thy strength, Thou Mighty One!
Ah, Thou my God, my heart's desire, I pray
Grant me Thy mercy; turn Thee not away.

Be Thou revealed, Dearest of mine!
And spread o'er me Thy canopy of peace;
Soon with Thy glory all the earth shall shine;
And we shall know a joy that shall not cease.
Hasten, Belovéd, for the time is nigh,
And have compassion as in days gone by.

Author Unknown
(Translated by Nina Davis)

Hymn of Glory
(Abridged)

Sweet hymns shall be my chant and woven songs,
For Thou art all for which my spirit longs—

To be within the shadow of Thy hand
And all Thy mystery to understand.

The while Thy glory is upon my tongue,
My inmost heart with love of Thee is wrung,

So though Thy mighty marvels I proclaim,
'Tis songs of love wherewith I greet Thy name.

* * *

I have not seen Thee, yet I tell Thy praise,
Nor known Thee, yet I image forth Thy ways.

For by Thy seers' and servants' mystic speech
Thou didst Thy sov'ran splendour darkly teach,

And from the grandeur of Thy work they drew
The measure of Thy inner greatness, too.

They told of Thee, but not as Thou must be,
Since from Thy work they tried to body Thee.

To countless visions did their pictures run,
Behold through all the visions Thou art one.

* * *

Truth is Thy primal word; at Thy behest
The generations pass—O aid our quest

For Thee, and set my host of songs on high,
And let my psalmody come very nigh.

My praises as a coronal account,
And let my prayers as Thine incense mount.

Deem precious unto Thee the poor man's song,
As those that to Thine altar did belong.

Rise, O my blessing, to the lord of birth,
The breeding, quickening, righteous force of earth.

Do Thou receive it with acceptant nod,
My choicest incense offered to my God.

And let my meditation grateful be,
For all my being is athirst for Thee.

Judah He-Hasid
(Translated by Israel Zangwill)

II. SONGS OF REDEMPTION

Belovéd, Hasten to Thy Hallowed Dwelling

Belovéd, hasten to Thy hallowed dwelling,
And though our wanton ways have vexed thy face,
Behold our woe, all other woe excelling,
Thou art our only strength and resting-place;
With hope in Thee our hearts are daily swelling,
O make us watered gardens of Thy grace.

Belovéd, hasten to our shrine all-holy,
And though Sin claims us almost for its own,
Behold how bound in chains we cower lowly,
Thou art the sacred Saviour, Thou alone;
To Thee we give ourselves in prayer wholly,
O grant redemption from Thy lofty throne.

Belovéd, hasten to our righteous city,
And though we lent no ear to lore divine,
Behold us now consumed, a thing of pity,
Thou art our Judge, we make our burden Thine.
Our Legislator, hear our mournful ditty,
O send the strength and peace for which we pine.

Belovéd, hasten to Thy habitation,
And though impatiently we spurned Thy reign,
Behold the measure of our tribulation,
Thou art the comforter of every pain;
We look to Thee to free our captive nation,
And in our boundaries be hymned again.

Belovéd, hasten to Thy seat uplifted,
And though presumption did our duty whelm,
Behold to what distresses we have drifted,
Thou art the liberator of our realm;
Our pleading trust in Thee hath never shifted,
O place upon our head salvation's helm.

Simeon ben Isaac ben Abun
(Translated by Israel Zangwill)

All the World Shall Come to Serve Thee

All the world shall come to serve Thee
  And bless Thy glorious Name,
And Thy righteousness triumphant
  The islands shall acclaim.
And the peoples shall go seeking
  Who knew Thee not before,
And the ends of earth shall praise Thee,
  And tell Thy greatness o'er.

They shall build for Thee their altars,
  Their idols overthrown,
And their graven gods shall shame them,
  As they turn to Thee alone.
They shall worship Thee at sunrise,
  And feel Thy Kingdom's might,
And impart their understanding
  To those astray in night.

They shall testify Thy greatness,
  And of Thy power speak,
And extol Thee, shrined, uplifted
  Beyond man's highest peak.

And with reverential homage,
  Of love and wonder born,
With the ruler's crown of beauty
  Thy head they shall adorn.

With the coming of Thy Kingdom
  The hills shall break into song,
And the islands laugh exultant
  That they to God belong.
And all their congregations
  So loud Thy praise shall sing,
That the uttermost peoples hearing,
  Shall hail Thee crownéd King.

Author Unknown
(Translated by Israel Zangwill)

Hymn of Welcome to the Sabbath

Come, my beloved, with chorus of praise,
Welcome Bride Sabbath, the Queen of the days.

"Keep and Remember!"—in One divine Word
He that is One, Alone, made His will heard;
One is the name of Him, One is the Lord!
  His are the fame and the glory and praise!

Sabbath, to welcome thee, joyous we haste;
Fountain of blessing from ever thou wast—
First in God's planning, though fashioned the last,
  Crown of His handiwork, chiefes of days.

City of holiness, filled are the years;
Up from thine overthrow! Forth from thy fears!
Long hast thou dwelt in the valley of tears,
Now shall God's tenderness shepherd thy ways.

Rise, O my folk, from the dust of the earth,
Garb thee in raiment beseeming thy worth;
Nigh draws the hour of the Bethlehemite's[1] birth,
Freedom who bringeth, and glorious days.

Wake and bestir thee, for come is thy light!
Up! With thy shining, the world shall be bright;
Sing! For thy Lord is revealed in His Might—
Thine is the splendor His Glory displays!

'Be not ashamed,' saith the Lord, 'nor distressed;
Fear not and doubt not. The people oppressed,
Zion, My city, in thee shall find rest—
Thee, that anew on thy ruins I raise.'

Spoiled shall thy spoilers be; banished afar,
They that devoured. But in thee, evermore,
God shall take joy; as the bridegroom, what hour,
Blushing, the bride lifts her veil to his gaze.

Stretch out thy borders to left and to right;
Fear but the Lord, Whom to fear is delight—
The man, son of Perez,[2] shall gladden our sight,
And we shall rejoice to the fullness of days.

Come in thy joyousness, Crown of thy Lord;
Come, bringing peace to the folk of the Word;
Come where the faithful in gladsome accord,
Hail thee as Sabbath-Bride, Queen of the days.

[1] Messiah.
[2] Messiah (Perez is an ancestor of King David).

Come where the faithful are hymning thy praise;
Come as a bride cometh, Queen of the days!

Solomon Alkabiz
(Translated by S. Solis-Cohen)

God of Might

God of Might,
God of Right,
Thee we give all glory,
Thine the praise
In our days
As in ages hoary.
When we hear,
Year by year,
Our redemption's story,
Now as erst,
When Thou first
Mad'st the proclamation,
Warning loud
Ev'ry proud,
Ev'ry tyrant nation,
We Thy fame
Still proclaim,
God of our salvation.

Author Unknown
(Translated by G. Gottheil)

A Song of Love
(Abridged)

My noble love!
O dove of wondrous grace!
What aileth thee that thou dost weep in woe?
Messiah cometh unto thee: then go,
Fly to thy resting-place.

I am thy Saviour Who will ransom thee,
Thy hope from ancient day;
Know that in truth I say:
I, thy Redeemer, I will set thee free,
My noble love!

My Mighty Love!
Where is Thy troth of yore,
The vision of the seers in ages gone,
Proclaiming to the lone, the outcast one,
Whose glory is no more,
That she shall yet be sought, again shall shine
A very great delight?
Thine is redemption's right,
Yea, and the power of sole possession Thine,
My Mighty Love!

My noble love!
Tried in the furnace blaze
Of dire affliction; thou with shackled feet
Shalt yet adorn thy form with joy complete,
Gird on thy song of praise.
The crown of beauty,—diadem divine,—
It seemeth good to Me
To give it unto thee,
That sanctified perfection may be thine,
My noble love!

My Mighty Love!
Naught of my fame is left,
Though erst I dwelt in regal robes of grace;
My sons lie slain, the scions of my race,
Of kin I stand bereft.

Behold me wrapt in darkness deep and fell,
Sunk in the loathsome pit,
By ray of light unlit;
The great stone lieth heavy o'er the well,
My Mighty Love!

My noble love!
I by Myself have sworn
To summon thee, My servant, unto Me;
And shall not kings bring presents unto thee,
Thy glory to adorn?
A witness have I made My holy one,
For nations to behold,
For peoples manifold,
For lo! of Jesse have I seen a son,
My noble love!

Author Unknown
(Translated by Nina Davis)

III. PENITENTIAL HYMNS

Supplication

Our sins are many, and we sigh
For that we hearkened not to Thee
When all the time we knew Thee nigh,
But proud in our prosperity
We went our ways with head on high.

Now wasted is our strength, and we
Are like an armless soldier grown;
All that our fathers wrought for Thee
Is nought, and now we stand alone
In shame and dire infirmity.

We are like stubble on the plain
That no one seeks to gather in
Or load upon the harvest wain—
Consuming fire will purge our sin
And lead us pure to Thee again.

O Lord, Thy seal accounts us Thine;
Of yore when in our dire distress
We craved Thy charity divine,
Thou didst us with Thy mercy bless;
O be Thou in this hour benign!

The driven leaf let healing cure,
Repent Thee for this human dust.
O cleanse us that we may be pure,
Let all our sins from Thee be thrust—
Thy mercy is for ever sure!

Jose ben Jose

Lord, I Remember

(Abridged)

Lord, I remember, and am sore amazed
To see each city standing in her state,
And God's own city to the low grave razed;
Yet in all time we look to Thee and wait.

Send us Thy mercy, O Redeemer! Make,
O thou my soul, to Him thy mournful plaint;
And crave compassion for my people's sake;
Each head is weary and each heart is faint.

O Thou who hearest weeping, healest woe,
Our tears within Thy vase of crystal store;
Save us, and all Thy dread decrees forego,
For unto Thee our eyes turn evermore.

Amittai ben Shephatiah
(Translated by Nina Salaman)

Lo! As the Potter
(Abridged)

Lo! as the potter mouldeth plastic clay
To forms his varying fancy doth display;
So in Thy hand, O God of love, are we:
Thy bond regard, let sin be veil'd from Thee.

Lo! as the mason's hand the block doth hew
To shapes sublime, or into fragments strew;
So in Thy hand, O God of life, are we:
Thy bond regard, let sin be veil'd from Thee.

Lo! as the smith the rigid steel hath bent,
Soften'd with fire and wrought with strength unspent;
So in Thy hand, O God of might, are we:
Thy bond regard, let sin be veil'd from Thee.

Lo! as the seaman's hand doth cast or weigh
The pond'rous anchor in the foaming spray;
So in Thy hand, O God of pardon, we:
Thy bond regard, let sin be veil'd from Thee.

Lo! as the smelter fuseth silv'ry vein,
Removing dross, that naught impure remain;
So in Thy hand, O God of healing, we:
Thy bond regard, let sin be veil'd from Thee.

Lo! as the potter mouldeth plastic clay
To forms his varying fancy doth display,
So in Thy hand, O God of love, are we:
Thy bond regard, let sin be veil'd from Thee.

Author Unknown
(Translated by Elsie Davis)

Even as the Daily Offering

Judge of the earth, who wilt arraign
The nations at Thy judgment seat,
With life and favour bless again
Thy people prostrate at Thy feet.
And mayest Thou our morning prayer
Receive, O Lord, as though it were
The offering that was wont to be
Brought day by day continually.

Thou who art clothed with righteousness,
Supreme, exalted over all—
How oft soever we transgress
Do Thou with pardoning love recall
Those who in Hebron sleep,[1] and let
Their memory live before Thee yet,
Even as the offering unto Thee
Offered of old continually.

[1] The Patriarchs

Trust in God's strength, and be ye strong,
My people, and His laws obey,
Then will He pardon sin and wrong,
Then mercy will His wrath outweigh.
Seek ye His presence and implore
His countenance for evermore,
Then shall your prayers accepted be
As offerings brought continually.

Solomon ben Abun
(Translated by Alice Lucas)

O Lord, Save We Beseech Thee

O Lord, save we beseech Thee.
O Lord, prosper we beseech Thee.
O Lord, answer us on the day that we call.

God of spirits, save we beseech Thee.
Searcher of hearts, prosper we beseech Thee.
O strong Redeemer, answer us on the day that we call.

Utterer of righteousness, save we beseech Thee.
Clad in glory, prosper us we beseech Thee.
Omnipotent and gracious, answer us on the day that we call.

Pure and upright, save we beseech Thee.
Thou who pitiest the poor, prosper we beseech Thee.
Good and bountiful Lord, answer us on the day that we call.

Diviner of thoughts, save we beseech Thee.
Mighty and resplendent, prosper we beseech Thee.
Thou that art clothed in righteousness, answer us on the day that we call.

King of worlds, save we beseech Thee.
Thou that art girt with light and majesty, prosper we beseech Thee.
Thou who supportest the falling, answer us on the day that we call.

Helper of the poor, save we beseech Thee.
Redeemer and Deliverer, prosper we beseech Thee.
O everlasting Rock, answer us on the day that we call.

Holy and revered, save we beseech Thee.
Merciful and compassionate, prosper we beseech Thee.
Keeper of the covenant, answer us on the day that we call.

Stay of the perfect, save we beseech Thee.
Sovereign of Eternity, prosper we beseech Thee.
Thou who art perfect in thy ways, O answer us on the day that we call.

Author Unknown
(Translated by H. M. Adler)

IV. DIRGES

The First Crusade

Yea, they slay us and they smite,
Vex our souls with sore affright;
All the closer cleave we, Lord,
To Thine everlasting word.
Not a word of all their Mass
Shall our lips in homage pass;
Though they curse, and bind, and kill,
The living God is with us still.

We still are Thine, though limbs are torn;
Better death than life foresworn.
Noblest matrons seek for death,
Rob their children of their breath;
Fathers, in their fiery zeal,
Slay their sons with murderous steel,
And in heat of holiest strife,
For love of Thee, spare not their life.
The fair and young lie down to die
In witness of Thy Unity;
From dying lips the accents swell,
'Thy God is One, O Israel';
And bridegroom answers unto bride,
'The Lord is God, and none beside',
And, knit with bonds of holiest faith,
They pass to endless life through death.

Kalonymus Ben Judah
(Translated by E. H. Plumptre)

The Burning of the Law
(Abridged)

Ask, is it well, O thou consumed of fire,
With those that mourn for thee,
That yearn to tread thy courts, that sore desire
Thy sanctuary;
That, panting for thy land's sweet dust, are grieved,
And sorrow in their souls,
And by the flames of wasting fire bereaved,
Morn for thy scrolls;

And thou revealed amid a heavenly fire,
By earthly fire consumed,

Say how the foe unscorched escaped the pyre
  Thy flames illumed!

O Sinai! was it then for this God chose
  Thy mount of modest height,
Rejecting statelier, while on thee arose
  His glorious light?

Moses; and Aaron in the mountain Hor;
  I will of them inquire:
Is there another to replace this Law
  Devoured of fire?

In sackcloth I will clothe and sable band,
  For well-beloved by me
Were they whose lives were many as the sand—
  The slain of thee.

I am astonished that the day's fair light
  Yet shineth brilliantly
On all things:—it is ever dark as night
  To me and thee.

E'en as thy Rock has sore afflicted thee
  He will assuage thy woe;
Will turn again the tribes' captivity,
  And raise thee low.

My heart shall be uplifted on the day
  Thy Rock shall be thy light,
When He shall make thy gloom to pass away,
  Thy darkness bright.

Meir of Rothenberg
(Translated by Nina Davis)

The Ten Martyrs
(Abridged)

When I call to mind the days of old,
The embers of sorrow are fann'd into flame
For the martyr'd Ten who proved so bold,
Slaughter'd like sheep by the sons of shame.
As the jackal I wail their woes untold,
I mourn, as the bird of dolorous fame,
The Ten Mighty Martyrs of glorious name.

They were brought before Caesar, and Simon arose,
Rabbi Simon the Good, who held himself least;
"Slay ye me first," he entreated his foes,
"Ere by Ishmael's death our band be decreas't—
Me first, ere befalls the direst of woes,
When Israel's Light shall have utterly ceas't,
And torture toucheth our Blessed High Priest."

"Nay," murmur'd the Priest, and besought in like strain—
So vied they for death, brave men ill bestead—
"Heaven spare me but this, to behold him slain,
Israel's loved Prince, our people's Head!"
"Cast lots," cried Caesar, "betwixt the twain."
Ishmael, God's servant, to Simon then said:—
"Come, brother, let both to the lot be led."

The twain there awaited whatso might betide,
As the lots, 'twixt the Prince and the Priest, they shook.
On Simon it fell; he first should be tried;
He, the first, should be marred with murderous hook.
Caesar, foul serpent, among them did glide,
As venomous adder that killeth with look;
Simon, the Good, from their midst he took.

Then Rabbi Akiba harshly they plied;
The heart quakes at his pangs, and the tongue it is still;
His flesh they scraped, and the dust was dyed
With his holy blood, as they work'd their will.
How scourged they Akiba, the sages' pride!
How passed he hence from this world of ill,
This world where holiest blood men spill!

Chaninah ben Tradyon next was their prey;
All Israël's tears could not quench the glare
Of the faggots they fired on that festal day;
With water-drenched wool made they fiercer the flare.

"Come, death," wail'd his comrades, "why dost thou delay?
Our Father in Heaven, hear Thou our prayer!
Fire and water for Thee we dare."

The twilight darken'd, and Sabbath Eve
Shed its peace o'er Chaninah, hoary, dim-eyed,
Four-score and ten. "Let me, sirs, but receive
With joyous blessing the Sabbath—the Bride,
E'en now," he craved, "ere your toils I leave
For the Sabbath of Sabbaths, the Lord beside.
'Tis sunset—longer I would not abide."

And he spake from the song of Creation's Days,
Bending as vassal before the Throne:—
"Thus He ended His work, 'mid Creation's praise;
The Heavens and Earth He had wrought alone;
And the seventh He hallow'd"—with that did they raise
Their weapons of death—and he ceased without moan;
As he breathed forth "hallow'd," his soul had flown.

For these I weep, and my heart it is sad,
These thrice-three Martyrs of deathless name:
Yet grief thereto a tenth must add,

Equal in sorrow, nor less in fame—
Rabbi Ben Baba. His soul was glad,
When death crown'd with glory the life without blame;
From the dark North drear destruction came.

Here endeth my dirge. Israel's glory and pride
Are these martyr'd Sages—the Ten Wise Men,
O'erwhelm'd by Iniquity's on-rushing tide,
As its noisome waters swept fastness and glen.
Their merit be ours when we are tried!
Lord! May Thy erring folk hear then,—
"I will not destroy, for the sake of the Ten!"

Joseph Ezobi
(Translated by Herman Gollancz)

The Prophet Jeremiah by the Cave of Machpelah

The Prophet standing by the fathers' graves,
With soul o'erwhelméd speaks, for solace craves:
"How can ye lie at rest, beloved ones,
While sharpened swords consume your captive sons?
Where now, O fathers, lurks your merit rare
In that vast wilderness of land laid bare?"
They cry each one with lamentation sore
For children banished, sons that are no more;
They pray imploring with a cry for grace
To Him who dwelleth in the realms of space;
Ah! where is now God's promise made of old:
'I will not my first covenant withhold'?

Changed is My glory,
From them departed;
They have not feared Me;
Dread have they known not;
From them I hid Me,

And still they turned not,
Nor to Me yearned they;
Shall I restrain Me,
Hearing them utter:
"Our God He is not"?

Then Father Abraham with bitter cry
Implored, a suppliant lowly, God on high:
"Ten times, in vain for them great trials I bore,
For woe! mine eyes have seen destruction sore;
Ah! where is now Thy promise made of old:
'Abram, thou shalt not fear, thy shield behold'?"

Far have they wandered,
Erred after strange gods,
And they have hewn them
Cisterns which hold not;
Shall I restrain Me,
When they regard not
My sacred mandates?

And thus did Isaac all his sorrow tell
Unto the Lord who high in Heav'n doth dwell:
"Wherefore was I appointed to be slain?
My seed is crushed and low in bondage lain;
Ah! where is now Thy promise made of old:
'My covenant with Isaac I will hold'?"

Unto My prophet
Sorely rebellious,
They have polluted
My holy mountain:
Lo, I am weary
With ever hearing

Their cry which riseth
From the earth upwards;
Shall I restrain Me,
Seeing the slaughter
Of Zechariah?

And then spake he with learning deep endowed,[1]
His form with shame and bitter sorrow bowed:
"My little ones I reared with holy care,
How are they caught within the fatal snare!
Ah! dearly have I paid a thousandfold
My erring children's debt of guilt untold."
Thus spake the faithful shepherd in his woe,
Covered with ashes and in dust laid low:
"My tender sheep in genial shelter reared,
Lo! how are they before their season sheared!
Ah! where is now Thy promise made of old:
'There shall not be one widowed in the fold'?"
With grievous voices all the air is rent;
With sobs doth Leah to her despair give vent,
And Rachel weeping for her children dead,
Zilpah with face of anguish, heart of dread,
And Bilhah grieving for the evil day,
Her hands to God uplifted in dismay.

Turn, O ye perfect ones,
Unto your rest again;
I will fulfil for you
All that your hearts desire:
Down unto Babylon
With you My Presence went;
Surely will I return
Your sons' captivity.

Eleazar Kalir
(Translated by Nina Davis)

[1] Jacob (According to the Midrash, Jacob was distinguished for his scholarship.)

V. MISCELLANEOUS POEMS

The Angels Came A-mustering

The Angels came a-mustering,
A-mustering, a-mustering,
The Angels came a-clustering
Around the sapphire throne.

A-questioning of one another,
Of one another, of one another,
A-questioning each one his brother
Around the sapphire throne.

Pray who is he, and where is he,
And where is he, and where is he,
Whose shining cast—so fair is he—
A shadow on the throne?

Pray, who has up to heaven come,
To heaven come, to heaven come,
Through all the circles seven come,
To fetch the Torah down?

'Tis Moses up to heaven come,
To heaven come, to heaven come,
Through all the circles seven come,
To fetch the Torah down!

Author Unknown
(Translated by Israel Zangwill)

Why Should I Wander Sadly?

Why should I wander sadly,
My harp within my hand,
O'er mountain, hill, and valley?
What praise do I command?

Full well they know the singer
Belongs to race accursed;
Sweet *Minne* doth no longer
Reward me as at first.

Be silent, then my lyre,
We sing 'fore lords in vain,
I'll leave the minstrels' choir,
And roam a Jew again.

My staff and hat I'll grasp, then,
And on my breast full low,
By Jewish custom olden
My grizzled beard shall grow.

My days I'll pass in quiet,—
Those left to me on earth—
Nor sing for those who not yet
Have learned a poet's worth.

Süsskind Von Trimberg

Chapter III

PHILOSOPHIC LITERATURE

When people of two conflicting cultures meet, their genius is usually stimulated to attempt either a defense of their respective cultures or a reconciliation of their differences. If these attempts are executed by well-sustained logical and systematic argumentation, they become contributions to their national philosophic literatures.

The Jews, as long as they were not exposed to foreign ideas, produced no philosophic literature. In Palestine, in Babylonia, and in the European Ghettos they lived their own life, free from the encroachments of conflicting ideas, and therefore free from the vexing problems that give rise to a philosophic literature. But between the tenth and the fifteenth centuries many Jews found themselves faced with complex and disturbing problems. Through the medium of the Arabs they came into contact with Greek philosophic thought. They could not resist the flawless arguments of the Greek philosophers, nor could they doubt the truths of the Bible. Unfortunately, the two sources of truth—the divine revelations of the Bible and the rational speculations of the Greeks—often ran counter to each other. Thus some of the keenest Jewish minds felt themselves called upon either to defend Judaism against the encroachments of secular learning, or to prove that essentially the two cultures were not at variance.

In addition to its conflict with philosophy, Judaism also became conscious of another challenge, more irritating than perplexing. Through the free exchange of ideas with their Mohammedan neighbors, and through the forced disputations with their Christian opponents, the Jews became aware of the arrogant claims to superiority on the part of the two daughter religions. This overbearing attitude incited the Jews to refute the presumptuous claims of the Mohammedans and Christians and to prove the abiding truth and superiority of Judaism. This impulse to defend Judaism against the attacks of foreign philosophies and theologies made the Jewish philosophic literature essentially apologetic.

Of the many books written by Jewish philosophers the four best known and most representative are *The Cusari* by Judah Halevi, *The Book of Doctrines and Beliefs* by Saadya Gaon, *The Guide for the Perplexed* by Moses Maimonides, and *The Book of Principles* by Joseph Albo.

The Cusari, though philosophically superficial, has exerted a profound influence on the Jewish people. Its popularity was due largely to its defense of traditional Judaism against the inroads of philosophy, and to its form of presentation. Its author, Judah Halevi, one of the most distinguished Hebrew poets of all time, was fortunate in finding a romantic setting for his treatise. He availed himself of the Platonic method of presenting philosophic thought through the medium of dialogue—a dialogue between a learned rabbi and a king of the Khazars. In this dialogue the rabbi systematically expounds the traditional teachings of Judaism, and thus succeeds in convincing the King and his people of the superiority of the Jewish religion.

Whereas the author of *The Cusari* denies the validity of philosophic speculation and upholds the truth of divine revelation, Saadya Gaon, author of *The Book of Doctrines and Beliefs*, and Moses Maimonides, author of *The Guide for the Perplexed*, attempt a reconciliation between the two—between philosophy and the Bible. This is especially true of Maimonides who proves himself to be a most original and logical thinker. His originality is particularly evidenced in his attempt at a rational explanation of the Biblical laws. His method of approach makes him the first student of comparative religion. He shows courage in his brilliant though unorthodox conclusions in regard to some of the origins of Biblical laws. He claims, for instance, that the whole sacrificial cult of the Bible was a mere concession on the part of God to the forms of worship of a primitive people. No wonder *The Guide for the Perplexed* became the center of a controversy which, for a time, divided Judaism into two hostile camps.

The Book of Principles by Joseph Albo represents the decadence of the creative impulse in Jewish philosophy. This work, like *The Cusari*, was popular because of its simple style. But the author is more often preacher than philosopher. He contributes nothing new to Jewish philosophy and merely repeats the views of his predecessors. His work is also more apologetic than that of the others because of his open attempt to refute Christian dogma. This open attack on Christianity was a result of the most trying experience of his life—the famous disputation at Tortosa, where he was forced to defend Judaism before an imposing assembly of non-Jews for almost twenty-two months.

The present chapter will undoubtedly prove to be one of the least adequate in this anthology. Whereas a poet's work can be adequately represented by a few well-culled selections, philosophy, which, by definition, must be sustained argument, necessarily loses by a disruption of its continuity. But if these few excerpts succeed in arousing the curiosity of some readers to acquaint themselves with the full texts, this chapter will have served its purpose.

I. THE BOOK OF DOCTRINES AND BELIEFS

by Saadya Gaon

The Purpose of the Book

I saw men sunk, as it were, in a sea of doubt and covered by the waters of confusion, and there was no diver to bring them up from the depths and no swimmer to come to their rescue. But as my Lord has granted unto me some knowledge which I can use for their support, and endowed me with some ability which I might employ for their benefit, I felt that to help them was my duty, and guiding them aright an obligation upon me, . . . although I confess to the shortcomings of my knowledge, which is far from being perfect, and admit the deficiency of my understanding, which is far from being complete. . . . Nevertheless, I maintain the hope that He who knoweth my intentions and the desire of my heart will grant me success and sustain me according to my purpose, not according to my gifts and abilities. . . .

In the name of God, the Creator of the universe, I implore any learned man who may read this book and find in it some mistake, to correct it, or if he finds a doubtful letter, to put it right. Let him not be prevented from doing so by the fact that the book is not his, or because I preceded him in shedding light on matters which were not clear to him. For the wise have compassion on wisdom and feel kindness for it as members of one family feel kindly towards each other, as is said, "Say unto wisdom: thou art my sister" (Prov. 7. 4). . . .

I further implore in the name of God (may He be exalted) all those of my readers who strive after wisdom to read this book with an open mind, to try honestly to see my point of view, and to clear their minds of obstinacy, hasty judgment and confused thinking so that they may derive from it the maximum of profit and advantage with the help of Him who has taught us wherein our benefit lies and on what it depends. . . . If both the scholar and the learner follow this path in reading this book, the certainty of him that feels certain will increase; the doubt of him that is in doubt will vanish; the believer who blindly relies on tradition will turn into one basing his belief on speculation and understanding; those who put forward erroneous arguments will be silenced; those who are obstinate and haughty will be ashamed; and the righteous and upright will rejoice, as is said, "The upright see it and are glad; and all iniquity stoppeth her mouth. Whoso is wise, let him observe these things, and let them consider the mercies of the Lord" (Ps. 107. 42–3).

The Freedom of the Will

. . . I maintain further that the Creator (be He exalted) does not allow His power to interfere in the least with the actions of men, nor does He compel them to be either obedient or disobedient. I have proofs for this doctrine founded on sense perception, Reason, Scripture and Tradition.

In regard to sense perception, I have found that a man observes from his own experience that he has the power to speak and to be silent, the power to seize a thing and to abandon it; he does not notice any other force that would hinder him in any way from exercising his will-power. The simple truth is that he directs the impulses of his nature by his Reason, and if he follows the bidding of Reason, he is prudent, if he does not, he is a fool.

As to the proof based on Reason, our previous arguments have already shown how untenable is the idea that one action can be attributed to two agents. Now one who thinks that the Creator (be He exalted and glorified) interferes with the actions of men, does in fact ascribe one single action to God and Man together. Furthermore, if God used compulsion against man, there would be no sense in His giving him commandments and prohibitions. Moreover, if He compelled him to do a certain action, it would be inadmissible to punish him for it. In addition, if men acted under compulsion, it would be necessary to mete out reward to believers and infidels alike, since each of them did only what he was ordered to do. If a wise man employs two workmen, the one that he may build, and the other that he may destroy, it is his duty to pay wages to both. . . .

As to the proofs based on Scripture, we have already mentioned the verse, "Therefore choose life" (Deut. 30. 19). The sinners are told, "This has been of your doing; will He accept any of your persons?" (Mal. 1. 9). Moreover, the Creator explains clearly that He is innocent with regard to their sins, as He says, "Woe to the rebellious children, saith the Lord, that take counsel, but not of Me" (Isa. 30. 1). He makes it clear that He is innocent with regard to the doings of the false prophets, saying, "I have not sent these prophets, yet they ran; I have not spoken to them, yet they prophesied" (Jer. 23. 21), and other similar pronouncements.

As to the proofs based on Tradition, our ancient Teachers have told us (b. Ber. 33b), "Everything lies in the hands of God except the fear of God, as it says, 'And now, Israel, what doth the Lord thy God require of thee, but to fear the Lord thy God'" (Deut. 10. 12).

Providence and Free Will

All this explanation brings me to the following question, which will no doubt be asked: "If what you have said is true, viz., that the will of God has no share in the disobedience of those who disobey Him, how is it possible that there should exist in His world anything which does not find His approval, or to which He does not give His consent?" The answer to this is not far to seek. It is this: *we* regard it as strange that a wise man should tolerate within the realm of his power anything which is undesirable from his point of view, and to which he cannot give his consent. This is intelligible in the case of a human being since he dreads those things which cause him harm, but our Lord does not dread disobedience on account of Himself, since it is impossible to assume that any sort of accident should affect Him. He abhors disobedience for our own sakes because it has a harmful effect on us. For if we sin against Him and fail to acknowledge His Truth, we act foolishly, and if we sin against each other, we endanger our lives and positions. Since this is quite clear and manifest, it is not strange that there should exist in His world things which we consider to be strange. When He explains to us that He abhors certain things, He does so for our own sakes in His way of mercy, as He made it clear in Scripture by saying, "'Do they provoke Me?' saith the Lord; 'do they not provoke themselves, to the confusion of their own faces?'" (Jer. 7. 19).

Perhaps, someone will ask further: "If God knows that which is going to be before it comes into being, He knows in advance if a certain person will disobey Him; now that person must by necessity disobey God, for otherwise God's foreknowledge would not prove to be correct." The fallacy underlying this question is even more evident than that underlying the previous one. It is this: He who makes this assertion has no proof that the knowledge of the Creator concerning things is the cause of their existence. He merely imagines this to be so, or chooses to believe it. The fallacy of this assumption becomes quite clear when we consider that, if God's knowledge of things were the cause of their existence, they would have existed from eternity, since God's knowledge of them is eternal. We do, however, believe that God knows things as they exist in reality, i.e., of those things which He creates, He knows in advance that He is going to create them, and of those things which are subject to man's free will He knows in advance that man is going to choose them. Should one object: "If God knows that a certain person will speak, is it possible for that person to be silent?" we answer quite simply that if that person was to keep silent instead of speaking we should have said in our original statement that God knew that this man would be silent, and we were not entitled to state that God knew that this person would speak. For God knows man's ultimate action such as it will be whether sooner or later after all his planning; for God knows man's nature, as is said, "The Lord knoweth the thoughts of man" (Ps. 94. 11), and furthermore, "For I know their inclination how they do even now" (Deut. 31. 21).

II. THE CUSARI

by Judah Halevi

Introduction to *The Cusari*

(The King of the Khazars, a man of piety and of fervent devotion to his religion, having been told in a dream that his intentions were agreeable to God, but not his actions, obtained an interview with a philosopher in order to ascertain his opinions about God, the world, and mankind. The explanations of the philosopher, based as they were upon the eternity of the world, the perfection to be attained by man through philosophic meditation, and the exaltation of God above all individual providence, did not satisfy him; and he decided to seek for further enlightenment from a Christian and a Mohammedan, thinking in himself that one of these two must be right—as for the Jew, it was sufficient to notice in what a depressed condition the Jews were, reduced in numbers and despised by every one. He accordingly called one of the most learned Christians and asked him about the belief and practices of his religion.)

The Christian replied: I believe that all things are created; that God is eternal, and that he created the whole world in six days, and that all men are descended firstly from

Adam, and secondly from Noah, to whom they are accordingly related. God provides for all his creatures, but entertains special relations towards man: with him is wrath, mercy, and favour: he speaks with his prophets and his saints: he appears and reveals himself to them, dwelling amongst those that please him. I believe in general all that is written in the law, and all the traditions of the children of Israel, facts which it is impossible to doubt since they are so fully known, so imperishable, and were so loudly proclaimed before a great multitude. Then (afterwards), however, the Godhead was incarnate, and took flesh in the womb of a virgin, one of the noblest women in Israel, who bore him in semblance human, in mystery divine—in semblance a prophet, in mystery God. This was the Messiah, called the Son of God, and this is the mystery of Father, Son and Holy Ghost, although when we proclaim the Trinity it is really the Unity only which we believe. I believe further that the Messiah dwelt amongst Israel for their glory, so long as they adhered to the idea of the Godhead (manifest in him), but that at last they rebelled against him and crucified him. From that time till now, the wrath of God has continued against the multitude of the rebellious, but (His) grace has been upon every one of those who followed the Messiah, as well as upon the nations which have followed them, and to which we belong. We are not, indeed, descendants of the family of Israel, but we are worthier than they are to bear their name, because we have followed the Messiah, and the twelve apostles who represent the twelve tribes. A great number of Israelites followed the Twelve: these formed the nucleus of the Christian people, and well did they deserve the rank and title of Israel's sons. We have become powerful in different lands: and all nations are invited to attach themselves to this creed, and enjoined to glorify the Messiah and his cross. Our laws and customs are derived partly from the commandments of the Apostle Simon (Peter), partly from the Torah, which we read, and the truth of which is beyond question: for the Gospel itself relates what the Messiah said:—I came not to destroy one tittle of the law of Moses, but to confirm and explain it.

The king replied: To argue on this subject is quite useless: for reason rejects most of what thou hast said. Only when the evidence and proof of a fact is so manifest to all that every man, from utter inability to confute it, is bound to accord belief, can reason come in to explain any part of it which may appear strange. In fact this is the method pursued by scientific men for explaining the wonderful occurrences of nature which, so long as they are simply related without having been seen, they ignore: but after having examined them, they express a definite opinion and try to assign their causes, either in the stars or in the winds, inasmuch as the evidence for them cannot be denied. Moreover, the words are new to me: and as I have not been trained up in them I am disinclined to accept them without a thorough investigation.

The king called next a learned Mohammedan to enquire concerning the belief and practices of Mohammedanism. His answer was as follows: We affirm the unity and eternity of God, the creation of the world, and the descent of the whole human race from Adam and from Noah. We deny in general the corporeality of God, endeavouring to explain any difficulty which may here meet us by saying that the expression which occasions it is only metaphorical or approximately true. We are bound to confess that the Koran is the Word of God: for the Koran is in itself a miracle, inasmuch as no man could compose such a book as it is, or even a single chapter of it, and we are therefore of course compelled to accept it even for its own sake. I believe further that our prophet is the last of the prophets, that he annulled all the laws in existence before him, and that he invites all nations to attach themselves to Islam. The recompense of the obedient will be that in Paradise his soul will return to his body, and that there he will live in the midst of delights, with plenty to eat and to drink, and every other pleasure he may desire: the punishment of the rebellious will be the condemnation to dwell after death in a fire where his pains will never cease.

The King of the Khazars answered: one who undertakes to guide a man in the right way concerning the knowledge of God, and to convince him of what he denies, namely, that God has held intercourse with flesh, can only do so successfully by the help of irrefragable evidences: only thus I repeat, could one who doubts be persuaded that God has held intercourse with flesh. If your book is a miracle because it is written in Arabic, it certainly cannot be regarded as such by a foreigner like myself: if read to me, it makes no other impression upon me than any other book in the same language.

The Mohammedan replied:—Miracles were indeed wrought by the Prophet, but they are not given as areas on for accepting his law.

The Khazar said:—A man can only be led to believe that God entertains relations with flesh through some miracle by which the nature of a thing is changed, and in which he may be enabled to perceive that the change could only have been caused by him who created all things out of nothing: moreover, this change must have been seen by a multitude, and not known merely from traditions and tales: and it must have been submitted to a searching examination, else it might be accounted for by the power of the imaginations or by collusion. These great principles, viz., that God who has created both this world and the next, the angels, the heavens and the light, entertains relations with man, who is a piece of impure clay, that he speaks with him and answers his requests and wishes, might be believed on the evidence of miracles (but in no other way).

The learned Mohammedan answered:—Is not our book filled with narratives respecting Moses and the children of Israel? No one is able to deny what God did unto Pharaoh; how he divided the sea, and saved those whom he loved, but drowned those with whom he was wroth; how he gave them manna and quails by the space of 40 years, and spoke with Moses upon Sinai; how he made the sun stand still for Joshua, and helped him against the giants. Neither, again, is it possible to deny what he did at the time of the deluge, and how he destroyed the people of Lot.[1] All this is sufficiently clear, and there can be no suspicion of the operation of imagination or of collusion.

The King of the Khazars then said:—There can be no longer any doubt that I must enquire of the Jews, who are the remnant of the ancient Israelites: for I see that all the proofs for the existence of God's law upon earth are derived ultimately from them. He accordingly called a learned Jew and quesioned him about the principles of his faith.

The Dangers of Abandoning the Traditional Law

In religious matters follow not your own inclinations lest they lead you into doubts which in turn lead to heresy. Following your own inclinations will also cause you to be out of harmony with all your friends, for every individual

[1] The inhabitants of Sodom and Gomorrah are called by Mohammedan writers "the people of Lot."

has his own inclinations and opinions on any given problem. One should only investigate the sources of the traditional and written laws . . . in order to be enabled to trace them to their sources. Where these laws lead you, there put your faith, though your mind and heart shrink from it.

That personal inclinations are misleading may be proven from the fact that men are inclined to deny the non-existence of a vacuum, while logic rejects its existence. Similarly, appearance denies the infinite divisibility of a body, while logic makes it an axiom. Appearance denies that the earth is a globe . . . while astronomy establishes it. It is for these reasons that whatever our Sages decreed, they did not base on personal inclinations, but on inherited knowledge, handed down to them . . . and any one who, because of his inability to grasp their wisdom, proceeds to judge them on the basis of his own conception is bound to misunderstand them, just as people often misunderstand the words of natural philosophers and astronomers.

The Jewish Attitude to Asceticism

According to our view a servant of God is not one who detaches himself from the world, lest he be a burden to it, and it to him; or hates life, which is one of God's bounties granted to him . . . On the contrary, he loves the world and a long life, because it affords him opportunities of deserving the world to come. The more good he does the greater is his claim to the next world.

The divine law imposes no asceticism on us. It rather desires that we should keep the middle path, and grant every mental and physical faculty its due, as much as it can bear, without overburdening one faculty at the expense of another . . . Prolonged fasting is no act of piety for a weak person who, having succeeded in checking his desires, is not greedy. For him feasting is a burden and self-denial. Neither is diminution of wealth an act of piety, if it is gained in a lawful way, and if its acquisition does not interfere with study and good works.

The Pious Man, a Prince Over His Passions

The pious man is nothing but a prince who is obeyed by his senses, and by his mental as well as his physical faculties, which he governs . . . He is fit to rule, because if he were the prince of a country he would be as just as he is to his body and soul. He subdues his passions, keeping them in bonds, and at the same time giving them their share in order to satisfy them as regards food, drink, cleanliness, etc. . . If he, then, has satisfied each of them (giving to the vital organs the necessary amount of rest and sleep, and to the physical ones waking, movements, and worldly occupation), he calls upon his community as a respected prince calls his disciplined army, to assist him in reaching the divine degree.

The Voluntary Aspect of Jewish Suffering

The Rabbi: I see thee reproaching us with our degradation and poverty, but the best of other religions boast of both. Do they not glorify him who said: He who smites thee on the right cheek, turn to him the left also; and he who takes away thy coat, let him have thy shirt also. He and his friends and followers, after hundreds of years of contumely, flogging and slaying, attained their well-known success, and just in these things they glory. This is also the history of the founder of Islam and his friends, who eventually prevailed, and became powerful. The nations boast of these, but not of these kings whose power and might are great, whose walls are strong, and whose chariots are terrible. Yet our relation to God is a closer one than if we had reached greatness already on earth.

Al Khazari: This might be so, if your humility were voluntary; but it is involuntary, and if you had power you would slay.

The Rabbi: . . . Yet the majority may expect a reward, because they bear their degradation partly of their own free will. For whoever wishes to do so can become the friend and equal of his oppressor by uttering one word,[1] and without any difficulty. Such conduct does not escape the just Judge. If we bear our exile and degradation for God's sake, as is meet, we shall be the pride of the generation which will come with the Messiah.

Israel amidst the nations is like the heart amidst the organs of the body.

Why the Bible Speaks of God in Human Terms

We see that the human soul shows fear whenever it meets with anything terrible, but not at the mere report of such a thing. It is likewise attracted by a beautiful form which strikes the eye, but not so much by one that is only spoken of. Do not believe him who considers himself wise in thinking that he is so far advanced that he is able to grasp all metaphysical problems with the abstract intellect alone, without the support of anything that can be conceived or

[1] Agreeing to be baptized.

seen, such as words, writing, or any visible or imaginary forms. Seest thou not that thou art not able even to collect the burden of thy prayer in thought alone, without reciting it? . . In this way, prophets' images picture God's greatness, power, loving-kindness, omniscience, life, eternity, government, and independence, the dependence of everything on Him, His unity, and holiness, and in one sudden flash stands revealed this grand and majestic figure with its splendour, its characteristics, the instruments which typify power, etc., the uplifted hand, the unsheathed sword, fire, wind, thunder and lightning which obey his behest, the word which goes forth to warn, to announce what has happened, and to predict. . . .

III. THE GUIDE FOR THE PERPLEXED
by Moses Maimonides

Object of the Treatise
(A Selection From the Author's Introduction)

The object of this treatise is to enlighten a religious man who has been trained to believe in the truth of our holy law, who conscientiously fulfils his moral and religious duties, and at the same time has been successful in his philosophical studies. Human reason has attracted him to abide within its sphere; and he finds it difficult to accept as correct the teaching based on the literal interpretation of the Law . . . Hence he is lost in perplexity and anxiety. If he be guided solely by reason, and renounce his previous views which are based on those expressions, he would consider that he had rejected the fundamental principles of the Law; and even if he retains the opinions which were derived from those expressions, and if, instead of following his reason, he abandon its guidance altogether, it would still appear that his religious convictions had suffered loss and injury. For he would then be left with those errors which give rise to fear and anxiety, constant grief and great perplexity . . .

The "Image of God"

Some have been of the opinion that by the Hebrew *zelem* (image), the shape and figure of a thing is to be understood, and this explanation led men to believe in the corporeality (of the Divine Being); for they thought that the words "Let us make man in our *zelem*" (Gen. I, 26), implied that God had the form of a human being, i. e., that He had figure and shape, and that, consequently, He was corporeal. They adhered faithfully to this view, and thought that if they were to relinquish it they would *eo ipso* reject the truth of the Bible: and further, if they did not conceive God as having a body possessed of face and limbs, similar to their own in appearance, they would have to deny even the existence of God. The sole difference which they admitted, was that He excelled in greatness and splendour, and that His substance was not flesh and blood. Thus far went their conception of the greatness and glory of God. . .

As man's distinction consists in a property which no other creature on earth possesses, viz., intellectual perception, . . . it has been compared . . . to the Divine excellency . . . On this account, i.e., on account of the Divine intellect with which man has been endowed, he is said to have been made in the form and likeness of the Almighty, but far from it be the notion that the Supreme Being is corporeal, having a material form.

Creatio ex Nihilo [1]

As to the proofs of Aristotle and his followers for the Eternity of the Universe, they are, according to my opinion,

[1] Maimonides' full exposition of the principle of *Creatio ex Nihilo* is too technical to be of interest to the average reader. This excerpt, however, is quoted to show Maimonides' unbiased and objective method of approach.

not conclusive; they are open to strong objections, as will be explained. I intend to show that the theory of the Creation, as taught in Scripture, contains nothing that is impossible; and that all those philosophical arguments which seem to disprove our view contain weak points which make them inconclusive, and render the attacks on our view untenable. Since I am convinced of the correctness of my method, and consider either of the two theories—viz., the Eternity of the Universe, and the Creation—as admissible, I accept the latter on the authority of Prophecy, which can teach things beyond the reach of philosophical speculation . . . When I have established the admissibility of our theory, I will, by philosophical reasoning, show that our theory of the Creation is more acceptable than that of the Eternity of the Universe; and although our theory includes points open to criticism, I will show that there are much stronger reasons for the rejection of the theory of our opponents. . . .

The Prerequisites of Prophecy

Every man possesses a certain amount of courage, otherwise he would not stir to remove anything that might injure him. This psychical force seems to me analogous to the physical force of repulsion. Energy varies like all other forces, being great in one case and small in another. There are, therefore, people who attack a lion, whilst others run away at the sight of a mouse. One attacks a whole army and fights, another is frightened and terrified by the threat of a woman. . .

The same is the case with the intuitive faculty; all possess it, but in different degrees. Man's intuitive power is especially strong in things which he has well comprehended, and in which his mind is much engaged. Thus you may yourself guess correctly that a certain person said or did a certain thing in a certain matter. Some persons are so strong and sound in their imagination and intuitive faculty that, when they assume a thing to be in existence, the reality either entirely or partly confirms their assumption. Although the causes of this assumption are numerous, and include many preceding, succeeding, and present circumstances, by means of the intuitive faculty the intellect can pass over all these causes, and draw inferences from them very quickly, almost instantaneously. This same faculty enables some persons to foretell important coming events. The prophets must have had these two forces, courage and intuition, highly developed, and these were still more strengthened when they were under the influence of the Active Intellect. Their courage was so great that, e.g., Moses, with only a staff in his hand, dared to address a great king in his desire to deliver a nation from his service. He was not frightened or terrified, because he had been told, "I will be with thee" (Exod. III, 12). The prophets have not all the same degree of courage, but none of them have been entirely without it. Thus Jeremiah is told: "Be not afraid of them", etc. (Jer. I, 8), and Ezekiel is exhorted, "Do not fear them or their word" (Ezek. II, 6). In the same manner, you find that all prophets possessed great courage. . .

The true prophets undoubtedly conceive ideas that result from premisses which human reason could not comprehend by itself; thus they tell things which men could not tell by reason and ordinary imagination alone; for (the action of the prophets' mental capacities is influenced by) the same agent that causes the perfection of the imaginative faculty, and that enables the prophet thereby to foretell a future event with such clearness as if it was a thing already perceived with the senses, and only through them conveyed to his imagination. This agent perfects the prophet's mind, and influences it in such a manner that he conceives ideas which are confirmed by reality, and are so clear to him as if he deduced them by means of syllogisms.

This should be the belief of all who choose to accept the truth. . .

The Meaning of "God Commanded," "God Sent," etc.

It is clear that everything produced must have an immediate cause which produced it; that cause again a cause, and so on, till the First Cause, viz., the will and decree of God is reached. The prophets therefore omit sometimes the intermediate causes, and ascribe the production of an individual thing directly to God, saying that God has made it. This method is well known; . . . it is the belief of our co-religionists.

After having heard this remark, listen to what I will explain in this chapter; direct your special attention to it more than you have done to the other chapters of this part. It is this: As regards the immediate causes of things produced, it makes no difference whether these causes consist in substances, physical properties, freewill, or chance—by freewill I mean that of man—or even in the will of another living being. The prophets (omit them and) ascribe the production directly to God and use such phrases as, God has done it, commanded it, or said it; in all such cases the verbs "to say," "to speak," "to command," "to call," and "to send" are employed. What I desired to state in this chapter is this: According to the hypothesis and theory accepted, it is God that gave will to dumb animals, freewill to the human being, and natural properties to everything; . . . it can consequently be said of everything which is produced by any of these causes, that God commanded that it should be made, or said that it should be so . . . Note this, and apply it everywhere according to the context. Many difficulties will thereby be removed, and passages apparently containing things far from truth will prove to be true.

The Sources of Evil

Men frequently think that the evils in the world are more numerous than the good things; many sayings and songs of the nations dwell on this idea. They say that a good thing is found only exceptionally, whilst evil things are numerous and lasting. Not only common people make this mistake, but even many who believe that they are wise. Al-Razi[1] wrote a well-known book "On Metaphysics" (or Theology). Among other mad and foolish things, it contains also the idea, discovered by him, that there exists more evil than good. For if the happiness of man and his pleasure in the times of prosperity be compared with the mishaps that befall him,—such as grief, acute pain, defects, paralysis of the limbs, fears, anxieties, and troubles,—it would seem as if the existence of man is a punishment and a great evil for him. This author commenced to verify his opinion by counting all the evils one by one; by this means he opposed those who hold the correct view of the benefits bestowed by God and His evident kindness, viz., that God is perfect goodness, and that all that comes from Him is absolutely good. The origin of the error is to be found in the circumstance that this ignorant man, and his party among the common people, judge the whole universe by

[1] A famous physician of the 10th century, the author of some metaphysical treatises.

examining one single person. For an ignorant man believes that the whole universe only exists for him; as if nothing else required any consideration. If, therefore, anything happens to him contrary to his expectation, he at once concludes that the whole universe is evil. If, however, he would take into consideration the whole universe, form an idea of it, and comprehend what a small portion he is of the Universe, he will find the truth. For it is clear that persons who have fallen into this widespread error as regards the multitude of evils in the world, do not find the evils among the angels, the spheres and stars, the elements, and that which is formed of them, viz., minerals and plants, or in the various species of living beings, but only in some individual instances of mankind. They wonder that a person, who became leprous in consequence of bad food, should be afflicted with so great an illness and suffer such a misfortune; or that he who indulges so much in sensuality as to weaken his sight, should be struck with blindness! and the like. What we have, in truth, to consider is this:— The whole mankind at present in existence, . . . forms an infinitesimal portion of the permanent universe. . . Man's existence is nevertheless a great boon to him, and his distinction and perfection is a divine gift. The numerous evils to which individual persons are exposed are due to the defects existing in the persons themselves. We complain and seek relief from our own faults: we suffer from the evils which we, by our own free will, inflict on ourselves and ascribe them to God, who is far from being connected with them! . . .

I explain this theory in the following manner. The evils that befall man are of three kinds:—

(1) The first kind of evil is that which is caused to man by the circumstance that he is subject to genesis and destruction, or that he possesses a body. It is on account of the

body that some persons happen to have great deformities or paralysis of some of the organs. This evil may be part of the natural constitution of these persons, or may have developed subsequently in consequence of changes in the elements, e.g., through bad air, or thunderstorms, or landslips. We have already shown that, in accordance with the divine wisdom, genesis can only take place through destruction, and without the destruction of the individual members of the species the species themselves would not exist permanently. Thus the true kindness, and beneficence, and goodness of God is clear. He who thinks that he can have flesh and bones without being subject to any external influence, or any of the accidents of matter, unconsciously wishes to reconcile two opposites, viz., to be at the same time subject and not subject to change. If man were never subject to change there could be no generation; there would be one single being, but no individuals forming a species. . . You will, nevertheless, find that the evils of the above kind which befall man are very few and rare; for you find countries that have not been flooded or burned for thousands of years; there are thousands of men in perfect health, deformed individuals are a strange and exceptional occurrence, or say few in number if you object to the term exceptional,— they are not one-hundredth, not even one-thousandth part of those that are perfectly normal.

(2) The second class of evils comprises such evils as people cause to each other, when, e.g., some of them use their strength against others. These evils are more numerous than those of the first kind; their causes are numerous and known; they likewise originate in ourselves, though the sufferer himself cannot avert them. This kind of evil is nevertheless not widespread in any country of the whole world. It is of rare occurrence that a man plans to kill his neighbour or to rob him of his property by night. Many

persons are, however, afflicted with this kind of evil in great wars; but these are not frequent, if the whole inhabited part of the earth is taken into consideration.

(3) The third class of evils comprises those which every one causes to himself by his own action. This is the largest class, and is far more numerous than the second class. It is especially of these evils that all men complain,—only few men are found that do not sin against themselves by this kind of evil. . . This class of evils originates in man's vices, such as excessive desire for eating, drinking, and love; indulgence in these things in undue measure, or in improper manner, or partaking of bad food. This course brings diseases and afflictions upon body and soul alike. The sufferings of the body in consequence of these evils are well known; those of the soul are two-fold:—First, such evils of the soul as are the necessary consequence of changes in the body, in so far as the soul is a force residing in the body; it has therefore been said that the properties of the soul depend on the condition of the body. Secondly, the soul, when accustomed to superfluous things, acquires a strong habit of desiring things which are neither necessary for the preservation of the individual nor for that of the species. This desire is without a limit, whilst things which are necessary are few in number and restricted within certain limits; but what is superfluous is without end—e.g., you desire to have your vessels of silver, but golden vessels are still better: others have even vessels of sapphire, or perhaps they can be made of emerald or rubies, or any other substance that could be suggested. Those who are ignorant and perverse in their thought are constantly in trouble and pain, because they cannot get as much of superfluous things as a certain other person possesses. They as a rule expose themselves to great dangers, e.g., by sea-voyage, or service of kings, and all this for the purpose of obtaining

that which is superfluous and not necessary. When they thus meet with the consequences of the course which they adopt, they complain of the decrees and judgments of God; they begin to blame the time, and wonder at the want of justice in its changes; that it has not enabled them to acquire great riches, with which they could buy large quantities of wine for the purpose of making themselves drunk, and numerous concubines adorned with various kinds of ornaments of gold, embroidery, and jewels, for the purpose of driving themselves to voluptuousness beyond their capacities, as if the whole universe existed exclusively for the purpose of giving pleasure to these low people. . .

The virtuous and wise, however, see and comprehend the wisdom of God displayed in the Universe. Thus David says, "All the paths of the Lord are mercy and truth unto such as keep His covenant and His testimonies" (Ps. xxv, 10). For those who observe the nature of the Universe and the commandments of the Law, and know their purpose, see clearly God's mercy and truth in everything; they seek, therefore, that which the Creator intended to be the aim of man, viz., comprehension. Forced by the claims of the body, they seek also that which is necessary for the preservation of the body, "bread to eat and garment to clothe," and this is very little. . .

Observe how Nature proves the correctness of this assertion. The more necessary a thing is for living beings, the more easily it is found and the cheaper it is; the less necessary it is, the rarer and dearer it is. E.g., air, water, and food are indispensable to man: air is most necessary, for if man is without air a short time he dies; whilst he can be without water a day or two. Air is also undoubtedly found more easily and cheaper (than water). Water is more necessary than food; for some people can be four or five days without food, provided they have water; water also exists in every country in larger quantities than food, and is also cheaper. The same proportion can be noticed in the different kinds of food; that which is more necessary in a certain place exists there in larger quantities and is cheaper than that which is less necessary. No intelligent person, I think, considers musk, amber, rubies, and emerald as very necessary for man. . . This shows the kindness of God to His creatures, even to us weak beings. . . It is no wrong or injustice that one has many bags of finest myrrh and garments embroidered with gold, while another has not those things, which are not necessary for our maintenance; he who has them has not thereby obtained control over anything that could be an essential addition to his nature, but has only obtained something illusory or deceptive. The other, who does not possess that which is not wanted for his maintenance, does not miss anything indispensable: "He that gathered much had nothing over, and he that gathered little had no lack: they gathered every man according to his eating" (Exod. XVI, 18). This is the rule at all times and in all places; no notice should be taken of exceptional cases, as we have explained. . .

In accordance with this correct reflection the chief of the wise men[1] says, "All his ways are judgment" (Deut. XXXII, 4). . .

The Efficacy of Prayer

Even if the Universe existed for man's sake and man existed for the purpose of serving God, . . . the question remains, What is the end of serving God? He does not become more perfect if all His creatures serve Him and

[1] Moses.

comprehend Him as far as possible; nor would he lose anything if nothing existed beside Him. It might perhaps be replied that the service of God is not intended for God's perfection; it is intended for our own perfection,—it is good for us, it makes us perfect. . .

The Origin and Purpose of the Sacrificial Cult

Now God sent Moses to make (the Israelites) a kingdom of priests and a holy nation (Exod. XIX, 6) by means of the knowledge of God. . . But the custom which was in those days general among all men, and the general mode of worship in which the Israelites were brought up, consisted in sacrificing animals in those temples which contained certain images, to bow down to those images, and to burn incense before them. . . It was in accordance with the wisdom and plan of God, as displayed in the whole Creation, that He did not command us to give up and to discontinue all these manners of service; for to obey such a commandment it would have been contrary to the nature of man, who generally cleaves to that to which he is used; it would in those days have made the same impression as a prophet would make at present if he called us to the service of God and told us in His name, that we should not pray to Him, not fast, not seek His help in time of trouble; that we should serve Him in thought, and not by any action. For this reason God allowed these kinds of service to continue; He transferred to His service that which had formerly served as a worship of created beings, and of things imaginary and unreal, and commanded us to serve Him in the same manner; viz., to build unto Him a temple; . . . to have the altar erected to His name; . . . to offer the sacrifices to Him; . . . to bow down to Him and to burn incense before

Him. . . By this Divine plan it was effected that the traces of idolatry were blotted out, and the truly great principle of our faith, the Existence and Unity of God, was firmly established; this result was thus obtained without deterring or confusing the minds of the people by the abolition of the service to which they were accustomed and which alone was familiar to them. . . .

Regarding the Details of the Sacrificial Cult

The law that sacrifices should be brought is evidently of great use; . . . but we cannot say why one offering should be a lamb, whilst another is a ram; and why a fixed number of them should be brought. Those who trouble themselves to find a cause for any of these detailed rules, are in my eyes void of sense; they do not remove any difficulties, but rather increase them. Those who believe that these detailed rules originate in a certain cause, are as far from the truth as those who assume that the whole law is useless. . .

The Origins of Some Biblical Prohibitions

We have explained in our large work [1] that it is prohibited to round the corners of the head, and to mar the corners of the beard, because it was the custom of idolatrous priests. For the same reason, the wearing of garments made of linen and wool is prohibited; the heathen priests adorned themselves with garments containing vegetable and animal material, whilst they held in their hand a seal made of a mineral. This you find written in their books.

[1] The Mishneh Torah—the famous code of Maimonides.

The same is also the reason of the precept, "The woman shall not wear that which pertaineth unto a man" (Deut. xxii, 5). You find it in the book Tomtom,[1] that a male person should wear coloured woman's dress when he stands before Venus, and a female, when standing before Mars, should wear a buckler and other armour. I think that this precept has also another reason; namely that the interchange of dress creates lust and leads to immorality.

[1] An Indian author of several works on magic.

IV THE BOOK OF PRINCIPLES
by Joseph Albo

The Three Basic Principles of the Divine Law

The principles of divine laws in general are three: existence of God, divine revelation, and reward and punishment. There is no doubt that these three are essential principles of divine law *qua* divine. For if we assume the removal of one of them the law will fall entirely. This is obvious from the nature of the principles. Thus if we do not believe in the existence of God who commands the law, there is no divine law. And if we do believe in the existence of God, and do not believe in divine revelation, there is no divine law. And if there is no corporeal reward and punishment in this world and spiritual in the next, what need is there of a divine law? If it is in order to maintain a proper order in human affairs and relations so as to have a perfect political society, the conventional law is sufficient for this purpose. It is clear therefore that if there is a divine law, it is for the purpose of leading mankind to such perfection as a human code cannot attain to, viz., human perfection which depends upon perfection of the soul, as will appear later. It is clear therefore that spiritual reward and punishment is a fundamental principle of divine law without doubt. And the corporeal reward which the righteous man obtains from God in this world for his observance of the commandments is a proof of the future spiritual reward. It follows, then, that reward and punishment in general is a necessary principle of divine law.

Man, the Noblest and Most Perfect of All Creatures

We must not say that the animal species are more perfect in their organization than man because they require no shade or shelter from the heat and the storm, nor preparation of the food they need, which nature provides ready for their use. Moreover they have certain instincts, like the beasts and birds of prey, which they use in hunting their prey to sustain life. Among the ancients there was one who maintained this very thing. He said that man is an inferior creation in comparison with the other animals. For the latter do not need other animals to ride on, in order to go from place to place, being more swift of movement than man. Similarly they do not have to prepare weapons with which to fight against their enemies, for they are provided with natural weapons, the ox has horns, the boar has tusks, the porcupine has quills, the turtle has a shell, and so on. Nor do they need to make themselves any garments, for their garments too are given them by nature, and they do not have to prepare their food, for they use it as found in nature; whereas man is devoid of all these things. . .

But on reflection we shall find this idea quite erroneous. If we consider the various forms . . . we find that they form an ascending series in regard to quality. The later form is superior to the prior one, as though matter in receiving forms proceeds from imperfection to perfection, first receiving a lower form and then a higher form, and thus gradually ascending from an inferior grade of existence to a more perfect one. Thus matter first receives the forms of the elements, then it rises to the stage of minerals, . . . then it attains to the grade of plants, . . . then it ascends to the degree of animals, . . . and then it rises to the grade of man. . . Here the process comes to an end. . . And as a given motion ends up with a result which is the final cause of all the partial motions, so the genetic process rises gradually until it attains finally to the human form, where it stops, because this is the end of all the lower genetic processes.

That matter always moves from a less perfect to a more perfect form of existence, as the character of the composition rises in quality, is proved by the coral, which is intermediate so to speak, between mineral and plant; by the marine sponge which has only the sense of touch, and is intermediate as it were between plant and animal; and by the ape, which stands midway between the animal species and man where the process stops. It follows necessarily, therefore that man, who is the end of all the lower creatures, is nobler and more perfect than all, since in him are combined all the earlier forms. . . Therefore he is greater than all the others, and subdues all the animals and rules them, because he has the power of comprehending the general, whereas the lower animals perceive only the particular, having no power to comprehend the universal . . .

The Grades of Prophecy

All the words of the prophets are true without doubt Nevertheless there is a difference in degree. The greater the dignity of the prophet and the higher the degree of his prophetic inspiration, the greater the truth value of his words. Some prophets, by reason of their weakness o comprehension, do not apprehend things with sufficient clearness. Prophetic apprehension has certain similarities to sensible apprehension. If a sense faculty or organ is healthy and strong, it apprehends the objects clearly; whereas if it is weak, it does not apprehend them clearly. It may apprehend the species to which the object belongs, or it may apprehend the genus only without being able to tell to what species it belongs. Thus a person who has powerful vision apprehends color correctly, as, for example, red or green. But he also apprehends the degree of redness or greenness. On the other hand a person with weak vision will apprehend the genus only, i.e., he will know it is a color, and no more. Or he may know the species too; that it is red or green, but will not know what degree of redness or greenness it is. The same thing is true in hearing and other sensibilia.

The same thing applies to the prophetic apprehension. The prophet who has a strong power of apprehension perceives the thing as it is without imagination and his words come out clear and not obscure; hence they may be understood in their literal meaning. On the other hand, a prophet who is inferior in degree to the one mentioned, will express himself in obscure language, in riddles and parables which are not clear. Hence the truth is not in the literal meaning, but in the allusion. If his words are taken literally, one gets an idea different from the one intended. Thus Ezekiel, prophesying after the exile, speaks in parables and riddles, which can not be understood literally; so much so that he complains about this to God, "They say of me: Is he not a maker of parables?" (Ezek. XXI, 5). Similarly Zechariah, coming toward the end of the prophetic period, experienced his prophetic inspiration in visions, the truth of which lay not in the vision itself as it appeared, but in the ideas which it suggested. Thus when he says that he saw horses and women and a golden candelabrum and two olives upon it, the candelabrum and the olives are not to be taken as real things, but only as alluding to a certain idea.

Jeremiah, on the other hand, who lived before the destruction of the temple, spoke always plainly and clearly. God Himself made clear the difference between Moses' prophecy and that of the others. In relation to the prophecy of Moses He says, "With him do I speak mouth to mouth, even manifestly and not in dark speeches" (Num. XII, 8). From this we infer that the other prophets spoke in dark speeches which were not clear, and saw visions which were not real. For this reason their prophetic messages must be interpreted so as to agree with the words of Moses. . .

From all this it is clear that an inferior prophet must not oppose the words of a prophet who is superior to him, but that his words must be so interpreted that they should not conflict with the words of the superior. Now since it is clearly stated in the Torah that the prophecy of Moses stands on a higher plane than that of any other prophet, it follows that we can not accept the words of any other prophet in opposition to and refutation of the words of Moses. . .

The Efficacy of Prayer

The reason which leads men to doubt the efficacy of prayer is the same as that which leads them to deny God's knowledge. Their argument is as follows: Either God has determined that a given person shall receive a given benefit, or He has not so determined. If He has determined, there is no need of prayer; and if He has not determined, how can prayer avail to change God's will that He should now determine to benefit the person, when He had not so determined before? For God does not change from a state of willing to a state of not willing, or vice versa. For this reason they say that right conduct is of no avail for receiving a good from God. And similarly they say that prayer does not avail to enable one to receive a benefit, or to be saved from an evil which has been decreed against him. . . .

But this opinion is not true, for the influences from above come down upon the recipient when he is in a certain degree and state of preparation to receive them. And if a person does not prepare himself, he withholds the good from himself. For example, if it has been determined from on high that a given person's crops shall prosper in a given year, and he neglects to plow or sow his land that year, then God may bring the most abundant rain upon the land, but his crops will not prosper, seeing that he has not plowed or sowed. He withheld the good from himself because he did not prepare himself to receive it.

Our idea therefore is that when a benefit is determined in favor of any one, it is conditional upon a certain degree of right conduct. This must be taken to be a general principle as regards the promises in the Bible. In the same way when a certain evil is determined upon some one, it is also conditional upon his being wicked in a certain degree or of being predisposed to it. And if the degree of wickedness or predisposition thereto changes, the pre-determined event or fate changes also necessarily for the better or the worse. .

In this way repentance benefits a wicked man, for through repentance he becomes another person, as it were, concerning whom no such decree was made. . . .

In this way it is clear that prayer and right conduct help to prepare the person to receive the good influence or to nullify the evil that has been decreed concerning him, because he changes from the evil state in which he was. . .

As for the objection that the divine will can not be changed by prayer, the answer is that the divine will in the first place is that the decree should be realized if the person in question continues in the same state, and that the decree should be changed if the person's state changes.

The Success of Christian Nations Not a Proof of the Validity of Christianity

The proof they bring from the prosperity of those who believe in their faith is no proof at all. For more than two thousand years before the law of Moses was given, all the nations worshipped idols, except a few rare persons, like the patriarchs and the like, and yet every one of the nations prospered in its own government and lived in quiet and tranquillity. And after the law was given, too, all the nations worshipped idols except Israel, and yet they were all prosperous in their own states. Surely the fact that Sennacherib and Nebuchadnezzar and Alexander were successful in ruling over Israel is no sign that their faith was better than that of Israel. Even now the Christians maintain that the law of the Mohammedans is positive and conventional, not divine, and yet they are successful and rule over a great part of the world. It seems clear therefore that the prosperity of a nation is no proof of the truth of its faith. . .

The Contradictions and Errors of the New Testament

It is especially difficult for the Jew to believe in the things stated in the law of Jesus when he considers that the fact which they lay down as the basis of their belief, namely, that Jesus was Messiah the son of David, is uncertain. For chapter one of the Gospel of Matthew traces the ancestry of Joseph, the husband of Miriam, or as they say, her betrothed, to Solomon and David, and says that he was of royal descent, whereas in the third chapter of the Gospel of Luke it is said that he was not of royal descent and was descended from Nathan the son of David. Both of these genealogies concern Joseph alone. For they say that Joseph never knew Miriam either before the birth of Jesus or after. This despite the fact that in the Gospel of Matthew (I, 25), the statement is made that Joseph did not know Miriam until Jesus was born, which would indicate that afterwards he did. We also find in the same Gospel that Jesus had brothers, which would lead to the same result. They explain, however, that brothers means relatives. The statement, too, that Joseph did not know Miriam until she gave birth to Jesus they explain like the verse, "For I will not leave thee, until I have done that which I have spoken to thee of" (Gen. XXVIII, 15), and as we explain the passage, "The sceptre shall not depart from Judah, nor the ruler's staff from between his feet, until he comes to Shiloh and unto him shall the obedience of the peoples be" (Gen. XLIX, 10), the meaning of which is that afterwards too the sceptre shall not depart. If this is so, Joseph's descent does not benefit Jesus at all, and how do we know the genealogy of Miriam?

Moreover, how can a Jew who is familiar with the Bible and sees that the biblical passages cited in the Gospels and in their other books as evidence do not prove the thing intended at all—how can such a person bring himself to believe in their ideas? Thus it says in Matthew (I, 22) that Jesus was born of a virgin to fulfil the words of the Bible, "Behold the young woman shall conceive." (Is. VII, 14). But every one who can read knows—even a child in school is aware— that this verse was said to Ahaz about six hundred years before the birth of Jesus as a sign that the kingdoms of Syria and Israel would be destroyed, and that the kingdom of Judah would remain under the kings of the house of David. How could Jesus' birth of a virgin be a sign to Ahaz?

In the second chapter of Matthew it says that Herod killed all the young males, whom it calls innocent, to fulfil the verse of the Bible, "Rachel weeping for her children" (Jer. XXXI, 15). But it is obvious from the context that the expression refers to the exile at the time of the first temple, for we read in the same place, "And they shall come back from the land of the enemy;" "And thy children shall return to their own border;" "I have surely heard Ephraim bemoaning himself . . . turn thou me, and I shall be turned" (Jer. XXXI, 16-18). There are other verses quoted in the Gospels and interpreted erroneously. All this prevents one believing that the law of Jesus is divine. One is rather inclined to believe that it is a conventional law laid down by persons who were not familiar with the Bible, and did not understand the meaning of the text. . .

Why the New Testament Cannot Supersede the Torah

The real and extraordinary wonder is that any one should say that the laws of the Torah of Moses, which is divine, are defective, and are completed by the law of Jesus. The law of Jesus has no civil laws governing human relations. The Christians follow in their civil life the rules of their learned men by order of the emperor or of the Pope. How is it possible that rules which are laid down by learned men on the basis of human opinion, should supply the defect of the rules in the law of Moses, which is divine? . . .

A still more important consideration is that a person should correct only that which he knows. But the Apostles, as it seems, were not familiar with the law of Moses. For we find in the seventh chapter of the Acts of the Apostles that according to Stephen, Joseph brought his father Jacob to Egypt with seventy-five souls. Then Jacob and his ancestors died and were buried in Shechem in the cave which Abraham bought with silver from the sons of Hamor, son of Shechem, all of which is different from the explicit account of the Torah. In the book of Genesis (XLVI, 8-27), . . . all the persons are enumerated by name who came to Egypt with Jacob. And together with Joseph and his sons, there are not more than seventy. And we have an explicit statement, "The fathers went down into Egypt with three score and ten persons (Deut. X, 22). The cave which Abraham bought was in Hebron and not in Shechem, and he did not buy it from the sons of Hamor, son of Shechem, but from Ephron the Hittite, as is explicitly stated (Gen. XXIII). Moreover, in the thirteenth chapter, Paul says that the Israelites asked Samuel for a King and he gave them the son of Kish, a Benjaminite, who reigned forty years. This contradicts the text (I Sam. XIII), according to which he reigned only three or four years. They can not answer these criticisms by saying that the Jews falsified the text, for the point does not affect religious belief. It seems therefore that they were not familiar with the words of the Torah and the Prophets.

But even if we suppose that, as they say, the Apostles had the authority to change the civil laws, who gave authority to the Pope to change the commandment of the Sabbath, which is not one of the civil laws? . . . No man can abolish it, especially since it is one of the ten commandments. Jesus and all his disciples observed the Sabbath, and it was only about five hundred years after Jesus that the Pope changed it and substituted Sunday for the Sabbath. This despite the fact . . . that the Sabbath is one of the ten commandments, which they admit to be free from defect. But it seems that their purpose was to destroy the law of

Moses on their own account without any reason or argument, for neither Jesus nor his disciples gave any such command. . . .

The charge of imperfection . . . on the ground that the Law of Moses prescribes only correct action, but not a pure heart, is the opposite of the truth. For do we not read, "Circumcise therefore the foreskin of your heart:" [1] "And thou shalt love the Lord thy God with all thy heart." "And thou shalt love thy neighbour as thyself;" "But thou shalt fear thy God;" "Thou shalt not take vengeance, nor bear any grudge against the children of thy people"? The reason it commands right action is because purity of heart is of no account unless practice is in agreement with it. The important thing, however, is intention. David says, "Create me a clean heart, O God." And there are many other passages of the same kind, more than we can enumerate here. . .

[1] The Biblical passages in this paragraph are, in the order of their quotation, from Deut. X, 16; VI, 5, Lev. XIX, 18; XIX, 14; XIX, 18, Ps. LI, 12; XIX, 8.

Chapter IV

ETHICAL LITERATURE

THE oft-repeated claim of many Christian theologians that Judaism is "legalistic," that it emphasizes the observance of the letter rather than the spirit of the law, has had far-reaching effects on the Jew. Sensitive as he is to public opinion and subject as he naturally is to the psychological effects of "suggestion," the Jew has subconsciously come to believe in the inferiority of Judaism. However, were he to examine, even casually, his ethical literature produced in the course of the centuries, he would discover that it abounds in the noblest sentiments and most humane precepts. This is particularly true of the vast ethical literature of the Middle Ages.

One of the most popular and most authoritative expositions of spiritual Judaism is the *Duties of the Heart* by Bachya Ibn Pakuda. This ethical treatise is a characteristic Spanish Jewish creation in that it combines "the ethical science of the West with the emotional and spiritual morality of the East."[1] The book is divided into ten sections, or "gates," wherein the author treats of all phases of man's life. Since he felt that man's ethical conduct depends largely on his convictions about God, he devoted the first "gate," entitled *The Gate of the Unity of God*, to a philosophical discussion of the nature of the deity. The other nine "gates," however, are of a purely ethical nature. They

[1] Collins, Edwin, *The Duties of the Heart by Rabbi Bachya*, p. 5, E. P. Dutton and Co., New York, 1909.

deal with such subjects as worship, trust in God, sincerity of purpose, humility, repentance, love of God, etc. The central theme of this logical and systematic book, as may be inferred from its title and from the titles of the ten "gates," is "that nothing is of so much importance as that our conduct be ruled entirely by most serious religious convictions and godlike holiness of purpose.[1]

The other ethical treatises which have enjoyed great popularity and have attained classic importance are the *Book of the Pious*, attributed to Judah He-Hasid of Regensburg, and the *Rokeach*, written by Eleazar ben Judah of Worms. These treatises, too, reflect the time and place of their authorship, for alongside of the noblest ethical teachings are to be found the rankest superstitious beliefs, a paradox characteristic of mediaeval German Jewish life. Moreover, these books lack system and intellectual profundity, but they more than make up for their philosophical superficiality by their singular moral depth. They teach meekness and humility, piety and devotion, loving-kindness and mercy. The Jew's life, according to these pious teachers, is to be a continuous process of sanctifying God's name, and, should circumstances demand it, even life itself is to be given for this noble purpose. Reading this mediaeval German Jewish literature, one begins to understand how it was possible for whole communities of mediaeval German Jewry to give their lives so courageously for their religious convictions. These ethical works have won the admiration of all who have read them, and because of their genuine piety and inspiring saintliness, will undoubtedly continue to arouse the enthusiasm of all readers for a long time to come.

[1] Graetz, H., *History of the Jews*, Vol. III, p. 271, The Jewish Publication Society of America, Philadelphia, 1894.

Another branch of ethical literature which is uniquely Jewish and uniquely interesting consists of ethical wills written by many Jews either for the guidance of their immediate families or for the instruction of the general public. Precedents for this practice may be found in Genesis XLIX, where Jacob before his death instructs his sons, and in the book of Deuteronomy, where Moses before his death instructs the whole people. This "literature of ethical wills is altogether a remarkable one and called forth the admiration and astonishment of a Christian professor of the eighteenth century, who suddenly made the discovery that the Jews actually knew something of morality and ethics."[1] "Indeed," says Israel Abrahams, "If one were writing apologetically, one could find in the confidential pronouncements which constitute these testaments, a most effective vindication of the Jewish character." [2]

[1] Schechter, Solomon, "Jewish Saints in Mediaeval Germany" in *Studies in Judaism*, Vol. III, p. 22, The Jewish Publication Society of America, Philadelphia, 1924.
[2] Abrahams, Israel, *Hebrew Ethical Wills*, Vol. I, p. XXVI, The Jewish Publication Society of America, Philadelphia, 1926.

1. DUTIES OF THE HEART

by Bachya Ibn Pakuda

The Danger of Pride

The man who does good works is more likely to be overtaken by pride in them than by any other moral mischance; and its effect on the conduct is injurious in the extreme. Therefore, among the most necessary of virtues is that one which banishes pride; and this is humility.

Aids to the Cultivation of Humility

Among the aids to the cultivation of proper humility are the contemplation of the greatness of man's obligation to the Creator and the thought of how small is his fulfilment of his duties, whether those commanded by his own Reason or by Scripture. Another is contemplation of the wonders of the universe and on the insignificance of man in comparison with even this earth, while, in comparison with the greatness of the Creator, the whole universe, even the highest sphere, is as nothing.

If a man fills his mind with these and similar thoughts, he will be continually humble, until humility has become a part of his very nature, and all pride and arrogance and haughtiness are removed from his heart, and this will deliver him from sin and error; as our sages, of blessed memory, say: "Think of three things and thou wilt never fall into sin; whence thou comest, whither thou goest, before whom thou hast to render an account."

The Hall-Marks of the Meek

First among the signs by which the meek are known is that they forgive all injuries and subdue their anger against those that treat them with contempt, even when they have the opportunity of avenging or resenting what has been done to them.

The second is, that when misfortunes come to them their endurance triumphs over their fear and grief, and they willingly submit to the decree of God, and own that His judgments are righteous.

On Trust in God

Of all things the most necessary to him who would serve God, is trust in God. . .

He who trusts in his own wisdom or abilities, or in the strength of his body and in his own efforts, will labour in vain, weaken his powers, and find his skill inadequate to the attainment of his desires; . . . and trust in wealth may be the destruction of the soul. He who trusts in God will be led to serve none other than Him, in that he will not build his hopes on a man, and will not wait, in anxious anticipation, for any human being; and he will not serve them, or try to curry favour with them; and he will not be hypocritical to please mankind, to the detriment of his service of God; and he will have no fear of man nor of human fault-finding. He will be independent, and strip off from himself the livery of human favours and benefactions. . .

He who trusts in God is able to turn his attention from worldly anxieties and devote it to doing what is right. For in the restfulness of his soul and the liberty of his mind, and in the diminution of his anxieties in regard to worldly affairs, he may be compared to an alchemist who knows how to turn silver into gold and brass and tin to silver. Only that he is better off; for he needs neither implements nor materials in his alchemy, and he needs not store up his gold in fear of robbers, nor restrict his production to what is only enough for the day and be in fear for the morrow. For he has confidence that God will supply his wants when and where it may be requisite.

If he who trusts in God is wealthy, he will hasten cheerfully to fulfil all the religious and ethical obligations of wealth; and if he is without wealth, he will look upon its absence as a blessing from God, relieving him from the responsibilities its possession involves, and from the anxiety of guarding and administrating it.

The wealthy man who trusts in God will not find his wealth a hindrance to this faith; for he does not place his reliance upon his wealth, which is, in his eyes, trust money assigned to him for a limited period that he may apply it in various appointed ways. He will not be proud, nor will he make any mention of his goodness to any one to whom he has been commanded to give some of this wealth, and he will not require any reward, or thanks, or praise; but he will render thanks to the Creator who has made him the agent of His beneficence. And if he loses his wealth he will not be anxious, or mourn its absence, but will be thankful to God at the taking away of what was only entrusted to him, just as he thanked God for the original gift; and he will rejoice in his portion, and not seek the injury of any one else, and not envy any other man his wealth.

The worldly advantages of trust in God include peace of mind from worldly anxieties, and rest for the soul from the disturbances of trouble caused by any want in the satisfaction of bodily appetites.

The Love of God

They who love God will do all that is right, without the hope of reward, and will forsake all that is evil, without the fear of punishment. They will also have no fear of anything, or of any person, in this or any other world, except of the Creator alone. And they will be indifferent to the praise and blame of men in doing the will of God. They will be pure in body as well as in mind, and fly from evil deeds of all kinds. They will serve the Creator not only in obedience to the laws of revelation, some of which are only binding in given circumstances, but also in the duties that are commanded by Reason and Conscience, and with every good spiritual quality.

Admonitions to the Soul [1]
(Abridged)

O my soul, set thy heart toward the highway, even the way by which thou didst go; for all was made of dust, and indeed unto dust shall all return. Every thing that was created and fashioned has an end and a goal to return unto

[1] This prose poem is not part of the *Duties of the Heart*, but is often printed as a supplement to this treatise. It has been incorporated for devotional purposes in many prayer books. The translation is by B. Halper in his *Post-Biblical Hebrew Literature* (English Translation), pp. 91-95, The Jewish Publication Society of America, Philadelphia, 1921.

the ground, whence it was taken. Life and death are brothers that dwell together; they are joined to one another; they cling together, so that they cannot be sundered. They are joined together by the two extremes of a frail bridge over which all created beings travel: life is the entrance, and death is the exit thereof. Life builds, and death demolishes; life sows, and death reaps; life plants, and death uproots; life joins together, and death separates; life links together, and death scatters. Know, I pray thee, and see that also unto thee shall the cup pass over, and thou shalt soon go out from the lodging-place which is on the way, when time and chance befall thee, and thou returnest to thine everlasting home. On that day shalt thou delight in thy work, and take thy reward in return for thy labor wherein thou hast toiled in this world, whether it be good or bad. Therefore hearken, I pray thee, and consider, and incline thine ear; forget thy people and thy father's house. Arise, and sing unto thy King all thy day and all thy night; lift up thy hands toward Him, and bow down unto Him with thy face to the ground; let thine eyelids gush out with waters, and kneel thou upon thy knees; the King may perchance desire thy beauty, and lift up His countenance unto thee, and give thee peace. He will be gracious unto thee in the days of thy affliction in this world, and also after thou hast returned to thy rest. For as long as thou didst live He dealt bountifully with thee.

O my soul, prepare provision in abundance, prepare not little, while thou art yet alive, and while thy hand has yet strength, because the journey is too great for thee. And say not: 'I shall prepare provision to-morrow'; for the day has declined, and thou knowest not what the next day may bring forth. Know likewise that yesterday shall never come back, and that whatever thou hast done therein is weighted, numbered, and counted. Nor shouldst thou say: 'I shall do it to-morrow'; for the day of death is hidden from all the living. Hasten to do thy task every day, for death may at any time send forth its arrow and lightning. Delay not to do thy daily task, for as a bird wanders from its nest, so does a man wander from his place. Think not with thyself that after thou hast gone forth from the prison of thy body thou wilt turn to correction from thy perpetual backsliding; for it will not be possible for thee then to do good or evil; it will not avail thee then to turn away from backsliding or to repent of wickedness, guilt, and transgression. . .

O my soul, if thou art wise, thou art wise for thyself; and if thou scoffest, thy error remains with thee. Hear instruction, and be wise, and refuse it not. Lay continually to thy heart the words of Koheleth the son of David: 'The end of the matter, all having been heard: fear God, and keep His commandments; for this is the whole man'. . . Seek the Lord thy Maker with all thy might and strength. Seek righteousness, seek meekness; it may be that thou wilt be hidden in the day of God's anger, and in the day of His fierce wrath, and that thou wilt shine as the brightness of the firmament and as the sun when it goes forth in its might. The sun of righteousness with healing in its wings shall shine upon thee. Now arise, go and make supplication unto thy Lord, and take up a melody unto thy God. Praise thou God, for it is good to sing praises to our God; for it is pleasant, and praise is comely.

II. BOOK OF THE PIOUS

Attributed to Judah He-Hasid

Be Honorable in Thy Dealings with All Men

Mislead no one through thy actions designedly, be he Jew or non-Jew; be not disputatious and quarrelsome with people, whatever be their faith. Be honorable in thy business dealings; do not say that such or such a price has been offered thee for thy wares when the thing is not true, and do not behave as though thou hadst a desire to sell what thou hast, when there is no serious thought of doing so in thy mind: such things are unworthy of an Israelite. If one, be he Jew or non-Jew, comes to borrow money from thee, and thou wilt not because of doubt of repayment, say not that thou hast no money.

If a contract be made between Jews and non-Jews, binding to mutual observance and performance, the first must fulfil it even if the last fail to perform that to which they are bound. If a Jew attempt to kill a non-Jew, and the latter only wishes to defend himself, but not in return to kill, we are bound to help him in his self-defense. Injustice must be done to none, whether he belong to our religion or to another. . .

In thy intercourse with non-Jews, be careful to be as wholly sincere as in that with Jews. . . If a non-Jew seek council of thee, tell him where he will find a true man and not a deceiver in the place whither he repaireth. If thou seest a strange man of another faith about to commit sin, prevent its coming to pass if it be in thy power, and herein let the prophet Jonah be thy model.[1] If an assassin take refuge with thee, give him no protection, even though he be a Jew; if one who bears a heavy burden on his shoulders meet thee on a narrow and difficult path, make way for him, even though he be no Jew. If one not a Jew observe the precepts of the natural (Noachian) moral law, restore to him whatsoever he may have lost, hold him in higher honor than the Israelite who neglects the truth given him by God.

Place Thy Confidence in God Alone

If any one offer thee an amulet, alleging it to be useful in helping to favor or wealth, carry it not, but place thy undivided confidence in God alone. If, when thy plans fail, thou wouldst seek any other Lord than the Eternal thy God, it would be apostasy. If thou canst possibly support thyself with the little thou hast, take not aught from another in order that thou mayest be rich; for few of those who take from others have any happiness in life. No blessing rests on the money of people who clip coin, make a practice of usury, use false weights and measures, and are in general not honest in business; their children and their friends' friends lose their homes at last and have to beg their bread.

[1] Jonah prophesied to the people of Nineveh, who were not Jews.

But many a one falls into poverty because he has looked down upon poor people or has repulsed them with harsh words. If one is able to work, I give him nothing, nothing. It is better to spend on poor people than to lavish in keeping useless foolish things, as birds or other such trifles.

Ingratitude, the Blackest of Faults

To him who is merciful and good to man, God is merciful and good: the pitiless man is like the cattle of the field which are indifferent to the sufferings of their kind.

There are three sorts of people for whom we ought to feel especial pain and sympathy; a reasonable, prudent creature subjected to a crazy fool; a good man who has to take orders from a bad; and a noble being dependent upon one of vulgar nature. There are three to whom we should sternly close our hearts: a cruel person who does pitiless wrong and vile things, the fool who rushes on ruin in spite of warning, and the ingrate. Ingratitude is the blackest of faults; it is not to be endured even towards the dumb creatures whom we use.

Worthy of punishment is he, too, who heaps excessive burdens on the carrying beast, beats and tortures it, twitches a cat by its ears to hurt it, or plunges his spurs too deep into a horse's flank. A sick or breeding beast ought to be tenderly dealt with; if a not dangerous dog runs into thy house, hunt him out with a small whip that hurts not, but see that thou strike him not with a heavy stick or pour boiling water over him, or jam him in the doors, or madden him by any ill-usage. Even worse hath he to answer for, who deals harshly with serving man or woman.

Prefer an Uneducated Man of Generous Soul to a Learned One Close-Fisted

When thou speakest concerning one, tell the good thou knowest of him; but do not so in presence of his enemies, for they would make it opportunity to vent themselves concerning his faults. Praise not one rich man in presence of another rich man; one author in presence of another author, and as a rule, never one man of any business in presence of another whose business is the same; only thou mayest freely give all glory to a God-fearing man in presence of another who fears his God. Make not reply in high-pitched self-asserting tones, but with moderate and sweet, and when thou findest thyself among people who have nothing better to do than to jeer and gibe, leave them as soon and as quickly as thou canst; for mockery leads to want of respect for one's self and others, and that is the high road to an unchaste life. Insist not upon having explanations by word of mouth with one who, aş you ought to know, will turn a deaf ear to thy side of the question or who is likely to become embittered and vengeful owing to such talk.

If a rich man and a poor man be sick, and thou seest all the world going to see the rich man, go thou to the poor one, even though he be ignorant and unlettered. But when thou hast to choose between supplying the needs of a learned man, or counseling the susceptibilities of a poor man, the first case is of the greater urgency; and if it should be that the scholar is also devout and God-fearing, but the poor man not so, then disregard the poor man's feelings altogether, if need be, to mark thy respect for learned piety. Be intimate and work with rather an uneducated man of generous soul than a learned one close-fisted. If thou art in debt, pay they debts before thou givest alms. If thou requirest one to join with thee in fellowship of study, and knowest of a worthy, reserved and modest disciple of the schools of whom others in reckless high spirits are wont to make mockery, choose and take him to thee, that one who is undeservedly set down may be lifted up to his right place. Make no sign of visible disgust when thou meetest people afflicted with loathsome visible disease; for they are God's creatures, remember, and healthy as well as sick are all alike dependent upon Him.

Expel All Envy and Hatred From Thy Breast

Say not, "I will avenge that wrong." Place thy trust in God; He will keep thee. If any one hath deceived thee by false weights, stolen from thee, borne false witness against thee, be not so misguided as to avenge thyself by doing the like. When insult is poured on thee, be thou unmoved, and never permit thy pupils, or those of thy household, to assail with injurious words or blows, when they meet him, one who is doing injury to thee. Expel all envy, all hatred from thy breast; if a fund be making up, and thy name be put down for more than thy possessions warrant, so that richer men pay less than they strictly should, breed not quarrel and mortification for thyself and others by remonstrance and reproach; hold thy peace and busy thyself more than ever with the study of divine things. When thy wife makes thy life heavy for thee, and hatred for her threatens to take possession of thee, then implore the Lord not to give thee another wife, but to turn that one's heart once more back to thee in love.

Let no one be troubled in mind or take up wrong ideas because of the prosperity of wicked people or of such as hold parents in little honor; their end is bad. The reason why good men have an ill lot in life is, lest men should fancy that the good man can only then be good when the world goes well with him. If a congregation has bad men at its head, that is a punishment for not valuing as they should the good men among them. The children of noble, righteous converts to the faith are to be preferred for the marriage tie to children of Jews of nature or conduct not so high.

The ancients of our nation composed works and sent them forth without their names; they disclaimed to seek recompensing delight for their labor in this lower earthly life. And if there be any one who of pure vanity is minded to perpetuate the memory of himself in some work, very surely he will miss his aim.

III. ROKEACH[1]

by Eleazar ben Judah of Worms

Cherish a Good Heart When Thou Findest It in Any One

No crown carries such royalty with it as doth humility; no monument gives such glory as an unsullied name; no worldly gain can equal that which comes from observing God's laws; the highest sacrifice is a broken and contrite heart; the highest wisdom is that which is found in the law; the noblest of all ornaments is modesty; the most beautiful of all the things man can do is to forgive wrong. Cherish a good heart when thou findest it in any one; hate, for thou mayest hate it, the haughtiness of the overbearing man, and keep the boaster at a distance. There is no skill or cleverness to be compared to that which avoids temptation; there is no force, no strength that can equal piety.

All Honor to Him Who Thinks Continually of His Maker

All honor to him who thinks continually and with an anxious heart of his Maker; who prays, reads, learns, and

[1] *Rokeach* (mixer of ointments or spices) has the same numerical value as "Eleazar," the author's name.

all these with a passionate yearning for his Maker's grace. Such a one bears about with him unrepiningly the burden of his nation's faith, holds worldly delights in contempt, is moderate in all the workings of his mind, is master of his passions, and, in sooth, has God continually before his eyes. The path which his feet tread is straight-forward, and the words which he utters to others are soft and sweet; he educates his children for a worthy life, infuses love and righteousness into all his works, seeks to lead others into the right way; he reverences his wife and is inflexible in fidelity to her; he sees that his children take to themselves husbands and wives as soon as may be, after age fits them for wedlock; is of a contented mind, and rejoices when the world goes well with other men. Such a one loves his neighbors and friends, lends to the needy, gives alms secretly, and does good purely and simply for God's sake; such a one you will find early and find late in the house of study and prayer, where he may add to the store of his knowledge and may pray from the depths of his reverent heart. God's blessing be on him and on his children.

Let Thy Dealings Be Such That a Blush Need Never Visit Thy Cheek

Let thy dealings be of such sort that a blush need never visit thy cheek; be sternly dumb to the voice of passion; commit no sin, saying to thyself that thou wilt repent and make atonement at a later time. . . Be not weakly pleased at demonstration of honor; strive not anxiously for distinction; never let a thought of envy of those who do grave wrong cross thy mind; be never enviously jealous of others, or too eager for money. Honor thy parents; make peace whenever thou canst among people, lead them gently into the good path; place thy trust in, give thy company to those who fear their God. If the means of thy support in life be measured out scantily to thee, remember that thou hast to be thankful and grateful even for the mere privilege to breathe, and that thou must take up that suffering as a test of thy piety and preparation for better things. But if worldly wealth be lent to thee, exalt not thyself above thy poor brother; for both of ye came naked into the world, and both of ye will surely have to sleep at last together in the dust.

My Son, Cling to Humility

My son, shake off all haughtiness of mind and cling to humility, cease to exalt thyself in thine own estimation, and be of lowly mind and temper; let none of thy failings appear small or trifling in thine own eyes, but all of them weighty and great; remember whence thou camest and whither thou goest; repent, atone, and serve thy Maker with love; free thyself from passion and desire before thy light is quenched, before thy soul is required of thee, before the book of thy deeds is opened for judgment.

The thoughts of thy heart and the imaginations of thy soul remain pure if the work of thy hands be pure. Fly from all unseemly things; close thine eyes, thy ears to them with stern decision; for there be desires which cause the soul to be apostate from God. Therefore in the days when thou art still young, think of Him who made thee, of the heavenly Father who supported thee, clothed thee, and requite him not ungratefully by delivering up thy soul to impurity. Bear well thy heart against the assaults of envy which kills even sooner than death itself; and know no envy at all, save such envy of the merits of virtuous men as shall lead thee to emulate the beauty of their lives. Surrender not thyself a slave to hate, that ruin of all the heart's good resolves, that destroyer of the very savor of food, of our sleep, of all reverence in our souls. Keep peace both within the city and without, for it goes well with all those who are counselors of peace; be wholly sincere; mislead no one by prevarications, by words smoother than intention, as little as by direct falsehood.

Fight with Evil Desire, Fight and Conquer

If thou hadst lived in the dread days of martyrdom, and the peoples had fallen on thee to force thee to apostatize from thy faith, thou wouldst surely, as did so many, have given thy life in its defense. Well then; fight now the fight laid on thee in the better days, the fight with evil desire; fight and conquer, and seek for allies in this warfare of your soul, seek them in the fear of God and the study of his law. Forget not that God recompenses according to the measure wherewith ye withstand the evil in your heart. Be a man in thy youth; but if thou wert then defeated in the struggle, return, return at last to God, however old thou mayest be.

Be Not Ashamed to Fulfil the Commandments of God in the Sight of Men

Be not ashamed to fulfil the commandments of God in the sight of men; reckon up aright, make no foolish mistake as to what thou owest to God, what to man. Murmur not because the world goes well with the powerful and wicked. The ways and the leading of God are wonderful and admirable, even though our poor eyes may sometimes not be able to see the good things which, be sure, He always does for Israel. Remain faithful to the law; deny thyself even many things that are permitted; be, so far as thou canst, ever of cheerful and ever joyous temper; and forget not that it is to God, God Eternal, God the Only One, to whom thy soul returns in death.

IV. HEBREW ETHICAL WILLS

Professional Advice

(From the Will of Judah Ibn Tibbon)

My son! Make thy books thy companions, let thy cases and shelves be thy pleasure-grounds and gardens. Bask in their paradise, gather their fruit, pluck their roses, take their spices and their myrrh. If thy soul be satiate and weary, change from garden to garden, from furrow to furrow, from prospect to prospect. Then will thy desire renew itself, and thy soul be filled with delight! . . .

Let thy countenance shine upon the sons of men; tend their sick, and may thine advice cure them. Though thou takest fees from the rich, heal the poor gratuitously; the Lord will requite thee. Thereby shalt thou find favor and good understanding in the sight of God and man. . .

My son! Examine regularly, once a week, thy drugs and medicinal herbs, and do not employ an ingredient whose properties are unknown to thee. I have often impressed this on thee in vain when we were together.

My son! If thou writest aught, read it through a second time, for no man can avoid slips. Let not any consideration of hurry prevent thee from revising a short epistle. Be punctilious as to grammatical accuracy, in conjugations and genders, for the constant use of the vernacular sometimes leads to error in this regard. . . Endeavor to cultivate conciseness and elegance, do not attempt to write verse unless thou canst do it perfectly. Avoid heaviness, which spoils a composition, making it disagreeable alike to reader or audience.

The Gate of Instruction
(Attributed to Maimonides)

Hear me, my children! Blessed be ye of the Lord, who made heaven and earth. . . Be strong and show yourselves men! Fear the Lord, the God of your father, the God of Abraham, Isaac, and Jacob; and serve Him with a perfect heart, from fear and from love. For fear restrains from sin, and love stimulates to virtue. . .

I entreat you to recognize the excellency of light over darkness. Reject ye death and evil, choose ye life and good, for the free choice is given unto you! Accustom yourselves to habitual goodness, for habit and character are closely interwoven, habit becoming as it were second nature. Again, the perfection of the body is an antecedent to the perfection of the soul, for health is the key that unlocks the inner chamber. When I bid you to care for your bodily and moral welfare, my purpose is to open for you the gates of heaven! Conduct yourselves with gravity and decency; avoid association with the wanton; sit not in the streets, sport not with the young, for the fruit thereof is evil. Be found rather in the company of the great and learned, but behave modestly in their presence, occupying the lower seats. Incline your head, and open the ears of your heart to listen and to understand their words, and what they praise and blame; weigh their opinions and thus will ye be set in the right way. Guard your tongue from wearying them, measure your words with judgment, for the more your words the more your errors. Be not supercilious or conceited when with them; be not ashamed to ask explanations, but do so at the right moment and in fitting terms. Ponder well over every word before you utter it, for you cannot recall it afterwards.

Love wisdom, seek her as silver, search for her as for hidden treasures. Be found on the threshold of the wise, those that learn and those that teach. There obtain your recreation; there take delight in hearing discourse of science and morals, as well as the new thoughts and ingenious arguments of the students. Emulate those who seek knowledge, despise those who have no intellectual curiosity. Whether you ask a question or answer one, speak without haste or obscurity, softly and without stammering. Use refined phrases, let your utterance be clear, tranquil, and apt to the point. Behave as one who wishes to learn and to discover the truth, not as one whose aim is to dispute and win a wordy victory. Attend there in a receptive frame of mind, determined to profit by your attendance; then will study be pleasant and facile. . .

When you find in the Law of the Prophets, or the books of the Sages, a deep text or an obscure saying, which you cannot understand nor can penetrate into its secret; which appears subversive of the corner-stones of the Torah or altogether absurd; do not budge from your faith, let not your mind be confounded. Stand fast in your stronghold, and attribute the fault to yourselves, for it is not a vain thing, and if it be vain, it is because of your lack of understanding. Place it "in a corner" and do not abominate the whole of your faith because you are incompetent to solve a single problem of philosophy. . .

Love truth and righteousness, and cleave to them. Prosperity so obtained is built on a sure rock. Hate falsehood and injustice, lust not after their dainties, for such happiness is built on sand. . .

Therefore, let truth and righteousness, by which ye may seem to lose, be more lovely in your sight than falsehood and unrighteousness, by which ye may seem to gain. . . Know that truth and righteousness are adornments of the soul and givers of strength and durability to the body. I have found no remedy for weakness of heart comparable to an infusion of truth and righteousness. Nor could the company of friends, the deep shelter of Ashteroth Karnayim, javelin or coat of mail, give me the same sense of security as the helmet of truth and the shield of righteousness!

Stand by your words, let not a legal contract or witnessed deed be more binding than your verbal promise, whether publicly or privately given. Disdain reservations and subterfuges, tricks, sharp practices, and evasions. Woe to him that builds his house thereon! For if one getteth riches and not by right, "in the midst of his days he shall leave them and at his end he shall be a fool." Live in sincerity, integrity, innocency! . . . Let your moral life be your pride of lineage, and your loyalty to truth your sufficient wealth, for there is no pedigree noble as virtue, no heritage equal to honor.

Bring near those who are far off, bow to the lowly, and show the light of your countenance to the downcast. Be pitiful to the poor and the sorrow-stricken. See to it that they share your joys! Help them in your feasts, according to the good hand of the Lord upon you. But beware lest they be put to the blush by reason of your gifts. Never cease to do good to all whom it is in your power to serve, and be on your guard against working ill to any man whatsoever.

Pious Admonitions
(From the Will of Judah Asheri)

Now, therefore, ye children, hearken unto me—for happy are they that keep my ways. Come, listen unto me, I will teach you the fear of the Lord. Look unto the rock whence ye were hewn, and to the hole of the pit, whence ye were digged. Why, forsooth, were ye brought into this world? Not to eat and drink and wear fine linen and embroideries, but for the service of the God who hangeth the earth over nothing. And since His wisdom has ordained that the body cannot be sustained without food and raiment, He permitted man to eat, drink and clothe himself for the sustenance of the body, that body and soul might be associated to perform God's behests so long as their association continues. Food to a man is like oil to a lamp; if it have enough it shines, if little it is quenched. Yet sooner is the lamp extinguished by redundancy than deficiency of oil. Therefore be diligently on your guard against over-feeding. More heinous than homicide is suicide. Gross eating is as dangerous to the body as a sword, besides that it bars one from occupation with the Law of God and the reverence due to Him. . .

Read ye every rule (*halakah*) 101 times, and appoint hours for studying *halakah* from the codifiers every day, and also strive to read a tractate with Rashi's commentary. In fine, you must consider yourselves as laborers hired by the day to do the work of God. . . See to it that ye do your tasks faithfully, and faithful is your employer to pay your wage, nay your reward is already with you, for he has paid it in advance.

Think not in your heart that the Torah is an inheritance from your fathers, and needs no personal effort to win it. The matter is not so. If ye toil not therein, ye shall not acquire, and more than ordinary will be your punishment, in that ye forsake your family tradition. . .

Be punctilious in honouring all men, for therein shall you find your own honour, for God Himself has declared: "them that honour Me will I honour." People remarked to a Sage: "We have observed that thou ever showest honor to every man;" and he replied: "I have never come across one in whom I failed to recognize superiority over myself; therefore have I shown him respect. Were he older, I said he has done more good than I; were he richer, I said he has been more charitable. Were he younger, I said I have sinned more; were he poorer, I said he has suffered heavier tribulations; were he wiser, I honoured him for his wisdom; were he not wiser, I said his fault is the lighter." Take this to heart and understand it.

Take heed to love and respect him that reproves you. For thus we read in Tractate 'Arakin: R. Johanan said: I call heaven and earth to witness that many a time was 'Akiba punished through me, for I complained of him before Rabban Gamaliel; all the more did he augment his love for me, to fulfil what is written: "Reprove a wise man and he will love thee" (Prov. IX, 18). As the Sage said: Love thy critic, and hate thy eulogist, the former helps, the latter hurts thee.

The Ideals of an Average Jew

(From the Testament of Eleazar of Mayence)

These are the things which my sons and daughters shall do at my request. . .

Their business must be conducted honestly, in their dealings both with Jew and Gentile. They must be gentle in their manners, and prompt to accede to every honourable request. They must not talk more than is necessary, by this will they be saved from slander, falsehood, and frivolity. They shall give an exact tithe of all their possessions; they shall never turn away a poor man empty-handed, but must give him what they can, be it much or little. If he beg a lodging over night, and they know him not, let them provide him with the wherewithal to pay an innkeeper. Thus shall they satisfy the needs of the poor in every possible way.

If they can by any means contrive it, my sons and daughters should live in communities, and not isolated from other Jews, so that their sons and daughters may learn the ways of Judaism. Even if compelled to solicit from others the money to pay a teacher, they must not let the young, of both sexes, go without instruction in the Torah. Marry your children, O my sons and daughters, as soon as their age is ripe, to members of respectable families, and let no child of mine hunt after money by making a low match for that object. . .

I earnestly beg my children to be tolerant and humble to all, as I was throughout my life. Should cause for dissention present itself, be slow to accept the quarrel; seek peace and pursue it with all the vigor at your command. Even if you suffer loss thereby, forbear and forgive, for God has many ways of feeding and sustaining His creatures. To the slanderer do not retaliate with counter-attack; and though it be proper to rebut false accusations, yet is it most desirable to set an example of reticence. You yourselves must avoid uttering any slander, for so will you win affection. In trade be true, never grasping at what belongs to another. For by avoiding these wrongs—scandal, falsehood, money-grubbing,—men will surely find tranquillity and affection. And against all evils, silence is the best safeguard.

Piety and Charity
(From the Testament of Elijah de Veali)

If your wealth increase, be not proud; unto the rich, more than other, is humility becoming. They that possess most should be the most lowly, gratefully recognizing that they have their all from God. Pride oft displays itself in men's dress; avoid this form of arrogance just as ye concern yourselves with your moral excellence. Be ye attired so that you and your garments harmonize. Let your dress be righteousness, wear modest stuffs, not embroideries or gold and silver. Grace is not shown by fine feathers, but is revealed by unobtrusive bearing.

Happy will ye be, my children, my disciples, and all who attend to my counsel, if ye keep strict account of your expenditure, avoiding all superfluities, acting parsimoniously to yourselves and generously to others. And what ye save from frivolous outlays, add bountifully to your charities, and to your loans to the poor in the hour of their need. So have I read of the brother of Obadiah of Bertinoro, the expounder of the Mishnah, that he was extremely rich, but lived on bare necessaries in order to support his famous brother who was settled in Jerusalem. It has been a lifelong sorrow to me to behold how, on the contrary, so many, of whatever station, spend extravagantly on themselves and their own pleasures, sparing nothing on their soul's desires, but acting the most miserly part towards others, to whom they yield no services at all; not among such should be the portion of Jacob!

Kiddush Ha-Shem [1]

(From the Testament of Alexander Suesskind)

I command you, my beloved children, that if ye be called upon to suffer actual martyrdom (from which may God deliver you and all the holy people!), ye shall go to your death with whole-hearted joy. And the Creator will delight in you throughout the realms above. He will say: "See ye what manner of a man I made in My world; he spared not his body, but bore chastisements for My honour, and delivered himself up for the sanctification of My Name!" And my heart knows, that if I were myself required to make this supreme sacrifice, it would not be for the wondrous reward which eye hath not seen in the worlds on high, but solely for the great Name of God, that it might be magnified and sanctified in all worlds below and above, by my act of voluntary martyrdom.

Love Thy Neighbor as Thyself

(From the Testament of Joel Son of Abraham Shemariah)

To be at peace with all the world, with Jew and Gentile, must be your foremost aim in this terrestrial life. Contend with no man. In the first instance, your home must be the abode of quietude and happiness; no harsh word must be heard there, but over all must reign love, amity, modesty, and a spirit of gentleness and reverence. This spirit must not end with the home, however. In your dealings with the world you must allow neither money nor ambition to disturb you. Forego your rights, envy no man. For the main thing is peace, peace with the whole world. Show all men every possible respect, deal with them in the finest integrity and

[1] Dying for the sanctification of God's name. For the laws regulating the Jew's obligation to die a death of martyrdom.

faithfulness. For Habakkuk (II, 4) summed up the whole Law in the one sentence: "The righteous shall live by his faith."

It was oft my way at assemblies to raise my eyes and regard those present from end to end, to see whether in sooth I loved everyone among them, whether my acceptance of the duty to love my fellow-men was genuine. With God's help I found that indeed I loved all present. Even if I noticed one who had treated me improperly, then, without a thought of hesitation, without a moment's delay, I pardoned him. Forthwith I resolved to love him. If my heart forced me to refuse my love, I addressed him with spoken words of friendship, until my heart became attuned to my words. So, whenever I met one to whom my heart did not incline, I forced myself to speak to him kindly, so as to make my heart feel affection for him. What if he were a sinner? Even then I would not quarrel with him, for I wonder whether there exists in this age one who is able to reprove another! On the other hand, if I conceived that he would listen to advice, I drew near to him, turning towards him a cheerful countenance. If, however, I fancied that he would resent my advances, I did not intrude on him. As there is a duty to speak, so is there a duty to be silent.

Chapter V

THE *ZOHAR*—THE "BIBLE" OF THE MEDIEVAL JEWISH MYSTICS

No single Jewish book has ever proved to be as harmful and at the same time as beneficial as *The Zohar*. On the one hand, it stimulated the imagination, stirred the emotions, and brought warmth and vigor into the hopeless existence of Mediaeval Jewish life; on the other, it has, through its fantastic speculations, confused the minds of many Jews, leading some into that dangerous self-delusion of Messiahship, and thousands of others into apostasy. One need only mention the Chassidic movement as an example of its happy influences, and the Sabbatai Zevi and Frankist movements as illustrations of its irreparable harmfulness.[1]

The Zohar, or *Book of Brightness*, is, paradoxically enough, unique in its obscurity of language and thought, and this obscurity has been the cause of the most diverse estimates of its value. There is hardly a book in any literature which has been praised as highly and denounced as bitterly as *The Zohar*. Among those who have praised it we find not only some prominent Jewish scholars but also a Pope (Sixtus IV), who sough to procure a Latin translation of it for the support of the Catholic faith. Such equally famous Christians as Pico de la Mirandola and John Reuchlin

[1] For a delightful, stimulating, yet scholarly account of the Chassidic movement see "The Chassidim" by S. Schechter in *Studies in Judaism*, First Series, pp. 1-45, The Jewish Publication Society of America, Philadelphia, 1896.

The Sabbatai Zevi and Frankist movements are adequately discussed by H. Graetz, *History of the Jews*, Vol. V, pp. 118-166; 274-289, The Jewish Publication Society of America, Philadelphia, 1895.

found in it profound ideas as well as many confirmations of Christian dogmas. Among the modern scholars who denounce *The Zohar* we find the famous historian, H. Graetz, who speaks of it in most derogatory terms. In his *History of the Jews* (Vol. IV, p. 14) he says that *The Zohar* gives occasionally "a faint suggestion of an idea but in a trice it evaporates in feverish fancies or dissolves in childish silliness." He also adds that it promulgates "a false doctrine, not only absurd, but sometimes even blasphemous and immoral." Strange to say, both those who sing its praises and those who cry its faults are right, for in it one finds a confusing mixture of the sublime and the ridiculous. Whatever its faults and virtues, however, it is worthy of our attention because it has influenced Jewish life most profoundly.

In order to understand *The Zohar*, it is important to realize that many of its ideas did not originate with its publication in the thirteenth century. Jewish mysticism, known as the Kabbalah, dates back to antiquity. There has always been in Jewish life a certain trend toward speculations about the mysteries of God and the universe. These speculations were kept secret among the few initiates because they were deemed dangerous for people unripe in age and understanding. According to a significant Talmudic account it may be inferred that such speculations were considered dangerous even for men who had attained both knowledge and understanding. The Talmud tells us that four sages entered Paradise (the garden of mystic speculation). Ben Zoma looked and became mad. Ben Azzai looked and died. Elisha ben Abuyah plucked up the plants, i.e., abandoned Judaism. Akiba alone entered in peace and departed in peace. This and many other references point to the presence of a secret mystic lore many centuries before the publication of *The Zohar*, and suggest that these mystic teachings were not considered safe for dissemination.

The Kabbalah, or Jewish mysticism, reached its greatest achievement in *The Zohar*. This book was compiled and published in Spain at the end of the 13th centruy by Moses de Leon, and was attributed by its compiler to Rabbi Simeon ben Yohai who lived in Palestine in the second century. The reason for this false attribution was Moses de Leon's desire to give the book the sanctity of age and the authority of a rabbi, famous for his mystic knowledge and miraculous deeds. Rabbi Simeon ben Yohai was compelled to hide thirteen years from the Romans who sought his life. In his lonely cave he is believed to have occupied himself exclusively with speculations of a secret nature and to have penetrated the mysteries of heaven and earth. In *The Zohar* Rabbi Simeon ben Yohai is pictured as having received heavenly revelations which he discusses with a small group of initiates. These discussions are arranged as a running commentary on the Pentateuch, and they constitute the major part of *The Zohar*.

Just as it is quite certain that Rabbi Simeon ben Yohai was not the author of *The Zohar*, so may it be assumed that Moses de Leon was not its sole author. Most probably the book represents the accumulated mystic knowledge of many generations, which Moses de Leon compiled and augmented by his own contributions. This theory accounts for the dissimilar nature of the various parts of the book.

The influence of *The Zohar* was not due solely to the prestige which it received from its attributed authorship. Much of its authority was derived from the fundamental mystic and human cravings with which it dealt. There have always been men who have sought to penetrate into the mysteries of heaven and earth. The Jewish mystics in particular yearned to understand the nature of God and His relationship to man. They were also anxious to find a solution of the more vexing philosophic problems, such as: How could a spiritual God create a material world? How could an infinite deity have intercourse with finite creatures? What is the destiny of human existence? In their search for the truth, the Jewish mystics turned to the Bible which was to them the source of all knowledge, especially in the field of divine problems. In the Bible they read the story of their forefathers, the ancient Hebrews, and the divine laws which were revealed to them through Moses. Since neither the historical accounts nor the legal injuctions satisfied their yearnings, the Jewish mystics concluded that there must be a deeper, an esoteric meaning which contained the answer to all their questions. Just as the essence of the human being is neither his garments nor his body but the invisible soul, so did the mystics conclude that the essence of the Torah is neither the historical accounts nor the legal portions, but the hidden teachings.

The Jewish mystics, therefore, proceeded to analyze the words and the letters of the Torah, and they thus evolved a complicated system which solved most of their problems. This Kabbalistic system dealt with the nature of God and His relationship to man through ten intermediary emanations (ten *Sefiroth);* the nature and the habits of the angels and spirits both good and evil; the nature of man and his destiny in this world and the next; and the coming of the Messiah and the new era which he was to inaugurate.

The several selections from *The Zohar* which are to be found in this chapter will, unfortunately, prove to be not only inadequate but to a certain degree misleading, for they are neither representative nor inclusive. They were culled from those portions which are understandable to the uninitiated and do not include anything about such basic teachings as the divine emanations or the speculations concerning the appearance of the Messiah. Neither do the selections include a single example of the confusing manipulations of numbers and letters, a method of great importance to the Kabbalists. The reasons for these omissions are obvious. The reader who has not been initiated into this secret lore would simply find it impossible to follow. However, the selections are offered in the hope that the reader will convince himself that in spite of its many absurdities the Kabbalah can be of some interest to the modern student, because intermingled with its fantastic speculations are to be found some portions of poetic beauty and genuine charm.

(NOTE: The excerpts of this chapter were chosen from the quotations in Adolph Franck's *The Kabbalah,* translated from the French by I. Sossnitz, The Kabbalah Publishing Co., New York, 1926; from the quotations in Isaac Meyer's *The Qabbalah,* published by the author, Philadelphia, 1888; and from *The Zohar,* translated by Harry Sperling and Maurice Simon, Vols. I, III, and IV, The Soncino Press, London, 1931–1933.)

I. THE KABBALISTIC METHOD OF INTERPRETING THE BIBLE

The Inner Meaning of Biblical Texts

If the law consisted of nothing but ordinary words and recitals, like the words of Esau, of Hagar, of Laban, of Balaam's ass, and of Balaam himself, why should it have been called the law of truth, the perfect law, the faithful testimony of God? Why should the wise man deem it more precious than gold and pearls? But it is not so. Every word hides a very high meaning; every recital contains more than the events it seems to contain. And that higher and more holy law is the true law.

Translation by Franck

The Soul of the Torah

There are foolish people who, when they see a man covered with fine clothes, look no further than the garment, and yet it is the body that lends value to the clothes; and still more precious is the soul. The law also has its body. There are commandments that may be called the body of the law, and the ordinary recitals which are mingled with them are the clothes which cover the body. The simple-minded take heed of nothing but the vestments or the recitals of the law; they know nothing else, and do not see what is hidden under this garment. The well-informed think not of the vestment, but of the body that the vestment covers. Finally, the wise, servants of the Supreme King, they who dwell upon the heights of Sinai, think of the soul only, which is the foundation of all the rest, and which is the law itself, and in time to come they will be prepared to contemplate the spirit of that spirit which breathes in the law.

Translation by Franck.

The Blindness of the Uninitiated

He who is unacquainted with that book,[1] is in this respect like a mountaineer who has always dwelt in the wilds of the mountains, and who is a stranger to the usages of civilized life. He sows wheat, but is accustomed to partake of the same, only in its natural condition. One day this barbarian came into a city, and whilst there, good bread, a food until then unknown to him, was placed before him. He asked: "What does one do with this?" He was told that it was bread to eat. He took it and tasted it with pleasure. He then inquired: "Of what material is it made?" It was answered that it was made of wheat. Afterwards a person offered to him a fine cake kneaded in oil. He partook of it, and again asked: "And this, of what is it made?" He was told of of wheat. Finally one placed before him, the royal pastry, kneaded with oil and honey. He again addressed the same question as at first and obtained the same reply. Then he said: "At my home I am in possession of all these things.

[1] The *Book of Mysteries*, or the Kabbalistic literature.

I partake daily of them in their root and cultivate the wheat from which they are made." In this crudeness he remained a stranger to the delights which one draws from the wheat. . . . It is the same with those who stop at the general principles of knowledge, because they are ignorant of the delights which one may draw from the further investigation and application of those principles.

Translation by Meyer

How the Mysteries of the Torah Reveal Themselves

Like unto a beautiful woman hidden in the interior of a palace, who, when her friend and beloved passes by, opens for a moment a secret window, and is only seen by him; then again retires and disappears for a long time: so the doctrine shows herself only to the elect (that is, to those devoted to her with soul and body), but also not even to these always in the same manner. In the beginning, deeply veiled, she only beckons to the one passing . . . Later she approaches him somewhat nearer, and whispers to him a few words, but her countenance is still hidden in the thick veil, which his glances can hardly penetrate. Still later she converses with him, her countenance covered with a thinner veil. After he has accustomed himself to her society, she finally shows herself to him, face to face, and intrusts him with the innermost secrets of her heart.

Translation by Meyer

II. GOD AND THE UNIVERSE

God, the Unknowable

Before having created any form in the world, before He produced any image, He was alone, without form, without resembling anything, and who could conceive Him as He was then, before the creation, since He was formless? It is therefore forbidden to represent Him by any image, by any form whatever, even by His holy name, even by a letter or by a point. That is the meaning of the words (Deut. IV, 15): "For ye saw no manner of similitude on the day that the Lord spake unto you." That is to say, you saw nothing that you can represent under any form or by any image. But after having produced the form of the Heavenly Man,[1] He used it as a chariot to descend; He wished to be called by that form which is the holy name of Jehovah; He wished to be known by His attributes, by each attribute separately, and let Himself be called the God of Mercy, the God of Justice, the All Powerful God, the God of Hosts, and the One Who Is. His intention was to make known His qualities, and how His justice and His mercy embrace the world as well as the work of man. Had He not shed His light over

[1] According to the Kabbalah, man was created in the image of the *Heavenly Man*, who is a sort of intermediary between God and man.

all creatures, how could we have known Him? How would it be true to say that the world is full of His glory? Woe to the man who dares compare Him even to one of His own attributes! Much less is He to be likened to man, born of earth and destined to death. He must be conceived as above all creatures and above all attributes.

Translation by Franck

How God May Be Known Through His Emanations

Man's soul cannot be known directly; save through the members of the body, which are . . . the instruments of the soul. The soul is thus known and unknown. So it is with the Holy One, blessed be He, since He is the Soul of souls, the Spirit of spirits, covered and veiled from anyone; nevertheless, through those gates,[1] which are doors for the soul, the Holy One makes Himself known.

Translation by Sperling and Simon

Why God Causes the Soul to Sojourn in This World

The souls of the just are above all His hosts and His forces Above. And if thou asketh wherefore from so elevated a place they come down to this world, and why did they leave that place? This is like the example of a king who has a son born to him, he sends him into a village to be nursed and brought up until he is grown up and learns the usages of the king's palace. When it is announced to the king

[1] The "gates" refer to the "*Ten Sefiroth,*" or emanations, through which God, who is transcendent and infinite, makes Himself known and immanent.

that the education of his son is finished, what does he do in his love for him? He sends the *Matroneethah*,[1] his mother, after him and brings him into his palace and rejoices with him all day. So the Holy, Blessed be He, has a son born to Him by the *Matroneethah*. Who is he? The holy soul Above. He sends him to the village, that is this world to grow up and learn the usages and customs of the King's palace. When the King knows that his son is grown up in that village (that is this world), and that it is time to bring him to His palace: What does He do for the love of His son? He sends the *Matroneethah*[2] after him and she brings him up to His palace. The soul does not leave this world until the *Matroneethah* comes after her and she brings her up to the King's palace and there she (the soul) remains forever. And nevertheless it is the custom of the people of the village, to weep because the son of the King is separated from them. A wise man who was there, said to them: "Why are you crying, is he not the son of the King and it would not be just that he should always live with you and not be in his Father's palace?" So it was with Moses who was wise. He has seen that the people of the village wept. On this said he: "Ye are the children of the Lord your God, ye shall not cut yourselves for the dead" (Deut. XIV, 1). Come, see! If all the just knew this they would rejoice on the day when it is their time to leave this world. And is it not the height of glory, that the *Matroneethah* descends in the midst of us, that she may bring us up into the palace of the King, that the King may rejoice with us.

Translation by Meyer

[1] Matron or Queen.
[2] *Shekinah*, God's presence.

How Repentance Reconciles Man to God

At the time the Holy, Blessed be He, created the world, He also desired to create a man. He took counsel with the Torah. She said before him: "Thou desirest to create a man, he will certainly sin before Thee, he will certainly provoke Thee. If Thou dealest with him according to his doings, the world cannot stand before Thee still less the man!" Said He to her: "Am I then in vain called, 'God, merciful, gracious and long-suffering?' " (Exod.XXXIV, 6)

Before the Holy, Blessed be He, created the world, He had already created Repentance, to whom He said: "I desire to create man in the world, but in such a way that thou art prepared to forgive and reconcile him, when he turns from his sins to thee.' Therefore Repentance is all the time prepared for men and when men turn from their sins, she (Repentance) returns to the Holy, Blessed be He, and reconciles them all. And the judgments are all wiped out and man is cleansed from his sins.

Translation by Meyer

God, the Gracious and Merciful

R. Simeon further discoursed as follows: "He who rejoices on the festivals but does not give to the Holy One, blessed be He, His due share, is selfish, Satan tries to injure him and accuses him before heaven, compasses his downfall, and causes him endless trouble. To give the portion of the Holy One, blessed be He, means to make glad the poor, according to one's ability. For on these days the Holy One, blessed be He, goes to look at those broken vessels of His.

He comes to them, and, seeing that they have nothing with which to rejoice on the festival, He weeps over them and reascends on high with intent to destroy the world. The members of the heavenly Academy then present themselves before Him and plead: 'O Lord of the universe, Thou art called gracious and merciful, let Thy compassion be moved upon Thy children.' The Lord makes answer: 'Verily I have made the world only on the foundation of mercy, as it is written: 'I have said, the world is built on mercy' (Ps. LXXXIX, 3), and the world is established on it.' Then the heavenly angels proceed: 'O Master of the universe, behold so-and-so, who eats and drinks and is in a position to give charity but neglects to do so.' Then the Accuser (Satan) comes and, having claimed and obtained permission, sets out in pursuit of that man. Whom have we in the world greater than Abraham, whose benevolence extended to all creatures? Once, we are told, he prepared a feast, as it is written: 'And the child grew, and was weaned. And Abraham made a great feast on the day that Isaac was weaned' (Gen. XXI, 8). To that feast Abraham invited all the great men of the age. Now we have been taught that whenever a banquet is given, the Accuser comes to spy out whether the owner has first dispensed charity and invited poor people to his house. If he finds that it is so, he departs without entering the house. But if not, he goes in and surveys the merry-making, and having taken note that no charity had been sent to the poor nor had any been invited to the feast, he ascends above and brings accusations against the owner. Thus, when Abraham invited to his feast the great men of the age, the Accuser came and appeared at the door in the guise of a poor man, but no one took notice of him. Abraham was attending on the kings and magnates; Sarah was giving suck to all their babes . . . The Accusing Angel was still standing at the door when Sarah said: 'God hath made laughter for me' (Ibid. 6). The Accusing Angel then presented himself before the Holy One, blessed be He, and said to Him: 'O Master of the world, Thou hast said 'Abraham is my friend'; behold, he has made a feast and has not given anything to Thee nor to the poor, nor hath he offered up to Thee so much as one pigeon; and further, Sarah said that Thou hast made mock of her.' The Lord made answer: 'Who in this world can be compared to Abraham?' Nevertheless the Accusing Angel did not stir from thence until he had spoilt all the festivity; and the Lord after that commanded Abraham to offer up Isaac as an offering, and it was decreed that Sarah should die from anguish on account of her son's danger—all this because Abraham did not give anything to the poor."

Translation by Sperling and Simon

Man's Deeds and Their Effects on the World

R. Hiya adduced the following text: "And God saw their works that they turned from their evil way" (Jonah III, 10). "See now," he said, "when the sons of men are righteous and observe the commands of the Torah, the earth becomes invigorated, and a fullness of joy pervades it, because then the *Shekinah* rests upon the earth, and there is thus gladness above as well as below. But when mankind corrupt their way and do not observe the commands of the Torah, and sin before their Master, they, as it were, thrust the *Shekinah* out of the world, and the earth is thus left in a corrupt state. For the *Shekinah* being thrust out, another spirit comes and hovers over the world, bringing with it corruption. It is in this sense that we say that Israel 'gives strength unto God,' that is, to the *Shekinah*, and thereby makes the world more secure. Should, however, Israel—God forbid—prove sinful, then, in the words of the Scripture, 'God withdraws himself above the heavens' " (Ps. LVII, 6).

Translation by Sperling and Simon

The Suffering of the Pious, an Atonement for the World

When the righteous are afflicted by illness or sufferings . . . it is that all the sinners of their generation may receive redemption. How is this proven? By all the members of the human body. At the time when all the members of the human body, suffer through an evil illness, then one member must be operated upon, so that all the remaining members may recover. Which member? The arm. It is operated upon and the blood is drawn from it, and from this results the convalescence of all the other members of the body. So it is with the children of the world, its members stand towards each other equally, like members of the human body each to the other. At the time that the Holy, blessed be He, desires to give health (sanctification) to the world, He afflicts a just (pious) one from the midst of the world with sickness and pain, and through him He gives health to all the world. How is this proven? It is written (Is. LIII, 5) "And he was wounded for our transgression, he was bruised for our iniquities . . . and by his stripes (wounds) are we healed," etc.

Translation by Meyer

The Power of Prayer

Prayer is spiritual worship. Deep mysteries are attached to it, for men wot not that a man's prayer cleaves the ethereal spaces, cleaves the firmament, opens doors and ascends on high. At the moment of daybreak, when light emerges from darkness, . . . the *Shekinah* descends whilst Israel enter the Synagogue to offer praise to their Master in song and hymn. It behooves, then, every man, after equipping himself with emblems of holiness,[1] to attune his heart and his inner being for that act of worship and to say his prayers with devotion. For the words that he utters ascend on high, for the scrutiny of angelic supervisors. These abide in ethereal space on the four sides of the world. On the eastern side there is the chief supervisor . . . who is attended by a number of other chieftains, all awaiting the word of prayer that is about to ascend to the ethereal realm on that side. The moment it does so the supervisor takes it up. If it be fitly uttered, he, together with all the other chieftains, kisses that utterance and carries it aloft into the supernal firmament, where other chieftains are awaiting it. When kissing the utterance of prayer they say: "Happy are ye; O Israel, who know how to crown your Master with holy crowns. Happy is the mouth from which issued this utterance, this crown." Then the letters of the Divine Name that abide in the ethereal space soar upwards . . .with the prayer utterance until Heaven is reached, where the prayer is taken in charge by another chief to carry it still higher.

Translation by Sperling and Simon

[1] The prayer shawl (*Tallith*) and the phylacteries (*T'filin*).

A Prayer to Be Said Before the Open Ark

R. Simeon said: "When the Book of the Law is taken out to be read before the congregation, the mercy-gates of heaven are opened and the attribute of Love is stirred up, and each one should then recite the following prayer:

'Blessed be the name of the Master of the universe, blessed by Thy crown and Thy place; may Thy favour accompany Thy people Israel for evermore, and manifest Thou to Thy people the redemption of Thy right hand in Thy Sanctuary so as to make us enjoy Thy goodly light and to accept our prayer in mercy. May it be Thy will to prolong our life in goodness, and may I, Thy servant, be counted among the righteous so that Thou have mercy upon me and guard me and all mine and all that are of Thy people Israel. Thou art He that nourisheth and sustaineth all, Thou art ruler over all, Thou art ruler over all kings, and the kingdom is Thine. I am the servant of the Holy One, blessed by He, and bow down before Him and before His glorious Torah at all times. Not in man do I put my trust, nor do I rely upon angels, but on the God of heaven, who is the God of truth and whose Torah is truth and whose prophets are true prophets: in Him do I put my trust and to His holy and glorious name do I sing praises. May it be Thy will to open my heart to Thy law, and grant me male children, such as will do Thy will, and mayest Thou fulfil the desires of my heart and that of Thy people Israel, for whatever is good, for life, and for peace. Amen'."

Translation by Sperling and Simon

III. THE MYSTERY OF MAN'S EXISTENCE

The Happy State of the Soul Before Its Birth

When the Holy One, praised be He, was about to create the world, the universe was already present in His thought. He then formed also the souls which were eventually to belong to man; these souls presented themselves to Him in exactly the same form which they were to take later in the human body. God examined them one by one, and found several which were to corrupt their ways (morals) in this world. When the time came each of the souls was summoned before God, Who said: "Go to that part of the earth and animate such and such a body." The soul replied: "O, Master of the universe, I am happy in this world and do not want to leave it for another where I shall be subjected and exposed to all kinds of contamination." The Holy One, blessed be He, then said: "From the day you were created you had no other destination but the world to which I send you." Seeing that it must obey, the soul sorrowfully took the earthly path and descended among us.

Translation by Franck

The Mystery of Terrestrial Man

Do not think that man is but flesh, skin, bones and veins; far from it! That which really constitutes man, is his soul; and the things we call skin, flesh, bones and veins are for us but a garment, a cloak, but they do not constitute man. When man departs (this earth), he divests himself of all the cloaks that cover him. Yet, the different parts of the body conform to the secrets of the supreme wisdom. The skin represents the firmament which extends everywhere and which covers everything, like a cloak. The flesh reminds us of the evil side of the universe (that is, as we have said above, the purely external and sensual element). The bones and the veins represent the celestial chariot, the forces that exist within the servants of God. However, all this is but a cloak; for the deep mystery of Celestial Man is within. All is as mysterious below as it is above. Therefore it is written: And God created Man in His image. The mystery of terrestrial man is according to the mystery of the Celestial Adam. Yet, as we see in the all-covering firmament stars and planets which form different figures that contain hidden things and profound mysteries, so there are on the skin that covers our body certain figures and lines which are the planets and stars of our body. All these signs have a hidden meaning and attract the attention of the wise who can read the face of man."

Translation by Franck,

The Soul During Man's Sleep

R. Simeon was once on a journey in company with his son R. Eleazar and R. Abba and R. Judah. As they were going along, R. Simeon said: "I marvel how indifferent men are to the words of the Torah and the problem of their own existence!" He proceeded to discourse on the text:

"With my soul have I desired thee in the night, yea, with my spirit within me will I seek thee early" (Is. XXVI, 9). He said: "The inner meaning of this verse is as follows. When a man lies down in bed, his vital spirit (*nefesh*) leaves him and begins to mount on high, leaving with the body only the impression of a receptacle which contains the heart-beat. The rest of it tries to soar from grade to grade, and in doing so it encounters certain bright but unclean essences. If it is pure and has not defiled itself by day, it rises above them, but if not, it becomes defiled among them and cleaves to them and does not rise any further. There they show her certain things which are going to happen in the near future: and sometimes they delude her and show her false things. Thus she goes about the whole night until the man wakes up, when she returns to her place. Happy are the righteous to whom God reveals His secrets in dreams, so that they may be on their guard against sin! Woe to the sinners who defile their bodies and their souls! As for those who have not defiled themselves during the day, when they fall asleep at night their souls begin to ascend, and first enter those grades which we have mentioned, but they do not cleave to them and continue to mount further. The soul which is privileged thus to rise finally appears before the gate of the celestial palace, and yearns with all its might to behold the beauty of the King and to visit His sanctuary. This is the man who ever hath a portion in the world to come, and this is the soul whose yearning when she ascends is for the Holy One, blessed be He, and who does not cleave to those other bright essences, but seeks out the holy essence in the place from which she (originally) issued. Therefore it is written, 'With my soul have I desired thee in the night', to pursue after thee and not to be enticed away after false powers."

(Translation by Sperling and Simon

How Souls Are Judged After Death

Thus it has been taught us and thus we have heard it; that man surely departs from this world through judgment. But before he obtains entrance into the dwellings of the just (righteous) he has to present himself before the tribunal and there he is judged by that Heavenly Council. And there stands the official of *gai-hinnom* (hell) to accuse him. Happy is he who leaves the tribunal acquitted! If not, then the official who has charge of the *gai-hinnom* seizes him, and casts him from there, Above; to down, Below; as a stone is cast from a sling, as it is written; "And the souls (*Nephesh*) of their enemies, them He shall cast, as out of a sling" (I Sam. XXV, 29). And he throws him into *gai-hinnom*, and according to the judgment passed upon him he receives his punishment.

Translation by Meyer

Why Sinners Are Punished by Fire

Said R. Judah: "Why are the sinners punished by the fire of *Gehenna?* Because the fire of *Gehenna*, which burns day and night, corresponds to the hot passion of sinfulness in man. There was once a period when for some time sin ceased to rule because it had been thrown into the iron ring in the abyss of the Ocean. During that period the fire of *Gehenna* went out and did not burn at all. When sinfulness returned, and again began to burn in the hearts of sinners, the fire of *Gehenna* was started again, for it is the heat of sinful passion in the hearts of sinners that kindles and keeps alight the fires of *Gehenna*, causing them to burn day and night without ceasing."

Translation by Sperling and Simon

IV. THE MIDRASHIC CHARACTER OF *THE ZOHAR*

The Lily, a Symbol of Israel

Rabbi Hizkiah opened his discourse with the text: "As a lily among thorns," etc. (S. S. II, 2). "What," he said, "does the lily symbolise? It symbolises the Community of Israel. As the lily among thorns is tinged with red and white, so the Community of Israel is visited now with justice and now with mercy; as the lily possesses thirteen leaves, so the Community of Israel is vouchsafed thirteen categories of mercy which surround it on every side. For this reason, the term *Elohim* (God) mentioned here (in the first verse of Genesis) is separated by thirteen words from the next mention of *Elohim*, symbolising the thirteen categories of mercy which surround the Community of Israel to protect it."

Translation by Sperling and Simon

Man's Inability to Hide From God

R. Hiya quoted . . . the verse: "Can any hide himself in secret places that I shall not see him? saith the Lord" (Jer. XXIII, 24). "How blind and obtuse are the sons of men who regard not and know not the honour of their Master, of whom it is written, 'Do not I fill heaven and earth?' (Ibid.) And yet men imagine that they can hide their sins, saying, 'Who seeth us? And who knoweth us?' (Is. XXIX, 15). Where, indeed, can they hide themselves?

"There was once a king who built a palace and constructed underneath it secret subterranean chambers. One day the courtiers rose in revolt against the king, who thereupon laid siege to the palace with his army. The rebels sought safety by hiding in the subterranean passages and chambers. Said the king: 'It was I who constructed these secret places, and do you think to escape from me by hiding there?' So God says to the wicked, 'Can anyone hide himself in secret places that I shall not see him?' As much as to say, 'I have created all chasms and caverns, I have made darkness and light; how, then, can you think to hide yourselves from Me?' "

Translation by Sperling and Simon

A Gentile Philosopher Is Converted to Judaism

"Once," Simeon continued, "a Gentile philosopher came to visit me and argued with me thus: 'You say that your God rules in all the heights of heaven, and that all the heavenly hosts and legions cannot approach Him and do not know His place. If so, then this verse, saying "For among all the wise men of the Gentiles, and in all their royalty there is none like unto thee," does not extol Him very highly, for what special glory is there for Him not to find among perishable men His like? And further, you infer from the passage which says "And there hath not arisen a prophet since in Israel like unto Moses"(Deut. XXXIV, 10), that only in Israel hath there not arisen, but among the other nations of the world there did arise one like him; and on this analogy I am justified in inferring [1] that only among the wise of the Gentiles there is none like Him, but among the wise of Israel there is. If that is so, such a God, the like unto whom is to be found among the wise men of Israel cannot be all-powerful. Look closely into the verse and you will find that it bears out my inference.' I replied to him: 'Indeed, what you say is actually true. Who raises the dead to life? Only the Holy One alone, blessed be He; yet Elijah and Elishah came and raised the dead to life. Who causes rain to fall? Only the Holy One alone, blessed be He; yet Elijah came and kept back the rain and then made it descend again, through his prayer. Who made heaven and earth? The Holy One alone, blessed be He; yet Abraham came and they were firmly established for his sake. Who regulates the course of the sun? None but the Holy One, blessed be He; yet Joshua came and ordered it to stand still in its place and it stood still, as it is written, "And the sun stood and the moon stayed" (Jos. x, 13). The Holy One, blessed be He, issues decrees, but similarly Moses issued decrees, and they were fulfilled. Further, the Holy One, blessed be He, pronounces judgments and the righteous of Israel annul them, as it is written, "The righteous ruleth the fear of God" (II Sam. xxiii, 3). And further, He commanded them to follow literally in His ways, and to be like Him in every way.' That philosopher then went to K'far Shekalim and became a proselyte, and was given the name of Jose Katina (humble), and he studied the Torah diligently until he became one of the most learned and pious men of that place."

Translation by Sperling and Simon

[1] Referring to the first verse.

The Righteous Among the Wicked

R. Abba then began to expound the verse: "My beloved is mine and I am my beloved's; he among the lilies tendeth his flock." We may explain this text as follows. As thorns are scattered among the lilies, so does the Holy One, blessed be He, permit in His world the wicked to be found among the righteous, for, as without the thorns the lilies could not exist, so would the righteous go unrecognized in the world were it not for the wicked, as R. Judah said: "How are the righteous recognized? By contrast with the wicked! If it were not for the one, the other would not be known."

Translation by Sperling and Simon,

Why the Poor Are Nearer to God

R. Hiya said: "I have often wondered at the words, 'For the Lord heareth the poor' (Ps.LXIX, 34). Does He then hear only the poor?" R. Simeon replied: "These words signify that the poor are indeed nearer to the King than all others, for it is written, 'A broken and a contrite heart, O God, thou wilt not despise' (Ps. LI, 18), and no one in the world is so broken in heart as the poor man. Mark this! Most human beings appear before the Holy One in body and in soul, but the poor man presents himself before the Throne of the Most High in soul only, and the Holy One is nearer to the soul than to the body."

Translation by Sperling and Simon

Chapter VI

LEGAL LITERATURE

IT is difficult for the non-rabbinic student to appreciate the important role played by the Jewish legal literature, technically known as the *Halakah.* In the eighteen centuries beginning with the common era and ending with the close of mediaeval Jewish history (1795), it has constituted fully seventy-eight per cent of the total literary output of the Jewish people.[1] But far more significant than the mere matter of quantity is the fact that it became the focal point of the genius of the Jewish people. And equally important is the telling fact that it never became the exclusive domain of a professional class of lawyers and judges. Despite its specialized nature, this vast literature remained the property of the whole people. Every Jewish male child, from the time he entered school, usually at the age of four or five, embarked on a narrow but exacting curriculum which paved the way for the study and mastery of the *Halakah.*

To understand this peculiar phenomenon one must realize that among the few dogmas forming the basis of the Jew's outlook on life was the precept that God, the Creator of the universe, had revealed His will concerning man's conduct and that this revelation was embodied in the Torah. It was therefore the prime duty of the Jew to study this Torah and to order his life in accordance with its teachings.

Since the Bible did not provide for the regulation of every phase of life, and since life itself was never at a stand-

[1] Ginsberg, Louis, *Students, Scholars and Saints,* pp. 112-113, The Jewish Publication Society of America, Philadelphia, 1928.

still, the Biblical regulations were soon found to be inadequate and often obsolete. It therefore became imperative not only to develop the Biblical legislation for the purpose of making it more inclusive, but also to reinterpret it and to adapt it to constantly changing conditions. About the year 500, these processes of reinterpretation and development were given definite literary expression in the huge folios of the Talmud. This vast literary creation, the product of many centuries of effort, was accepted by the Jew not merely as the practical elaboration of the Biblical law but as the authoritative expression of God's will.[1]

But the compilation of the Talmud only served to stimulate new activity in the field of the *Halakah*. "So vast is it (the Talmud) and so complicated, so much are its leading principles obscured by the way in which they have been stated, scattered here and there through the vast expanse of the 'sea of the Talmud', in an order peculiar to the latter, which is the perfection of disorder, that it presents itself to the learner as a most arduous study, a study indeed which only a few carry so far as to make themselves masters of the whole."[2] It was therefore quite natural for the scholars who were constantly called upon to expound the intricate discussions of the Talmud and to apply its legal judgments to the daily exigencies of life, not only to write numerous commentaries and analytical discussions upon the text, but to attempt the compilation of comprehensive and practical codes. The urgent need of such codes was further in-

[1] It is because of this attitude toward the Talmud and toward the whole literature of the *Halakah* that there is practically no distinction between law and ethics, for inwardness and spirituality were always recognized to be as much the will of God as was the outward observance of religious ritual.

[2] Ginsberg, Louis, *Students, Scholars and Saints*, p. 114, The Jewish Publication Society of America, Philadelphia, 1928.

tensified by purely practical considerations. The mediaeval Jews either formed a semi-independent state as in Babylonia, or, as in Christian Europe, were the outcasts of society. They therefore stood in need of a law of their own by which to govern themselves.

Beginning with the eighth century, codes began to multiply, but most of them, though useful and popular, were in reality little more than abstracts of the Talmudic discussions. It was not till Saadiah Gaon (882-942) that an attempt was made to codify the laws according to subject matter rather than according to the sequence of the Talmudic discussions. This activity was finally crowned by the compilation of several masterpieces, two of which are quoted in this chapter. The first and by far the most epoch-making code was the *Yad Hahazakah*, or *Mishneh Torah*,[1] by Moses Maimonides. This code was not only a logical, all-inclusive guide of conduct, but a harmonious compilation of Jewish ethics and philosophy. "It is impossible to give the uninitiated an idea of this gigantic work, in which he collected the most remote things from the vast mine of the Talmud, extracting the fine metal from the dross, classifying all details under appropriate heads, showing how the Talmud was based on the Bible, bringing its details under general rules, combining apparently unconnected parts into one organized whole, and cementing it into a work of art."[2]

[1] The word *Yad* of the title, *Yad Hahazakah* (strong hand), has in Hebrew the numerical value of fourteen, which corresponds to the fourteen books into which the code is divided. *Mishneh Torah* means Deuteronomy. This title is also appropriate in that the code was meant to be a comprehensive and logical restatement of the whole Torah, both the "written" and the "oral law."

[2] Graetz, H., *History of the Jews*, Vol. III, p. 466, The Jewish Publication Society of America, Philadelphia, 1894.

The second code is the *Shulhan Aruch* (Prepared Table) by Joseph Karo. This code, because of its scope and its excellence as a work of general reference, was soon accepted by the Jewish communities throughout the world as the sole authoritative code, making all further codification unnecessary. It is indeed "a model of the most perfect code of laws, . . . a monument of piety and learning, of penetrating intellect, of skill and devotion, an everlasting glory."[1]

Equally important in the field of Halakic literature is the Responsa literature, known in Hebrew as *She'eloth Uteshuboth* (Questions and Answers). It consists of written decisions by eminent rabbis, teachers, and heads of academies to questions addressed to them in writing. Hundreds of thousands of such repsonsa have been written and there are about one thousand collections of these in existence. In reading these responsa one is impressed with the piety of the authors, their painstaking search for the truth, and their deep concern for the execution of justice. Because of the authors' keen sense of righteousness the answers are marked by stern impartiality and a consistent attempt to apply the spirit as well as the letter of the law. This conscientiousness led to a thorough consideration and minute analysis of each case, and is responsible for the discursive nature of a great part of this literature.

The responsa literature may be traced back to the correspondence between the Babylonian and Palestinian authorities prior to the compilation of the Talmud. When the Talmud was compiled and became accessible to scholars outside of Babylonia, legal questions continued to be addressed to the heads of the Babylonian academies (*Gaonim*).

[1] Gaster, Moses. *Studies and Texts*, Vol. II, p. 709, London, 1925-1928.

There further developed the custom not to give mere decisions but to indicate their Talmudic bases and to refute all possible objections. Thus the responsa became scholarly treatises.

With the decline of the Babylonian academies (eleventh century), Jewish communities began to address their questions to local authorities. The questions during this period were almost exclusively practical legal problems that arose in the various communities. Since the Jews refused to submit their controversies to non-Jewish courts, there was a tremendous output of responsa on the part of all authorities.

Until recently these responsa were preserved because of their legal importance. Rabbis studied them in order to increase their knowledge of the law so that they might be the more efficient judges in their communities. In the last few decades these responsa have been attracting the historian because they form a well-nigh inexhaustible source of historic information. Whereas the answers are usually technical, attempting, by intricate reasoning, to bring the newer Jewish life into moral harmony with the principles of the Talmud, the questions are usually simple, dealing with the actual phases of Jewish life. The historic information thus recorded is in the nature of cursory notes not intended for the historian, but incidentally mentioned to give the background of the legal questions to which answers were being sought. This very cursoriness of the information gives it historicity and renders it of great value to the modern historian who seeks to reconstruct the life of mediaeval Jewry.

Of the many authoritative collections of medieval responsa, those of Moses Maimonides (RaMBaM) and of

Solomon Ibn Adret (RaShBA) have been chosen to illustrate this vast literature. The few responsa quoted in this chapter have been selected not for their legal importance but rather for their simplicity and terseness of expression, their relative conciseness and lucidity of style. But these qualifications which recommend themselves for the purposes of this anthology are necessarily limitations so far as the responsa in general are concerned. The very brevity and simplicity of these responsa render them unrepresentative of the literature as a whole, for most responsa are technical, discursive, and complicated, appealing to the specialist but hardly comprehensible to the uninitiated.

I. THE MISHNEH TORAH
by Moses Maimonides

Excerpt From the Author's Introduction to the "Mishneh Torah"

In our times disasters continually follow one another. The need of the moment sets aside every other consideration. The wisdom of our wise men is lost, and the learning of our learned men is hidden. Therefore all the interpretations, codes and responsa, which the *Gaonim* composed, and which they thought were easy of understanding, have become unintelligible in our days, and there are but few who are able to understand them properly. As to the Talmuds themselves, both the Babylonian and the Palestinian, and the other Talmudic literature, I have no need to say that they require wide knowledge and great intelligence, and that it takes a long time before anyone can find out the right way concerning all the things permitted and forbidden, and concerning all the other commandments of the Law.

On account of this, I, Moses, the son of Maimon, the Spaniard, have girded my loins and put my trust in the Lord, blessed be He, and studied all these works and made up my mind to collect the results derived from them, bearing on the regulations concerning things forbidden or permitted, pure or impure, and all the other commandments of the Torah—expounding them all in precise language and in a concise manner, so that the entire Oral Law may be made accessible to everyone, without any arguments or counter-arguments, but in clear and unmistakable terms, in entire accord with the decision which may be deduced from all the treatises and interpretations existing since the time of Rabbi Judah Hanassi, the compiler of the Mishnah, until the present day. In short, my intention is that no man shall have any need to resort to any other book on any point of Jewish law. . . For this reason I called the name of this work *Mishneh Torah*, "the second Torah," for all that a man has to do is to read first the Written Law (the Bible) and follow it up by this work, and he will know the entire Oral Law, without the need of reading any other book between them.

Laws Concerning the Sanctification of God's Name
(*Book of Knowledge*, Section on the "Foundation of the Law," v, 1-4)

All Israelites are commanded to sacrifice their lives for the sanctification of God's name, as it is written, "I will be hallowed among the children of Israel" (Lev. xxii, 32). They are also cautioned not to profane it, as it is written, "Ye shall not profane My Holy Name" (Lev. xxii, 32). For instance, should a Heathen compel an Israelite to transgress any of the commandments of the Torah on pain of death, the Israelite should transgress and not be killed, for it is written regarding the commandments, "If a man do (them), he shall live by them" (Lev. xviii, 5), signifying that he is to live by the laws and not die by them; and if a man sacrifices his life because of his refusal to transgress, he is guilty of suicide.

The above-mentioned, however, does not apply to the commandments regarding idolatry, adultery, and murder. If any one should order an Israelite to transgress any of these commandments on pain of death, he must choose death. . . .

These rules apply only to ordinary times and circumstances. In time of religious persecution, however, . . . the Jew must sacrifice his life and not transgress any of the commandments, whether he be compelled to do so publicly or privately.

Wherever the law commands that one should transgress and not sacrifice his life and a Jew sacrifices his life, he is guilty of suicide. On the other hand, wherever the law commands that one should sacrifice his life rather than transgress and a Jew acts accordingly, he has in truth sanctified the name of God, and if this act has been performed in the presence of ten Israelites, he has sanctified the divine name publicly like Daniel, Hananiah, Mishael, Azariah, and Rabbi Akiba and his colleagues, . . . concerning whom it is written, "For Thy sake are we killed all the day; we are accounted as sheep for the slaughter" (Ps. XLIV, 23).

The Duty to Teach Our Children

(*Book of Knowledge*, Section on the "Study of the Torah," I, 6-7)

When must a parent begin to teach his son the Torah? As soon as the child begins to talk the parent must begin to teach him the Biblical verses, "Moses commanded us a law, an inheritance of the congregation of Jacob" (Deut. XXXIII, 4), and "Hear, O Israel, the Lord our God, the Lord is One" (Deut. VI, 4). After that, the parent is gradually to teach the child other Biblical passages until the child reaches his sixth or seventh year, depending on the child's capacity, and then he is to take the child to the teacher.

If it is customary in the locality to pay the teacher, the father must pay for the instruction, and he must continue paying until his child is able to read the whole Bible. Where it is customary to accept payment for teaching the Bible, it is permissible for a teacher to be remunerated but he is definitely forbidden to teach the Oral Law (Talmud and other non-Biblical texts) for any remuneration, as it is written, "Behold, I have taught you statutes and ordinances, even as the Lord my God commanded me" (Deut. IV, 5). The Rabbis interpreted this text thus, "As I (Moses) have been taught gratuitously, so have I taught you gratuitously, and similarly, when you will instruct future generations, do so without remuneration in the same manner as you were taught by me."

Should one fail to find a teacher willing to teach without remuneration, the instruction must be paid for, as it is written, "Buy the truth" (Prov. XXIII, 23). Lest we infer from this that it is also permissible to teach others for remuneration, the verse cautions "and sell it not." We are therefore to infer that it is not lawful to teach for payment even if one has paid for his own education.

The Duty to Study the Torah

(*Book of Knowledge,* Section on the "Study of the Torah," I, 8-11)

Every Israelite is obligated to study the Torah, whether he is rich or poor, in good health or physically afflicted, very young or so old that his strength fails him. Even if one is so poor that he is supported by public or private charity, or if one is married and is the father of a large family, he is still bound to set aside a definite time for the study of the Torah both during the day and during the night, as it is written, "Thou shalt meditate therein (in the Torah) day and night" (Josh. I, 8).

Among the eminent sages of Israel there were hewers of wood, drawers of water, and some who were even afflicted with blindness. Yet they devoted themselves to the study of the Torah both by day and by night. These were the distinguished men who handed down the oral tradition from man to man as it was received from the mouth of Moses our Teacher.

How long is a man obligated to study the Torah? Till the day of his death, as it is written, "Lest they (the words of the Torah) depart from thy heart all the days of thy life" (Deut. IV, 9). For as soon as a man ceases to study he begins to forget. . .

Concerning Schools and Teachers

(*Book of Knowledge,* Section on the "Study of the Torah," II, 1-3, 5)

It is obligatory to appoint teachers in every province, in every district, and in every city. If there is a city which has no school for children, its inhabitants are to be excommunicated, and the ban is not to be lifted until teachers are appointed. If despite the excommunication, the inhabitants fail to appoint teachers, the city itself is to be put under the ban, for the foundation of the world rests on the education of our children.

A child is to be entered in the school at the age of six or seven, depending on his capacity for learning and his physical strength. But under no circumstances should a child be taken to school under the age of six.

The teacher may inflict slight corporal punishment for disciplinary purposes, but he may not beat the children cruelly or mercilessly. He is therefore to use neither whip nor cane, but a small strap.

The teacher should teach the children throughout the whole day as well as through part of the night in order to train them to study by day and by night. These studies must not be interrupted (by any vacations) except for the half days preceding Sabbaths and festivals, on the festivals proper, but not on the Sabbaths, when children may review their old lessons but may not begin new work. The general principle is that one is not to interrupt the children in their study even for the purpose of so holy a task as the building of the Temple in Jerusalem.

Any teacher of children who goes away and leaves the children alone, or attends to some other business while engaged in teaching the children, or carelessly neglects their studies is to be included among those concerning whom the prophet says, "Cursed be he that doeth the work of the Lord with a slack hand" (Jer. XLVIII, 10). It is therefore not proper to appoint teachers unless they be God-fearing, industrious, and conscientious.

A teacher may not teach more than twenty-five children. For classes from twenty-five to forty, the community must appoint an assistant teacher; for classes beyond forty, there must be two teachers.

The Reward of the Righteous in the Life Hereafter

(*Book of Knowledge*, Section on "Repentance," VIII, 6)

The bliss awaiting the righteous in the life hereafter will perchance be slighted by you, imagining that the reward for one's fulfilling the divine commandments, and for being perfect in the way of truth, consists in eating dainty food and drinking delicious beverages, in being arrayed in raiment of fine linen and embroidered work, in dwelling in pavilions of ivory, and in using vessels of silver and gold, or in similar luxuries, as those ignorant Arabs imagine, who are plunged in sensuality. But now, wise and intelligent men know that all these things are idle, vain, and futile; and that if with us, in this world, they are considered as something desirable, it is only because we consist of flesh and bone, and because all these things are cravings of the body. . . . But at a time when there will be no body (i.e. no corporeal existence), all these things must needs become vain.

With regard to that great bliss which the soul is to attain in the world to come—there is no possibility of comprehending or of knowing it whilst we are in this world; seeing that here beneath we are sensible of that only which is good for the body. But with respect to the celestial bliss, it is so exceedingly great, that all earthly good can bear no comparison with it, except by way of figure. So that truly to estimate the happiness of the soul in the world to come by the happiness of the body in this world, as for instance in eating or drinking, is utterly impossible. This is what David meant in exclaiming, "Oh how abundant is Thy goodness, which Thou hast laid up for them that fear Thee" (Ps. XXXI, 20).

The Motives for Obeying the Law

(*Book of Knowledge*, Section on "Repentance," X, 1-3)

A man must not say, "I will fulfil the commandments of the Torah, and I will devote myself to the study of its wisdom, so that I may obtain all the blessings which are written therein, or that I may attain unto the life of the world to come," and he must not say, "I will refrain from transgressing these laws of the Torah in order that I may be saved from the curses which are written therein, or that I may not be cut off from the life of the world to come." No, it is by no means becoming to serve God after this manner, for he who serves God thus does so out of fear, and consequently will never reach the state of the prophets or of the wise. Indeed no one serves the Lord after this manner except ignorant men and women, or children who are temporarily taught to serve God out of fear until they increase in knowledge and then learn to serve Him in love.

He who serves God out of love devotes himself to the study and to the performance of the divine commandments, and walks in the paths of wisdom not for the sake of any worldly advantage, nor because he fears evil, nor because he wishes to attain the bliss vouchsafed the righteous. He abides by its truth solely because it is truth, and good results will naturally follow. Such is an exceedingly high state which not every wise man can attain, this being the state which Abraham, our father, held, whom the Holy One, blessed be He, called "his friend," for he served Him out of love only. This is the degree which the Holy One, blessed be He, has commanded us through the medium of Moses to attain, for it is said, "And thou shalt love the Lord thy God" (Deut. VI, 5). When man succeeds in loving the Lord with that love which is due unto Him, he will as a matter of course fulfil all the commandments purely out of love.

But what is the nature of that love which is due unto Him? It is that a man should love the Lord with a love so fervent and so exceedingly strong that his soul shall be bound up in the love of the Lord, and be constantly absorbed therein, as He commanded us, "Thou shalt love the Lord thy God with all thy heart and with all thy soul" (Ibid.).

II. THE SHULHAN ARUCH
by Joseph Karo

The Blessings of the Charitable
(Article 247, Sections 1-4)

It is a positive Biblical command to give charity according to one's means. There are numerous positive commands as to charity; and also a negative command not to close one's eyes to charity, for it is written, "Thou shalt not harden thy heart nor shut thy hand (from thy poor brother)" (Deut. xv, 7). And he who closes his eyes to it is called "wicked" and is regarded as if he worshiped idols. One should take great heed in giving alms that he be not the cause of bloodshed, for the poor man in need may die before help reaches him if it is not offered quickly, as in the story of Nahum of Gimzo.[1]

No man is ever impoverished from giving alms, nor is evil or harm ever caused by it; as it is written, "And the work of righteousness shall be peace" (Is. xxxii, 17).[2]

Whosoever has compassion on the poor, the Holy One, blessed by He, has compassion on him.

RMI [3]*—Let man realize that he himself is forever*

[1] See *The Treatise Ta'anit of the Babylonian Talmud*, translated by Henry Malter, pp. 150-151, The Jewish Publication Society of America, Philadelphia, 1928.

[2] The Hebrew word for "righteousness" (*Tsedakah*) also means "charity."

[3] RMI (*R*abbi *M*oses *I*sserles), the annotator of the *Shulhan Aruch*, died in Cracow in 1572.

seeking sustenance at the hand of God, and just as God answers his prayer, so should he answer the prayer of the poor. Let him also realize that the world is a revolving sphere, and that eventually he or his son or his grandson may be reduced to such circumstances.

Charity prevents threatened punishment from Heaven, and in famine it delivereth from death, as in the story of the widow of Zarephath.[1]

The Obligation to Contribute to Charity

(Article 248, Sections 1, 7, 8)

Everyone is obliged to contribute to charity. Even a poor man who is himself maintained by charity should give a portion of what he receives. If one gave less than his due, the court used to bring pressure to bear and punish him for contempt of court until he gave the amount assessed; and if he persisted in his refusal, they would seize his goods to the amount (in his presence).

A man who gives more than his share to charity, or who straitens himself to pay the collector in order not to be embarrassed, from such a man it is forbidden to demand or claim his dues; and the *Gabbai* who humiliates him by asking for it, will be called to account in the future by the Holy One, blessed be He.

He who wishes to be deserving of divine reward, shall conquer his evil inclinations and open wide his hand, and everything (done or given) in the name of Heaven shall be of the best and the finest. If he build a house of worship, let it be more beautiful than his dwelling; if he feed a hungry one, let him give him to eat of the best and the sweetest

[1] See I Kings XVII.

on his table; if he clothe one naked, let him clothe him with one of his finest garments; if he consecrate anything, let him consecrate from the best of his property; and so, too, the Bible says: "All the fat is the Lord's" (Lev. III, 16).

The Amount of Charity One Should Give
(Article 249, Sections 1-2)

The amount of charity one should give is as follows: if one can but afford, let him give as much as is needed. Under ordinary circumstances, a fifth of one's property is most laudable. To give one-tenth is the average disposition. But to give less than one-tenth is niggardly. When the Rabbis said a "fifth" they meant a fifth of the property the first year only and a fifth of the profits in succeeding years.

RMI—But a man should not give more than one fifth for charity, so that he might not himself become a public charge. This refers only to his lifetime. Of course, at the time of death a man may leave for charity as much as he pleases.

One should never give less than one-third of a Shekel a year and if he gives less than this, he does not fulfil the command to be charitable.

The Spirit in Which Charity Should Be Dispensed
(Article 249, Sections 3-5)

Charity should be given with a friendly countenance, with joy, and with a good heart; the giver should sympathize with the poor man, and should speak words of comfort to him. If he gives with a displeased countenance he loses his reward.

If the poor man stretches out his hand and he has nothing to give him, he should not scold and raise his voice to him, but should speak gently to him and show him his goodness of heart; namely, that he wishes to give him something but cannot.

> *RMI—It is forbidden to turn away a poor man entirely empty-handed. Let him give something, if only a fig, for it is written, "Oh, let not the oppressed return ashamed"* (*Ps.* LXXIV, *21*).

If he can induce others to give, his reward is greater than the reward of the one who gives.

The Eight Grades of Charity [1]

(Article 249, Sections 6-13)

The following are eight grades of charity work, arranged in a descending scale. The noblest form is to strengthen the hand of an Israelite in need, to give him a gift or a loan, or to join him in partnership, or to find him work, that he may not become a public charge and beggar; and it is with reference to such a mode of charity that the Bible says, "Thou shalt uphold him" (Lev. XXV, 35).

The next highest form of doing charity is to give in such a way that the giver should not know to whom he gives; nor should the receiver know from whom he receives. Contributing to a charity fund is a close analogy; but one

[1] Joseph Karo took this section from Maimonides' Code, *Mishneh Torah* (Seventh Book, Chapter X, 7-14). Similarly he took the last paragraph of the section entitled *The Amount to Be Given to a Poor Man*, p. 299, from a responsum of Solomon Ibn Adret. This responsum is included in this chapter under the title, *How Should a Community Levy Taxes for the Support of Its Poor*, p. 311. The preceding observations illustrate the method that Joseph Karo pursued in compiling his code.

should not contribute to a fund unless he knows that the official in charge of it is trustworthy and knows how to manage it properly.

A somewhat lower form than that is when the giver knows to whom he gives but the receiver knows not from whom he receives; as the greatest of our sages used to do when they would secretly throw money into the doorways of the poor. This method is especially recommended where those appointed over the charities do not manage them properly.

It is a still lower form when the poor man knows from whom he takes, but the giver knows not to whom he gives; as when the sages would tie money in a corner of a sheet and throw it over the shoulder so that the poor might come and take it without humiliation.

A still lower form—to give before being asked.

Next, to give a sufficient sum after the asking.

Next, to give, even what is insufficient, but with a pleasing countenance.

> *RMI—On the other hand a man should not pride himself on the charity he gives; for if he does, he not only receives no reward but there is punishment in store for him. However, one may have his name inscribed on anything he donates, as a remembrance, in fact, it is the proper thing to do.*

The lowest form of charity is to give grudgingly.

The Amount to Be Given to a Poor Man
(Article 250, Sections 1-5)

How much is to be given to a poor man? Sufficient for his need in that which he lacks (Deut. xv, 8). Thus, if he is hungry, he should be fed; if he needs clothing, he should be clothed; if he lacks household utensils, they should be purchased for him; and even if he had been accustomed, before he was impoverished, to ride on horseback with a slave running before him, he should be furnished with a horse and a slave. And so each and every one should be supplied with what he needs. If it is fit to give him (merely) a slice of bread, give him a slice; if it is proper to give him dough, give him dough; if he ought to be provided with lodging, provide a bed for him. If it is fit to give him a warm meal, give him warm food; if cold lunch, then cold lunch. If he has to be fed (like an infant) then he must be fed. If he is unmarried and he comes to take a wife, the community should find him a mate; but first they should rent him a home, prepare him a bed and furnish him with necessary household utensils, and then marry him off.

RMI—It appears that all this applies to Gabbaim *over public funds or to many doing charitable work together, but every individual is not bound to satisfy all the needs of a poor man who may chance to come his way. What he ought to do is to arouse public interest in a worthy case; but if he lives far from men, he should give what he can afford.*

A poor woman who has an opportunity of marrying, shall receive not less than fifty *Zuz;* and if there is enough in the treasury, she should be maintained as honorably as is befitting her.

A pauper who begs from house to house should be given only a small sum from the *Kuphah.*[1]

A poor man, who goes from place to place, shall receive not less than a loaf of bread. . . [2] If he remains over night, he should be given a couch to sleep upon and a bolster under his head, and oil and small fruit; and if it is Sabbath, he

[1] See *How Charity Is to Be Collected*

[2] The omitted portion specifies the meaning of the phrase "loaf of bread."

should be provided with food for three meals, and oil, small fruit, fish and herbs; and if he is known (to be worthy), he should be given as much as is befitting his honor.

If the poor in a city are numerous, and the rich say they should go and beg, and the middle classes say they should not beg but be supported by the members of the community in proportion to their wealth, the law is as the latter say.

How to Distribute the Public Funds
(Article 251, Sections 8, 10, 12-14)

If a man and a woman ask for food, the woman is given the preference; and so, too, if they ask for clothing. So also, if two orphans, a man and a woman, come to be married, the woman is given the precedence.

If one comes and says, "Give me food," no investigation is made to see that he is not an imposter, but he is given food at once. If he is destitute and asks for clothing, the case is investigated, and if he is found worthy, he is immediately furnished with raiment.

Two poor men who are required to give to charity, may pay their obligations by giving alms to one another.

RMI—This refers to charity in the ordinary sense. But if, for some misdemeanor, the community imposes a fine upon them to give a certain sum to charity, they can not give it to one another; for that would not be paying a fine.

A Congregation in need of a rabbi and a public reader, but unable to engage both, should give the preference to the former, provided he is a distinguished rabbi ... Otherwise, a reader should be engaged.

RMI—The rabbi should not be maintained out of the charity fund, as it is a disgrace both for him and for the city; but the community should provide him with another source of income. However, gifts of individuals are perfectly honorable.

The community authorities may use even school funds if necessary, for the payment of the annual per-capita tax of thirty *Peshitim* [1] to the commander of the city's troops, because it is a matter of life and death; for if they will not come to terms with him now, many poor people, not having the wherewithal to pay, will be beaten and stripped naked.

The Duty to Ransom Captives [2]

(Article 252, Sections 1-12)

Ransoming captives comes before feeding or clothing the poor. There is no act of charity more meritorious than ransoming captives; therefore, money collected for any worthy purpose whatsoever may be used as ransom, even if originally collected for the erection of a synagogue. And further: even if the building materials have already been bought and the beams squared (which makes it a grave offense to sell them for any other purpose) nevertheless, it is permitted to sell them to raise a ransom. However, if the structure is already erected it should not be sold. . .

He who shuts his eyes against the ransoming of captives

[1] Small coins.

[2] Jewish soldiers captured in battle and Jews kidnapped by bandits or pirates were usually sold into slavery. Also debtors who could not meet their obligations were, as a rule, sold into slavery. The number of such captured and enslaved Jews was often considerable. The public fund for *Pidyon Shevuim* (The Redemption of Captives) was therefore one of the most important institutions of mediaeval Jewish life. It has survived to our own day under the same name, but the money is used to help Jewish prisoners and their families. Of course, the institution has lost its significance and in many Jewish communities has ceased to exist. For a concrete example of the functioning of such a fund in the Middle Ages, read *The Four Captives*

transgresses the negative precepts, "Thou shalt not harden thy heart," and "(Thou shalt not) shut thy hand"; also this, "Neither shalt thou stand against the blood of thy neighbor," and this, "He shall not rule with rigor over him in thy sight"; and he neglects the positive precepts, "Thou shalt surely open thy hand unto him," and "That thy brother may live with thee," and "Thou shalt love thy neighbor as thyself," and "Deliver them that are carried away unto death." [1]

Every moment that one delays unnecessarily the ransoming of a captive, it is as if he were to shed blood.

Captives are not to be ransomed at an unreasonable cost, for the safety of society; otherwise, the enemies would exert every effort to capture victims. But a man may ransom himself at any price. So also, a scholar should be ransomed at a greater price, or even a student who gives promise of becoming a great scholar.

Captives should not be aided to escape, for the sake of public safety; lest the enemies treat the captives with greater severity and confine them under closer custody.

He who sells himself as a slave to heathens, or who borrowed from them and is enslaved by them for non-payment, should be ransomed the first time and the second time, but not if it happens a third time. . . However, if his life is in danger, he must be ransomed immediately, no matter how many times it has happened before.

If a non-Jewish slave belonging to a Jew is made captive, he is to be ransomed like a captive Israelite, since he is regarded as a free-man after he takes the required ritual bath and assumes the obligations of certain Jewish laws.

A woman is redeemed before a man; . . . If a captive man

[1] The verses in this section are, in the order of their quotation, from Deut. XV,7; Deut. XV,7; Lev. XIX, 16; Lev. XXV, 53; Deut. XV, 8; Lev. XXV, 36; Lev. XIX, 18; and Prov. XXIV, 11.

and woman threaten suicide, the man is rescued first.

If a man and his father and his teacher are captives, he himself comes before his teacher; and his teacher before his father; but his mother comes before all.

If a man and his wife are captured, the wife is ransomed first, and court may seize his property to ransom her; and even if he protests, "Do not ransom her with my property," no attention is paid to him.

If a captive has property but does not wish to ransom himself, his ransom is paid against his will.

A father is obliged to ransom his son, if the father has the means and the son has not.

Who May Receive Charity
(Article 255, Sections 1, 2)

One should always avoid charity and rather roll in misery than to depend upon the help of man. And thus our Sages commanded, "Rather make thy Sabbath a week-day [1] than be dependent on men." [2] And even though he be scholarly and respectable, let him engage in some occupation, even an unpleasant occupation, so as not to need the help of man.

Whosoever is not in need of charity, but deceives the public and takes it, will be in actual need before his days are ended. And whosoever is so much in need of charity that he cannot live unless he receives it—as, for instance, a man who is old or sick or in constant pain,—but takes none out of pride, is guilty of bloodshed and is responsible for his own life; so that he has nothing for his suffering, save punishment and sin. But, whosoever is in need of charity and

[1] As regards festive meals.

[2] Babylonian Talmud, *Pesahim* 112a.

suffers patiently and leads a pinched and humble life, so as not to become a burden to society, will live to help others some day; and it is with reference to such a person that the Bible says, "Blessed is the man that trusteth in the Lord" (Jer. XVII, 7).

How Charity Is to Be Collected
(Article 256, Section 1)

Every city in which Israelites dwell must appoint charity *Gabbaim*,[1] —well-known and trustworthy men who should go about and collect from each one what he ought to give and what he as been taxed. This money they should divide among the poor once a week before the Sabbath, giving each one enough to suffice him for seven days. This fund is called *Kuphah*. The community should also appoint other *Gabbaim* to collect, day by day from every household, donations of bread and other victuals, or fruit, or money. This should be distributed among the poor daily towards evening, to each one enough food for the day. And this is what is called *Tamhuy*.[2] We have never seen or heard of a Jewish community that has no *Kuphah*, but in some places it is not customary to maintain a *Tamhuy*.[3]

[1] The term *Gabbai* (pl. *Gabbaim*) means "collector," but since the collector was usually also the "charities manager," the same word is used for both.

[2] "The *Tamhuy* (alms-basket) is meant for any poor people who may apply, while the *Kuphah* (charity fund) is intended for the poor of a particular city" Article 256, Section 3

[3] The other sections of this article deal with the technical details of collecting and distributing charity.

III THE RESPONSA OF MOSES MAIMONIDES

May a Proselyte Recite the Prayer "Our God and God of Our Fathers"?

Thus says Moses the son of Rabbi Maimon, one of the exiles from Jerusalem, who lived in Spain:

I received the question of the master Obadiah, the wise and learned proselyte, may the Lord reward him for his work, may a perfect recompense be bestowed upon him by the Lord of Israel, under whose wings he has sought cover.

You ask me if you, too, are allowed to say in the blessings and prayers you offer in private or in the congregation: "*Our* God" and "God of *our* Fathers," "Thou who hast sanctified *us* through Thy commandments," "Thou who hast brought *us* out of the land of Egypt," "Thou who hast worked miracles to *our* fathers," and more of this kind.

Yes, you may say all this in the prescribed order and not change it in the least. In the same way as every Jew by birth says his blessing and prayer, so shall you bless and pray, whether you are alone or pray in the congregation. The reason for this is that Abraham, our father, taught the people, opened their minds, and revealed to them the true faith and the unity of God; he rejected the idols and abolished their adoration; he brought many children under the wings of the Divine Presence; he gave them counsel and advice, and ordered his sons and the members of his household after him to keep the ways of the Lord forever, as it is written, "For I have known him to the end that he may command his children and his household after him, that they may keep the way of the Lord, to do righteousness and justice." Even since then whoever adopts Judaism and confesses the unity of the Divine Name, as it is prescribed in the Torah, is counted among the disciples of Abraham, our father, peace be with him. These men are Abraham's household, and he it is who converted them to righteousness.

In the same way as he converted his contemporaries through his words and teaching, he converts future generations through the testament he left to his children and household after him. Thus Abraham, our father, peace be with him, is the father of his pious posterity who keep his ways, and the father of his disciples and of all proselytes who adopt Judaism.

Therefore you shall pray, "Our God" and "God of our fathers," because Abraham, peace be with him, is *your* father. . . . As to the words, "Thou who hast brought us out of the land of Egypt" or "Thou who hast done miracles to our fathers"—these you may change, if you will, and say, "Thou who hast brought Israel out of the land of Egypt" and "Thou who hast done miracles to Israel." If, however, you do not change them, it is no transgression, because since you have come under the wings of the Divine Presence and confessed the Lord, no difference exists between you and us, and all miracles done to us have been done as it were to us and to you. . . . There is no difference whatever between you and us. You shall certainly say the blessing, "Who hast chosen us," "Who hast given us," "Who hast taken us for Thine own" and "Who hast separated us": for the Creator, may He be extolled, has indeed chosen you and separated you from the nations and given you the Torah. . . .

Do not consider your origin as inferior. While we are the descendants of Abraham, Isaac and Jacob, you derive from Him through whose word the world was created. . . .

Who May Be Called an Am Ha-Aretz (Ignoramus)?

I gather from the letter of the esteemed Mar Joseph called Ibn Gabir that he regrets being an *Am Ha-Aretz* (ignoramus), because he knows Arabic only but not Hebrew and that he, therefore, while studying our Commentary to the Mishnah with great zeal, is unable to read our code *Mishneh Torah*. He reports further in that letter that some scholars in Baghdad reject some of my decisions. I have been asked for the benefit of learning to give my opinion in my own handwriting. I am going to fulfil these requests herein.

First of all I must tell you, may the Lord keep and increase your welfare, that you are not justified in regarding yourself as an *Am Ha-Aretz*. You are our beloved pupil; so is everybody who is desirous of studying even one verse or a single *Halakah*. It makes also no difference whether you study in the holy language, or in Arabic or Aramaic; it matters only whether it is done with understanding. This is the important thing whichever language may be used in the commentaries or in the summaries. But of the man who neglects the development of his spirit it is said: " . . . he has despised the word of the Lord"; this applies also to a man who fails to continue his studies even if he has become a great scholar, for the advancement of learning is the highest commandment. I say, therefore, in general, that you must not belittle yourself nor give up the intention of improving. There are great scholars who did not begin their studies until an advanced age, and who became scholars of distinction in spite of this.

If you want to study my work you will have to learn Hebrew little by little. It is not so difficult, as the book is written in an easy style, and if you master one part you will soon be able to understand the whole work. I do not intend, however, to produce an Arabic edition, as you suggest; the work would lose its specific colour. How could I do this, when I should like to translate my Arabic writings into the holy language! In any case, you are our brother; may the Lord guard you, lead you to perfection and grant you the happiness of both worlds. . . .

Maimonides Comforts the Jews of Yemen

(From *Iggeret Teman*)

Moses son of Maimon sends greetings to the wise-hearted and much esteemed R. Jacob son of Nathaniel al Fayumi, and to the faithful brethren of South Arabia, whom may God take under His protection now and evermore. . . . May the Lord sustain you in your righteous endeavours, that ye may always be distinguished as adherents of His covenant. Amen. . . .

What you remark in your letter, that some of our brethren told me in high esteem, I consider a token of kind feelings on their part. But you, please, listen to me, and heed not what others say. I am among the least of the scholars that Spain has produced. Overwhelmed with cares, and exposed to frequent setbacks through our sore dispersion, I endeavoured nevertheless to gather knowledge, like the gleaner working slowly behind the reapers. Had it not been for the help obtained from on high, even the little I possess would not have been acquired. . . .

And now let me deal with the rest of the contents of your epistle. I reply to it in the Arabic language, in order that all may easily understand, for all are concerned in what I shall communicate. The news that the government under which you live ordered all Jews in South Arabia to apostatize, in the same manner as the ruling Powers in Western countries have acted towards us, made us turn pale with terror. . . .

Now, my Brethren! You must lend your attention, and hearken to what I am about to set forth, so that you may impart it to women and children, and they be confirmed in their belief. Let all doubts vanish, and confidence in the unchangeable word of the Lord take deep root in the hearts of all of us, through celestial assistance.

Know for certain, that what we believe in is the Law of God given through the father of the prophets. That by its teaching the heavenly Legislator intended to constitute us an entirely distinct people. The selection was not due to our inherent worth. Indeed we have been distinctly told so in the Scriptures. But because our progenitors acted righteously through their knowledge of the Supreme Being, therefore we, their descendents, reap the benefit of their meritorious deeds.

Be assured, my Brethren, that our three opponents, namely, the system of coercion, that of sophistry, and that which seeks to impress by claiming a high origin to which it is not entitled, will vanish. They may continue to prosper for a certain period, but their glory will be evanescent. We have the infallible promise of the Almighty, that decrees aiming at our apostasy or destruction will be brought to naught. . . . In fact, the Divine declaration to Jacob may be said to prefigure our chequered national life. He was told, "Thy seed shall be like the *dust* of the earth." Now, dust is trodden upon by all, and still increases in volume; dust is stamped upon at will, but it rises above him that treads it. Even so would it be with Israel. They would be levelled with the ground, yet augment in numbers. They would be pressed down, and still be uplifted beyond the reach of their oppressors. . . .

Our Brethren of the house of Israel, scattered to the remote regions of the globe, it is your duty to strengthen one another, the older the younger, the few the many. Raise your joint voices ever again in faithfulness which shall never fail, proclaiming that God is a Unity, that Moses is His prophet, who spoke with Him; that he is the master and most perfect of all prophets, that to him was given to attain a knowledge of the Supreme which none can ever reach; that the Torah is from beginning to end the communication of the Almighty to His faithful servant, as proved by the sentence, "Mouth to mouth do I speak with him"; that nothing was to be changed, nothing to be added to or diminished from it, and that no other Law than this will ever come from the Creator. . . .

My Brethren! Hold fast to the covenant, be immovable in your convictions, fulfil the statutes of your religion. . . . Rejoice ye that suffer trials, confiscation, contumely, all for the love of God, all to magnify His glorious name. It is the sweetest offering you can make. . . . Should ever the necessity of fleeing for your lives to a wilderness and inhospitable regions arise—painful as it may be to sever oneself from dear associations, or to relinquish one's property—you should still endure all, and be supported by the consoling thought that the Omnipotent Lord, who reigns supreme, can recompense you commensurately to your deserts, in this world and in the World-to-Come. . . . It often happens that a man will part from kindred and friends and travel abroad, because he finds his earnings inadequate to his wants. How much more readily ought we to follow the same course, when we stand in danger of being denied the means to supply our *spiritual* necessities. . . .

With regard to what you reported, that the adversary seeking your apostasy seduces people by trying to show that several words in the Torah can be explained as alluding to the rise of Mahomet, and that in the same book even his name is mentioned, you may rest assured that this theory is not only untenable and preposterous, but supremely ridiculous. . . . The apostates themselves laugh at the idea, but they wish to deceive the Gentiles by pretending to believe. . . . They know that proofs of such a character cannot stand the test of investigation. . . .

Let your hearts be filled with glowing hope, and strengthen one another in the belief that the redeemed *will* come and not delay. . . . The Almighty has announced through Isaiah, the herald of our national felicity, that because of the lengthy and sore captivity many will imagine that Providence has cast us away altogether, but he immediately endeavoured to correct that error, and to show that we shall never be rejected by our God. . . . And by the first prophet of our people, the Most High foretold us the same: "The Lord thy God will restore thy captivity, and have mercy on thee, and gather thee again from all the peoples whither the Lord thy God has scattered thee." This, my Brethren, is a cardinal point in our religion; I mean that there will rise a man of the direct descent of David, who will gather our outcasts, roll away our shame, and put an end to our exile. He will make the law of truth triumphant. He will cause those to perish who oppose it. . . .

I am not at all surprised to hear of the transactions in South Arabia of the man who proclaims himself the Messiah, nor of the credulity of his adherents. The man is beyond doubt demented. His actions are therefore the effect of his disease, over which he has no control, and those who put faith in him are benighted and cannot form a right idea of the character of the Messiah. . . . But I am surprised at you, who possess learning, and who must have read what the Rabbis have taught. Are you not aware that the personage who is to redeem Israel from their suffering must prove himself greater than all prophets, with the exception of Moses? . . .

Now, beloved Brethren, accept his adjuration, and act accordingly. And let me pray that the beneficent Creator may remember us and you, and gather His heritage and His portion to Himself; that suffering Israel may be drawn up out of the depth of misery, be restored from utter darkness to refulgent light, and again behold the splendour of Divinity and visit His temple. . . .

May peace be with you, dear and esteemed friend, who are noted for your learning and talents, and peace be with all our brethren, both learned and unlearned, for ever and ever. Amen.

And now I beg that you will send a copy of this letter to every congregation, to those who are possessed of knowledge in Israel and to others, so that they may be strengthened in their faith, and may remain unwaveringly steadfast. Read it publicly, and become one of those who bring many to righteousness. Only be exceedingly careful that the Gentiles do not hear a word of it, lest they use it as an opportunity for renewing their violent attacks from which may God always serve us. Indeed, after having written it, I became afraid that perhaps it might be attended with ill results. Yet the thought of confirming my co-religionists in their faith prevailed, and I overcame my apprehension. Nevertheless, I confide the letter to you as a secret; and I trust that, as our Rabbis, who received instruction from the prophets, said, even so will it happen in the present instance, namely that "Those who go on a meritorious errand, will not meet with harm." And surely there can be no greater merit than that attached to what you are about to undertake.

Peace to all Israel. Amen.

IV. THE RESPONSA OF RABBI SOLOMON IBN ADRET

What Shall Be the Status of People Who Claim to Be Jews?

(Responsum II, 16-17)

QUESTION: We have in our town several Jews who came from a distant country and have been living with us for some time as full-fledged Jews. They carry out all religious observances, but they do not know the Hebrew names of their fathers. Please inform us how they are to be named in official documents such as notes, marriage writs, etc. [1]

ANSWER: From the tone of your question, wherein you say "and they have been living with us for some time as full-fledged Jews, carrying out all the religious observances," it appears that since they do not know their fathers' Hebrew names, you doubt whether they are really Jews. But whatever their origin, their status is fixed. If they claim to be Jews, no one has the right to investigate their past record, and they are to be accepted as full-fledged Jews just as we accept Jews of most distinguished birth. No one has the right to say to a Jew, "Prove that you are a Jew." And in the case of these Jews, had they wanted to lie, what

[1] Official Hebrew documents bear the patronymic in place of the family name.

could have prevented them from inventing names for their fathers as they did for themselves? Who would challenge their fathers' names any more than their own? Even if a man claims that he is a proselyte, that is, that he has been converted by a properly constituted *Beth Din* (Rabbinical court), he is to be believed. If his word is taken in regard to the damaging part of his evidence (namely, that he was born a gentile), it is also to be accepted in regard to the favorable part of his evidence (namely, that he was converted). Had he wanted to lie, he might have said, "I am a Jew," and he would not have been required to bring evidence in support of his claim. . .

As to your question, "How are these people to be named in official documents?", please realize that it is not essential to have names recorded in documents. . . It is only necessary to designate in some clear way who the parties of the transaction are. . . Even in a writ of divorce it is not essential to mention the father's name. . . If it were otherwise, how could a proselyte or a man who had been a foundling be named in notes and writs of marriage and divorce?

How Should a Community Levy Taxes for the Support of Its Poor?

(Responsum III, 380)

QUESTION: The poor of the city are many and the government taxes are exorbitant. Therefore, a dispute has arisen among the well-to-do members of the community. The wealthy say, "Let the poor go begging at the doors and all will contribute toward their daily bread, for the middle class is just as obligated to support the poor as we, the rich." The middle class, however, insist that the poor should stay at home and not go begging at the doors, for they are our brothers, our own flesh and blood. The burden of their sustenance should rest upon the community as a whole and each should contribute according to his wealth. This is feasible because the *Beth Din* has the right to enforce the collection of its assessments in accordance with the precedent established by Rabba (Babylonian Talmud, Tractate Baba Bathra, 8b). On whose side is the law?

ANSWER: The law is on the side of the middle-class because charity and support of the poor is not to be borne equally by all members of the community, but is to be based on their relative possessions. . . Every poor man should be provided for according to his needs. Our Rabbis of the Talmud teach that if a man is too proud to accept charity, his needs are to be supplied in a subtle manner, either through "gifts" or "loans" . . . and that the charity is to be so dispensed as to rob no man of his dignity. Thus, if a man is of noble descent, he is to be given a larger grant. Under no circumstances is a poor man to be forced to go begging at the doors. . . The practice everywhere is to provide the poor from the community fund,[1] and the assessments for this fund are apportioned according to the possessions of the residents of the city. If the poor, after receiving their allowance, wish to go begging at the doors, they may do so and everyone is to give them according to his disposition.

How Is a Redemption Fund to Be Disposed of in Case of the Captive's Death Before Redemption?

(Responsum IV, 55)

QUESTION: Collectors of charity gathered money for the

[1] See *How Charity Is to Be Collected*,

redemption of a certain Jewish captive.[1] After the funds had been collected but prior to the redemption, the captive died. What is to be done with the money? Does it belong to the captive's heirs or not?

ANSWER: It is quite clear that this money belongs to the heirs of the captive, for the *Mishnah* (*Shekalim* II, 5) teaches that "the surplus of a fund collected for the redemption of a Jewish captive belongs to that captive. . ." I question whether there is anywhere a dissenting opinion regarding this matter, for the underlying principle is that at the time of the collection these funds were acquired for the benefit of the captive. Wherein is the difference between the surplus left after redeeming the captive and the money left because of the captive's death? In either case the money is no longer needed for the captive's redemption. If the surplus is not returned to the donors, neither should the entire sum be returned.

However, if the money was explicitly donated to be used exclusively for the captive's redemption, then the surplus must be returned to the donors. . .

To What Extent Must a Member of the Jewish Community Share Communal Responsibility?

(Responsum V, 183)

QUESTION: Reuben [2] and Simeon were exempted by the king from all government taxes. It happened that the Jewish community spent huge sums of money for communal

[1] By captives is usually meant slaves, though anyone kept for ransom, including the kidnapped and imprisoned, were included in the term. See *The Duty to Ransom Captives*,

[2] Names in the responsa are, as a rule, fictitious. Biblical names such as Reuben, Simeon, etc., are used in place of the actual names of the litigants.

needs, including the community's protection; viz., for bribes during the Christian holidays,[1] for city fortifications, for the elimination of the badges (because the king decreed that every Jew should wear a large badge), and for the mitigation of the King's decree absolving Christian debtors from the payment of their debts to Jewish moneylenders if the interest exacted exceeded the legal rate. Through this outlay of money the community succeeded in reducing by half the legal size of the badge and in exempting the Jews from wearing the badge on their overcoats. The community also succeeded in preventing the cancellation of debts, though the Jews were obliged to refund the interest collected illegally. Now Reuben and Simeon were asked to pay their share of the taxes because the expenditures had been incurred for the entire community, themselves included. The king's exemption, the community points out, was from government taxes only and not from local assessments. Reuben and Simeon, however, claim that they were exempted from these assessments too, and the proof offered is that the community has never taxed them, even in matters of personal benefit and local city repairs. Moreover, they contend, that even if they were duty bound to pay these assessments, they are now free from them because the community has already paid for all these expenditures. The case is therefore similar to that in which a person pays another's debt without the latter's knowledge. In such a case the debtor may refuse to reimburse the man who paid the debt. . .

The community, on the other hand, claims that this legal principle does not apply to communal matters, for the members of the community are mutually responsible and are therefore like people who have assumed each other's

[1] Probably for the protection of the Jewish community against outbreaks, particularly during the Easter season.

obligations unconditionally, who, according to law, do not suffer any loss if they pay for the persons whose surety they are. Moreover, the community had to pay for these expenditures without waiting for the collection of the assessments. In fact, it is the usual practice for the wealthy members of the community to defray all communal expenditures and then to be reimbursed from the subsequent collection of assessments. Please inform us on whose side is the law?

ANSWER: The law is on the side of the community. The king exempted these two men from paying the royal taxes which he exacts from the Jewish community. However, he did not obligate the Jewish community to save these people's money from confiscation, since they were among those who transgressed the king's decrees by accepting interest above the legal rate. Nor did the king obligate the community to remove from these people the evil of the badges, particularly since the decree of the badges affected all Jews without exemption. . . The same is true of the repairs of the city fortifications. . . Even if they are free from the king's taxes, they still need protection. Consequently, they must share the burden of all these expenditures.

As for their claim to exemption because the community, by paying for all the expenditures, has placed itself in the same category as one who, unauthorized, pays another's debt, it is altogether without foundation. On the basis of such reasoning it is possible for every member of the community to avoid the payment of taxes because the heads of the community usually pay before collecting the assessments. The leaders of the community are elected officials and are therefore not strangers acting without jurisdiction. Their status is that of official administrators or agents acting in behalf of the fellow-members of the community.

How the Jews Enforced the Authority of Their Own Courts
(Responsum VII, 142)

QUESTION: A community passed an ordinance that if a Jew takes a case to a non-Jewish court and thereby causes the defendant to suffer a loss of money, he is to be excommunicated until he makes good that loss. It happened that a Jew disregarded this ordinance and fell under the ban. Now he wishes to make good the loss incurred, but he insists that the loss suffered by the defendant was less than the amount claimed.

ANSWER: It is reasonable to state that this man is not to be freed from the excommunication until he pays the full sum claimed. The reason is that the excommunication has already taken effect and is therefore in the status of a "certainty," while his statement that the loss suffered was less than the amount claimed is in the status of a "doubt," and the accepted legal principle is that a "doubt" cannot set aside a "certainty.". . .

How the Jewish Communities Proscribed Gambling
(Responsum VII, 244)

QUESTION: A community agreed to excommunicate anyone who gambled. Later a part of the community wanted to lift the ban but the rest opposed them, some of the outstanding members of the community publicly voicing their opposition to such a procedure. But the former group paid no attention to this opposition and declared the ban lifted. On that very day one vile fellow took advantage of this lifting of the ban and was therefore punished and excommunicated.

Does this lifting of the ban (executed by a part of the community) have any validity?

ANSWER: The prohibition of gambling is not new. It is an important ordinance originating with our distinguished scholars of old. To allow gambling was therefore sinful to the extreme. Whoever attempts to permit it opens the way to lawlessness. . .

I wonder how it came about that a legal decision aiming at the sanction of gambling could have been accepted by anyone. Even if a whole community agreed to lift such a ban, gambling would still be prohibited by Rabbinic law. Now that there is an additional prohibition by a local ordinance and a ban of excommunication, how can anyone possibly permit it? . . . Whoever in your city agrees to permit this is like one who agrees to transgress a religious prohibition in the company of a crowd of accomplices. The larger the number of accomplices, the greater the sin and the greater the confusion.

Moreover, I contend that when part of a community opposes the lifting of a ban, even if the matter prohibited by the ordinance is otherwise legal, the excommunication still holds good because of the Biblical law that oaths and

Religious Disputation Between Jews and Christians.

(A Mediaeval Woodcut From *Das Judentum in der deutschen Vergangenheit,* by Georg Liebe)

bans can only be nullified if provisions for retracting them were made at the very outset, and then only through the agency of a scholar. . .

In our days, however, because of the general practice of lifting community bans when there is a unanimous demand, no loopholes are needed. This general practice has rendered each communal excommunication conditional. It is assumed that there is a tacit understanding that the excommunication become null and void whenever the whole community so desires. . . In any case the prevalent custom is that if even a single member dissents no retraction can take place. . . It is therefore clear that the lifting of the ban by a part of your community has no validity whatever. . .

Chapter VII

MEDIEVAL JEWISH CHRONICLES

THAT the Jews possessed historic consciousness even in ancient times becomes evident from a cursory glance at the contents of the Bible. Not only is this ancient literature replete with many historical accounts, but practically all of its writings betray a knowledge of and a concern with Israel's past. To a lesser extent this is also true of mediaeval Jewish literature, where one finds an interesting and varied store of historical material and works, the latter usually referred to as mediaeval Jewish chronicles. Like all mediaeval historical writings, they are devoid of a critical sense and are therefore made up largely of legends, miracles, and folk-lore.

This historical literature may be divided into four general groups. The first consists of books dealing with the splendor and glory of Israel's past. The wretched and intolerable conditions of the Middle Ages encouraged some writers to devote their talents to the re-writing and the embellishment of the Jewish past. These accounts became popular because they reminded the Jews of their glorious past and encouraged them to believe in a bright future. Among the most popular of such historical writings were the book *Josippon* and *The Book of Jashar*, the authors of which are unknown to us. The former was probably written in the tenth century[1] and was supposed to have been a con-

[1] The date of the authorship of *Josippon* is a highly controversial matter. Some scholars have claimed for the book as early a date as the fourth century. Most scholars, however, have accepted the tenth century as the most probable time of authorship.

densed history by Josephus, giving an account of the Jewish people from the creation to the year seventy. Its style is a pure and simple Hebrew, which made it readable and popular among the masses. *The Book of Jashar* was written in the twelfth century in Spain and pretends to be the lost *Book of Jashar* which is mentioned in the Bible (Josh. X, 13; II Sam. I, 18). It gives an account of the Jewish people from Adam to Joshua. Most of this account, however, is legendary, dealing with the exploits and victories of the Jewish people during this early period of their history. This book, too, was written in a pure and simple Hebrew and therefore enjoyed great popularity.

The second group of historical writings, though often polemical and apologetic in nature, is nevertheless much more trustworthy. These chronicles deal with schools, scholars, and scholarship. They often attempt to prove the continuity, validity, and authority of Jewish knowledge and tradition, thereby refuting the claims of those who challenged the binding character of the Talmud and other rabbinic teachings. Among the best known of these historical writings is the chronicle of Rabbi Nathan Ha-Babli entitled *Order of the Academies.* It was written in the tenth century and it vividly depicts the cultural life in the Babylonian academies. Of greater importance is *The Book of Tradition* by the famous Spanish Jewish philosopher of the twelfth century, Abraham Ibn Daud. The aim of his book is to refute the contention of the Karaites that the Talmud and the subsequent development of Jewish tradition were not binding upon the Jewish people. To prove the authenticity of Rabbinic tradition, Ibn Daud gives an account of Jewish life beginning with the last of the prophets and ending with his own day. He thus proves the continuity of Jewish life and thereby establishes the authority of Jewish tradition. *The Book of Tradition* is exceptionally well written and has been considered by succeeding generations an authoritative account of the Jewish past.

The third group of mediaeval historical writings consists of accounts of the persecutions, massacres, and individual martyrs of the Jewish people during the Middle Ages. The purpose of these chronicles is well summed up by Joseph Ha-Cohen in the preface to his *Chronicles of the Kings of France and Turkey*. The author states that the aim of his book is "to write how these Egyptians (Christian oppressors) have wronged us, as well as our fathers, that the remembrance thereof may not pass away from among the Jews, and the memory of our wrongs shall not come to an end, nor depart from their seed forever."

Among the best known chronicles of this type are those by Ephraim of Bonn, of the twelfth century, who wrote a touching and reliable account of the massacres and other miseries that befell the Jews during and after the second crusade. More comprehensive and therefore more valuable is the martyrology, *The Vale of Tears*, by Joseph Ha-Cohen of the sixteenth century. He drew his material from all preceding historians and therefore gives a fuller and also more heart-rending account of the suffering of the Jews in the Middle Ages. But the most touching is the epistle of Rabbi Shabbatoi Kohen, the brilliant Talmudist of the seventeenth century, who personally witnessed the horrible Cossack massacres of Polish Jewry in 1648–9.

Finally, there are several historical writings of a variety of types which may be grouped under the heading "miscellaneous." One of the most interesting and most valuable is *The Chronicle of Ahimaaz*, an eleventh century record of a prominent Jewish family of Southern Italy. This family history covers a period of two centuries and gives us an insight into the inner life of the Jews of Southern Italy. Other interesting documents are the letter of Hasdai Ibn Shaprut to the King of the Khazars and the King's reply. These two historical epistles contain reliable information about the Jewish kingdom of the Khazars and about the life of the Jews in Spain, particularly during Hasdai's time.

Since "the national self . . . is nothing but a combination of past and future—a combination, that is, of memories and impressions with hopes and desires,"[1] it is incumbent upon those who wish to know the "national self" of the Jewish people to become acquainted with the memories of that people, memories which have, in part, been preserved for us in the chronicles of the Middle Ages. The few excerpts which follow will illustrate their general character, and it is hoped that they will create in the reader a desire to acquaint himself more thoroughly with the records of the Jewish past.

[1] *Selected Essays by Ahad Ha-'Am*, translated from the Hebrew by Leon Simon, p. 82, The Jewish Publication Society of America, Philadelphia, 1912.

I. CHRONICLES DEALING WITH ISRAEL'S PAST GLORY

Mattathias Charges His Sons Before His Death and Appoints Judah in His Stead

(From *Josippon*)

Now the days of Mattathias drew nigh that he should die; and he called unto his five sons, and he encouraged them, and he strengthened them with his words. And he said unto them: "My sons, I know that now many wars will be waged among you, because we arose, and bestirred ourselves to fight for our people and for our remnant that escaped, and for the cities of our God. And now, my sons, be jealous for the sake of your God and for the sake of his sanctuary; and fear not death, for if ye die in the battle of the Lord, ye will receive your reward, and ye will be in the land of the living with our fathers. Moreover, ye will also inherit a portion and an inheritance in the lot of their inheritance; for all our fathers were jealous for the Lord, and our God gave them grace and honor. Know ye not that Phinehas [1] our father, because he was jealous for the God of Israel, when he slew Zimri with the Midianitish woman, received a covenant of salt for ever? And his priesthood was unto him, and unto his seed after him, an everlasting

[1] See Numbers XXV.

covenant; because he was jealous for his God, and made atonement for the children of Israel. And the Lord our God therefore raised him above all the sons of Aaron, our first father, and He gave him His covenant of peace. Also unto all our fathers who were jealous for our God did our God give their reward; and they found favor in the sight of God. Now, my sons, be strong and of good courage, fear not, and be not dismayed on account of these unclean nations; for they trust in their strength that perisheth and in their might that cometh to an end, but ye trust in the strength of the Lord our God which perisheth not and in the power of His might which cometh not to an end. For they trust in the multitude of their troops and in their army, but ye trust in the Lord with whom are strength and power to save by many or by few. And the power of the horse is a vain thing for deliverance, for deliverance is the Lord's. Assemble yourselves, my sons, and be like one man and of one heart; and be jealous for the God of Israel, as your pious fathers were; and the Lord, the God of your strength, will put the dread of you and the fear of you upon your enemies."

And he called unto Simon his eldest son, and charged him, and said unto him: "My son, I know that the Lord has put wisdom and understanding in thy heart. And now give, in perfect good will, thy counsel unto thyself and unto the holy people, and withhold not, I pray thee, thyself nor thy counsel from this people. And thou shalt be a father to thy brethren, and they will hearken unto thee in every matter; for the Lord our God has put in thee counsel, and wisdom, and strength."

And Mattathias said again: "Call to me Judah my son." And he was called unto him; and he stood before him. And he said unto him: "My son Judah, whose name is called Maccabee, because of thy strength, hearken to my counsel, so that whithersoever thou turnest, thou mayest have good success, and mayest be prosperous. I know that thou art a man of war, and that God has put in thee power and strength so that thy heart is as the heart of a lion, which melteth not and feareth not. And now honor the Lord with thy strength which He has given thee, for everything is from Him; and go, and fight His battles without slothfulness; and be not slothful to go to every side, and to every corner, in the east, and in the west, and in the north, and in the south, in the holy land, to take vengeance from the nations who defile it. And be thou unto the holy people captain of the host and war Messiah."[1]

And Judah answered his father, and said: "Behold, my lord my father, I will do according to all which thou hast commanded me."

And he commanded, and they brought unto him the vial of oil; and he poured it upon his head, and he anointed him leader and war Messiah. And all the people shouted with a great shout, and blew the trumpet, and they said: "Long live the leader," and "Long live the anointed."

And it came to pass, when Mattathias the priest finished charging his sons, that he expired and died, and was gathered unto his people. And Judah his son, who was called Maccabee because of his strength, arose in his stead from among his sons, to be leader and anointed. And his brethren and all his father's house and all the congregation of the pious helped him. And he buried his father with great honor. And after that Judah put on a coat of mail as a mighty man; and he girded his armor upon his loins; and he went down to the uncircumcised, who were encamped round the mountain. which they came to take. And he smote among them eight thousand and two hundred of their mighty men.

[1]The priest who is anointed to encourage the army.

And he judged Israel with his sword; and he purged out the violent from them, and he destroyed them. And he trod down to the earth the strangers that were in all the borders of Israel. And the wicked were discomfited through their dread of him. And the wrong-doers were dismayed through their fear of him. And it was that, when he shouted, his voice was as the voice of the roaring of a lion on the day he roars to tear the prey. And all Israel rejoiced in his deeds, and exulted in his work. And all the world was terrified because of his fame. Then were kings, greater and mightier than he, dismayed; and trembling seized hold upon the chiefs of the earth and the kings thereof. And his name went forth among the nations to the end of all the earth; and the tales of the wonders of his war and the terrors of his mighty deeds reached to the end of the earth. And when he was gathered unto his people, all the seed of Israel praised him, and honored him. And they spoke, saying: "May the spirit of the Lord cause him to rest, and may he dwell in the secret place of the Most High, and abide under the shadow of the Almighty, under the tree of life."

And he went from city to city, and slew all the wicked of the people of Judah, who were destroying the people of Israel.

Jacob and His Sons Wage War with the Amorites and Conquer the City Gaash

(From *The Book of Jashar*)

And the sons of Jacob . . . attempted again to enter the city, and to fight under the walls of the city, but they succeeded not. For all the inhabitants of Gaash, that were in the city, had surrounded the walls on either side and the sons of Jacob could not come near the city to fight with them. And as the sons of Jacob approached one corner, to fight under the wall, the people threw upon them arrows and stones like a rain storm, and they fled from under the wall. And when the people of Gaash saw that the sons of Jacob could not prevail, they taunted the sons of Jacob, saying: "What hath happened to you in the war that you can not succeed. Can you do to the mighty city of Gaash as you have done to the other cities of the Amorites which are less powerful? Verily to those feeble ones amongst us you could do those things to slay them in the gates of the city, for they had no strength, when you terrified them with your powerful shrieking, but will you be able to fight in this place? Verily here you must die all of you, and we will avenge on you the cause of the cities which you have destroyed."

And the inhabitants of Gaash taunted the sons of Jacob greatly cursing their God, and still casting stones and arrows upon them from the wall.

And when Judah and his brothers heard these words, their anger was greatly excited, and Judah became zealous of his God concerning that matter and he called out saying: "Oh Lord help us and our brethren." And he ran from the distance, sword in hand, and by reason of his great strength he sprang from the ground and mounted the wall and his sword fell from his hand. And Judah shouted tremendously upon the wall, so that many of the men that were upon the wall were terrified, and fell down from the wall and died, and those remaining upon the wall, seeing Judah's strength were greatly afraid of their lives and they fled into the city to save themselves. And some of them, seeing that Judah had no sword, became emboldened and they approached to slay him and to throw him from the wall to his brothers. And twenty men of the city came to their assistance, and they surrounded Judah, shouting at him and coming near him with drawn swords. And Judah became terrified and he cried out to his brothers from the top of the wall. And

Jacob and his sons drew the bows from under the wall and slew three men upon the top of the wall. And Judah continued crying, and he exclaimed, "Oh Lord help us, Oh Lord save us." And his loud crying upon the wall was heard at a great distance. And after thus crying, Judah shouted once more and the men around him were greatly terrified at Judah's voice, and they threw away the swords from their hands and fled. And Judah seized the swords which they had thrown away and he fought with them and slew twenty of their men that were upon the wall. And about eighty men and women ascended the wall, surrounding Judah; but the Lord filled their hearts with fear of Judah and they dared not approach him. And when the people upon the wall saw that twenty of their men were dead, they rushed all toward Judah with their drawn swords, but they could not approach him for fear of his great strength. And one of the most powerful men, by the name of Arud came near striking with his sword at Judah's head, but Judah placed his shield quickly against his head, and the sword struck the shield and flew in twain. And the powerful man, after having struck Judah, ran for his life, and he slipped and fell from the wall amongst the sons of Jacob under the wall, and the sons of Jacob smote him and killed him. And Judah's head pained him from the blow of that heroic man, and he was nearly dead from that blow. And Judah cried out in the agony of his pain, and when Dan heard him his anger kindled within him. And Dan also took a run from the distance and sprang from the ground upon the wall with his great strength and burning wrath. And when Dan mounted the wall all the men upon it that surrounded Judah fled hastily, and ascended the second wall, throwing stones and arrows at Judah and Dan from the second wall, in order to drive them away. And the arrows and stones struck Dan and Judah, and they were almost slain upon the wall, and whithersoever they turned they were attacked by stones and arrows from the second wall. And Jacob and his sons were still at the entrance of the city, under the first wall, but they could not use their bows against the people of the city, for they could not be seen by them from the second wall. And when Dan and Judah saw that they could no longer stand the attack of the stones and arrows from the second wall, they both jumped over to the top of the second wall. And when the people of the city, upon the second wall, saw that Dan and Judah were amongst them they cried out in their fear and descended between the walls. And Jacob and his sons heard the shouting from the people of the city, and they were in great anxiety concerning Dan and Judah on the second wall, whom they could not see. And Naphtali went with his strength, excited by wrath, and he jumped upon the first wall, to ascertain the cause of that great shouting heard from the city. And Naphtali sprang from the first wall to the second wall and came to his brothers' assistance. And when the people of Gaash, that were upon the second wall, saw that Naphtali was the third one who had come to assist his brothers, they fled and descended into the city, and Jacob with all of his young men came over them in the city. And Judah and Dan and Naphtali also descended from the wall into the city and they pursued the inhabitants of the city. And when the inhabitants of the city had all descended, the sons of Jacob came over them from all sides, and being surrounded and attacked from front and rear, the sons of Jacob smote them terribly, and they killed of them about twenty thousand men and women; not one could stand against the sons of Jacob. And the blood flowed terribly through the city even like a brook of water, and it flowed out of the city reaching the desert of Bethhorin.

II. CHRONICLES DEALING WITH SCHOOLS, SCHOLARS, AND SCHOLARSHIP

The Installation of an Exilarch

(From *The Order of the Academies* by Nathan Ha-Babli)

When the community agreed to appoint an exilarch, the two heads of the academies, with their pupils, the heads of the community, and the elders assembled in the house of a prominent man in Babylon, one of the great men of the generation, as, for instance, Netira, or a similar man. That man in whose house the meeting took place was honored thereby, and it was regarded as a mark of distinction; his esteem was enhanced, when the great men and the elders assembled in his house.

On Thursday they assembled in the synagogue, blessed the exilarch, and placed their hands on him. They blew the horn, that all the people, small and great, might hear. When the people heard the proclamation, every member of the community sent him a present, according to his power and means. All the heads of the community and the wealthy members sent him magnificent clothes and beautiful ornaments, vessels of silver and vessels of gold, each man according to his ability. The exilarch prepared a banquet on Thursday and on Friday, giving all kinds of food, and all kinds of drinks, and all kinds of dainties, as, for instance, different kinds of sweetmeats.

When he arose on Sabbath morning to go to the synagogue, many of the prominent men of the community met him to go with him to the synagogue. At the synagogue a wooden pulpit had been prepared for him on the previous day, the length of which was seven cubits, and the breadth of which was three cubits. They spread over it magnificent coverings of silk, blue, purple, and scarlet, so that it was entirely covered, and nothing was seen of it. Under the pulpit there entered distinguished youths, with melodious and harmonious voices, who were well-versed in the prayers and all that appertains thereto. The exilarch was concealed in a certain place together with the heads of the academies, and the youths stood under the pulpit. No man sat there. The precentor of the synagogue would begin the prayer "Blessed be He who spoke," and the youths, after every sentence of that prayer, would respond "Blessed be He." . . .

When all the people were seated, the exilarch came out from the place where he was concealed. Seeing him come out, all the people stood up, until he sat down on the pulpit, which had been made for him. Then the head of the academy of Sura came out after him, and after exchanging courtesies with the exilarch, sat down on the pulpit. Then the head of the academy of Pumbeditha came out, and he, too, made a bow, and sat down at his left.

During all this time the people stood upon their feet, until these three were properly seated: the exilarch sat in the middle, the head of the academy of Sura at his right, and the head of the academy of Pumbeditha at his left, empty places being left between the heads of the academies and the exilarch. Upon his place, over his head, above the pulpit, they spread a magnificent covering, fastened with cords of fine linen and purple. Then the precentor put his head under the exilarch's canopy in front of the pulpit, and with blessings that had been prepared for him on the preceding days he blessed him with a low voice, so that they should be heard only by those who sat round the pulpit, and by the youths who were under it. When he blessed him, the youths responded after him with a loud voice: "Amen!" All the people were silent until he had finished his blessings.

Then the exilarch would begin to expound matters appertaining to the biblical portion of that day, or would give permission to the head of the academy of Sura to deliver the exposition, and the head of the academy of Sura would give permission to the head of the academy of Pumbeditha. They would thus show deference to one another, until the head of the academy of Sura began to expound. The interpreter stood near him, and repeated his words to the people. He expounded with awe, closing his eyes, and wrapping himself up with his *tallith*, so that his forehead was covered. While he was expounding, there was not in the congregation one that opened his mouth, or chirped, or uttered a sound. If he became aware that any one spoke, he would open his eyes, and fear and terror would fall upon the congregation. When he finished his exposition, he would begin with a question, saying: "Verily, thou needest to learn." And an old man who was wise, understanding, and experienced would stand up, and make a response on the subject, and sit down. Then the precentor stood up and recited the *Kaddish*. When he reached the words "during your life and in your days," he would say: "During the life of our prince the exilarch, and during your life, and during the life of all the house of Israel."

The Four Captives
(From *The Book of Tradition* by Abraham Ibn Daud)

After the death of Hiskia, who was Head of the Academy and Prince of the Exile, the Academies and Gaons ceased to exist. But even before that time (about the year 960) the Holy One, blessed be He, had decreed the suspension of the subsidies which were being sent to the Academies from Spain, from Maghreb, from Africa, from Egypt and from Palestine. The thing came to pass as follows. There came from the city of Cordova a captain by the name of Ibn Damahin, whom Abd-el-Rahman, the Arab King of Spain, had placed at the head of a fleet. This commander of mighty ships went forth to conquer the ships of the Christians and to harass the cities on the coast. They went as far as the coast of Palestine, went round the islands of the Greek Archipelago, and there encountered a ship which was carrying four of our sages from the city of Bari to a city called Safsatin. These sages were travelling for the purpose of collecting funds for the Academies. Ibn Damahin captured the ship and made the sages prisoners. One of them was Rabbi Shushiel, son of Rabbi Chananel; the second was Rabbi Moshe, father of Rabbi Enoch (he was taken prisoner together with his wife and his son Enoch, who was then a young boy); the third was Rabbi Shemariah, son of Rabbi Elkanan; as to the fourth, I do not know his name. As the captain sought to violate the wife of Rabbi Moshe, for she was a very beautiful woman, she cried out to her husband in the sacred tongue, and asked him if those who are drowned will wake with the other dead on the day of the resurrection. He replied: "The Lord said: I will bring them again from Bashan, from the depths of the sea will I bring them again."[1]

[1] Psalm LXVIII, 23.

When she heard that she would be resurrected, she leapt into the sea and was drowned.

These sages spoke not concerning themselves and their learning. The Captain sold Rabbi Shemariah as a slave in Alexandria, Egypt; thence Rabbi Shemariah went to Cairo and founded a school there. Rabbi Shushiel was sold on the coast of Africa; and he made his way to the city of Kairouan, which was then the mightiest Arab city of the Maghreb. Rabbi Shushiel became the head of a school. . . Then the captain returned to Cordova, where he sold Rabbi Moshe and his son Enoch. They were bought into liberty by the people of Cordova, who knew not the great learning of these captives.

There was in Cordova a Synagogue called the Synagogue of the House of Study, and in it there was a judge by the name of Rabbi Nathan, who was a man of great piety. Nevertheless, those of Spain were not deeply versed in the words of our teachers, whose memory be blessed. However, with the little learning they commanded, they carried on discussions and interpreted the Law. One day Rabbi Nathan, the judge, was interpreting the law concerning the lustrations which are required for every sprinkling, concerning which it is spoken in the Tractate of the Talmud, *Yoma*, and they were not able to offer an explanation. Then Rabbi Moshe, who, as beadle, was seated in a corner, rose and said: "Master, that would make too many lustrtions." When the master and the pupils heard these words, they were astonished and they asked Rabbi Moshe to explain the law; and he explained the law in the correct way. Then they asked him to explain other difficulties, and they continued their questions, all of which he answered out of the abundance of his learning. There stood, outside the house of study, a number of plaintiffs who were not permitted to enter until the pupils had ended their lesson. On that day Rabbi Nathan, the judge, went out, and the plaintiffs followed him, but he said: "I am no longer the judge; this man, who is dressed in sackcloth and who is a stranger, he is my teacher and my master, and I am his pupil from to-day on." They did so. And the community set aside for him a generous recompense, and gave him precious raiment and a carriage. The Captain, learning of this, desired to annul his sale, but the King would not permit it, for he was greatly pleased to learn that the Jews of his Kingdom were no longer dependent on the people of Babylon.

III. CHRONICLES DEALING WITH THE SUFFERING OF THE JEWS IN THE MIDDLE AGES

The First Crusade

(From *The Vale of Tears* by Joseph Ha-Cohen)

In the reign of Philip, son of Henry, King of France, Peter the Hermit went to Jerusalem, saw the sufferings of the Christians who lived there and, on his return, related it to his brothers; this was in the year 4856, which is the year 1096. The Christian Kings then offered to go and conquer Judah and Jerusalem; from all countries there gathered an enormous concourse of men and women who would go with them, and with this year began a time of pitiless desolation for the Israelites in Christian countries, wherever they were scattered; and the times were such that they became sick of life; terrible and numberless were the afflictions which they bore, for there rose against them the multitude of France and of Germany which had gathered for the Crusade, an evil-faced multitude, which neither spared the aged nor took pity on children. Their cry was: "Let us avenge our Saviour on the Jews, let us wipe them out from among the peoples, unless they accept another god and become Christians like ourselves; and only when this is accomplished will we set out." When the Jews of Germany heard this, their hearts melted in them and became like water, and pain and trembling seized them as with a woman in labour; they lifted their eyes to heaven, set aside fast days and cried to the Eternal in their misery, but the Eternal had hidden himself behind clouds which no prayer could pierce. On the twenty-third day of the month the Crusaders descended like night wolves against the holy community of Worms, and many of the members took refuge in the house of the Bishop for fear of disaster. The attackers rushed into the houses and put to the sword whomsoever they found, sparing neither man nor woman; they sacked the houses, broke down the towers, and stretched out their hands to the plunder, and there was none to save from them in that day of divine wrath. They threw down the scrolls of the law, tore them to pieces and trampled them underfoot, and they shouted in the house of God as on a day of celebration, devouring Israel, and leaving alive but a small remnant, whom they forced to deny their God, the God of Israel, but who, when the fury was once passed, returned again to the God of their fathers. As to the slaughtered, they sanctified the Holy One of Israel in the open light, and chose death rather than life that they might not become faithless to God. Many immolated themselves, and this one slew his brother, or his friend, his beloved wife, his sons and daughters: tender mothers slaughtered with firm hand and heart their little children, and the little ones pronounced the Unity of God as they gave up their souls on the bosoms of their mothers. When the holy community of Mayence learned the dreadful news, they fled to the palace of the Bishop, thinking to find there a refuge from death. But the enemy rose against them on the third day of the month of Sivan, and put them to the sword. Age was not spared in that day of terror. When the enemy found them, they cried with one voice, "Hear, O Israel, the Lord our God, the Lord is One," and stretched out their hands against those that were the delight of their eyes, and slew their wives and their little ones. And in that day of horror the wives too dedicated themselves to death. Behold the warriors shout without and the angels of peace weep bitterly for this holy community, given over to the fierce destroyer. . . And for this I beat my bosom and weep aloud, and I run from place to place, naked and despoiled, because of the thirteen hundred souls who became a booty and a prey in that day of horror. Will this suffice for thine anger, O God of Israel? Sixty poor wretches hid themselves in the treasury, and the Bishop sent them out among the villages, that they might save themselves, but the enemy pursued them and put them to the sword. Whithersoever they fled from death, the very stones cried out to betray them, for people were given freedom on that day to sack and destroy. Two men escaped death—they were baptized by violence: the name of one was Uri, of the other Ben David. Ben David was the chief of the community, and his two daughters were with him. All of them turned back again to the God of their fathers: and Isaac Ben David slew his two daughters during the festival of Weeks, and, having set fire to his house, made a burnt offering to the Lord; and he and his friend Uri went to the synagogue and stood before the tabernacle. and they died there as the flames ascended, and their souls mounted to heaven. My heart, my heart is moved for those that have died, and my soul will not be comforted for those that died by fire. Almighty God, protect their souls, judge their cause, avenge the slaughter of Thy servants, as it is written: "But when I will make them innocent of all their sins, I shall not make them innocent of the blood which they have shed, and the Eternal shall inhabit Zion."

The Second Crusade
(From the *Book of Memorials* by Ephraim of Bonn)

In the year 1146 Israel's communities were terror-stricken. The monk Rudolph who shamefully persecuted Israel, arose against the people of God, in order, like Haman of old, to destroy, to slay, and to cause to perish. He travelled throughout Germany to bestow the cross of the crusaders upon all who consented to set out for Jerusalem to fight against the Moslems. In every place where he came he aroused the people, crying, "Avenge ye first the vengeance of our God on His enemies who are here before us, and then we will go forward." When the Jews heard this, their courage failed them by reason of the rage of their oppressor who sought their destruction. They cried to God, saying: "Alas, O Lord God! Behold fifty years, like the period of a jubilee, have not yet elapsed since we shed our blood like water to sanctify Thy holy, great, and revered Name, on the day of the great slaughter. Wilt Thou indeed forsake us for ever and extend Thy wrath against us unto all generations? Shall misery follow misery?"

The Lord heard our supplications, and turned unto us, and had pity upon us, according to His abundant loving-kindness. He sent one of their greatest and respected teachers the abbot Bernard, from the town Clairvaux in France, after this evil monk. And he also preached to his people according to their custom, crying "It is good that you are ready to go forth against the Moslems; but whosoever uses violence against the Jews commits a deadly sin."

All honoured this monk as one of their saints, neither has it ever been said that he received a bribe for his good service to us. Many desisted from any further murderous attacks against us. We gladly gave our possessions as ransom for our lives. Whatever was asked of us, silver or gold, we withheld not.

If our Creator in His great compassion had not sent us this abbot, there would have been none in Israel that would have escaped or remained alive. Blessed be He who saves and delivers. Praised be His Name.

The Spanish Expulsion
(From *The Vale of Tears* by Joseph Ha-Cohen)

Since the time of Brother Vincent, the New Christians (converted Jews) had multiplied in Spain; they had made alliances with the greatest families in the country and had acquired a mighty influence. On the other hand, the Jews had also multiplied greatly until the time of Ferdinand and Isabella. These two princes appointed inquisitors over the New Christians to find out whether they were not relapsing into their former ways, and they were made objects of scorn and contempt, and many of them were burned in those days. . . These two princes, seeing that multitudes of Jews were returning to the House of Israel, drove the Jews from their country, so that the New Christians would not go in their ways, as many had done until then. All the hosts of the Lord, the exiles of Jerusalem in Spain, left this accursed country in the fifth month of the year 5252, which is the year 1492, and were scattered to the four corners of the earth. From Carthaginia there went forth, on the 16th day of Ab, sixteen large ships laden with human cattle, and this took place in all the other provinces. The Jews went whither the winds carried them, to Africa, to Asia, to Greece and to Turkey, in which countries they live to this day. And they suffered greatly and many tribulations assailed them, and the Genoese sailors treated them with cruelty.

Many of them died of despair on the journey. The Mussulmans disembowelled some of them to get the gold which they had swallowed to hide it, and others they threw into the waves; and there were others who were devoured by pestilence and by famine; and others the captains set down naked on desert islands, and others were sold as slaves in the mighty city of Genoa and the cities which owed her sovereignty. Among those who had embarked for Italy there was a cantor by the name of Joseph Cibbon, who had a son and several daughters, and one of his daughters awoke the love of the captain. The mother was informed of this, and preferring death to dishonour she threw her daughters into the sea and leapt after them. The sailors, seeing this, were seized with horror, and they put boats out and succeeded in rescuing one of them. The name of one of the sisters was Paloma, which means a dove: and her father lamented her, saying: "And they took the dove and threw her into the waves." There were many Jews who remained in Spain, not having the strength to flee, and there were some whose hearts were untouched by God, and many at this time apostatized. See, O God, against whom Thou hast stretched out thine hand! Shall a man eat his own offspring? For there were some who were put down on islands near Provence, and there was one Jew whose old father lay dying of hunger, and who went begging a morsel of bread in this strange place, and no one would give it to him. Then this man went to sell his youngest son for a piece of bread, but when he returned he found only a dead body. He tore his raiment and went back to the baker to get his son, but the baker would not return him; and he uttered heart-rending cries and shed bitter tears, but there was none to help him. God, my God! All these miseries have befallen us, yet we have not forgotten Thee, nor have we betrayed our covenant. And now, O God, estrange thyself no longer from us, and deliver us soon, because it is for Thy sake we are slaughtered, and for Thy sake we are no better than sheep which are destined for the slaughter. Help us, God of our salvation, sustain our cause and save us for Thy Name's sake.

The Charge of Ritual Murder

(From *The Scourge of Judah* by Solomon Ibn Verga)

In the time of the just king, Alphonso the Great (13th century), it was told to the judges that, on the eve of Easter, a Christian had entered a Jewish house, and he had been heard to cry for help and had never been seen again. A search was made in the house of the Jew, but without any result. The king asked the accusers: "Why did you not go to the help of the Christian?" They answered: "We should have had to break in the door and were afraid of committing a crime." "But," the Jew said, "the door of my house has been broken these ten days, in order to capture a slave who had taken refuge in my house, and it is still broken." The king did not believe that the crime had taken place. "This Jew," he said, "is an old man. He has not even strength enough to kill a louse." But the accusers held firm and brought false witnesses who even gave the name of the Christian. "His name," they said, "was Pedro Guzman, the husband of Beatrice, the priest's servant." And they also gave his description; small in build, red hair, forked beard, and one-eyed. The Jew was put to the torture; he confessed, and was condemned to be executed. When the sentence was being cried through the town, the bishop was passing through to go to the king. "What is this I hear?" he said. "The sentence says that Pedro Guzman was killed by the Jew on January 1st, and only yesterday I saw this Guzman in a neighbouring village of the town, and he will be here to-day or to-morrow." "Why then," asked the king, "did the Jew confess?" "This was a confession extracted by torture," said the bishop, "and words spoken under torture are as false as the deeds of princes." They began to search for Guzman, and he was led before the king, who was overjoyed to know the truth, and praised God and thanked the bishop. "Your majesty may now see," said the bishop, "that words extorted by torture are false."

The Massacres of 1648–1649

(From the Epistle of Rabbi Shabbatai Kohen)

Know then, if you have not heard it before, you surviving communities of the Lord, you who pray to God and listen trembling to His word. . . . A great sorrow fell upon the Jews, fasting and weeping and bitter lamentation was to be seen everywhere . . . because their Israelite co-religionists, God's people, fell by the sword and the persecutions of impure and wicked Christians. Cursed criminals murdered thousands and myriads of honest and decent Israelites, pious men and women . . . learned Rabbis and eminent scholars who taught numerous pupils.

This has been done by that low and despicable mob of the Orthodox Church called Cossacks. (They) revolted against the king, his princes and vassals. . . . This king was Vladislav (IV), an honest regent, worthy to be counted among the righteous. . . . In the year 5408 (1648) after the creation of earth and heaven, in the first month, namely the month of Nisan, the tears of the oppressed began to flow because the reprobate started at that time to attack and to exterminate the Israelites. Many nobles and many of the Polish people marched against them, but when they approached their camp in the land called Ukraine the scoundrels fell upon them with cunning and treachery. . . .

All Israelites in the Ukraine left their homes and fled from their houses and their lands with nothing but their lives and what little of their belongings they could carry. . . . Many fled to Niemirow, a big and famous town and the first among the Jewish communities. . . . About fifty villains came to Niemirow under false pretenses and blew the trumpets and trombones so that all the people could hear them, as if the Poles had arrived with their horses, riders and bands of music in order to induce the inhabitants of the fortress to open the gates. . . . This devilish stratagem met, indeed, with full success and thus they performed new cruelties there. They killed about six thousand people in the city, pious, learned and erudite men, rabbis, old and young men, maidens, bridegrooms and brides, children and women, and above all the most learned and world-famous Rabbi R. Yehiel Michael. . . . Then they destroyed the Synagogue which resembled a small temple; the villains with shouts and roars pulled out the scrolls, cut them up and either let people and animals, horses and riders trample on them or made sandals, shoes or garments of them. . . .

The pious community of Niemirow was the first victim of the mad and savage mob which spread from there over the whole country. One of the gangs turned to the fortress Tulczyn, which they besieged for eight days and invested so closely that all the inhabitants, among them many Jews and nobles, suffered hunger and thirst. In spite of this they did not rest day or night and defended themselves against the villains. At last the latter sent the following message to the nobility: "Why do you fight against the Christian people for the benefit of those miserable Jews, who since the earliest days have been our enemies. . . . We do not want to do any harm to you, you nobles and brave men, deliver to us only the Jews, who reject our faith, that we may treat them according to our desire. . . ." After that the nobles fulfilled their request and delivered up the most esteemed Jews. Thus three thousand pious and decent men lost their lives. They were killed with various instruments of murder, with clubs, scythes and axes. . . .

On the same day, too, fifteen hundred people were killed in the city of Human in Russia. On the Sabbath the nobles, with whom the wicked mob had again made an alliance, chased the Jews from the city into the fields and vineyards, where the villains surrounded them in a circle, stripped them to the skin and ordered them to lie on the ground, where the Jews huddled themselves in shame and ignominy like cattle led to the butcher. The villains spoke then to the Jews with friendly and consoling words: "Why do you want to be killed, strangled and slaughtered like offerings for your God, who poured out His anger upon you without mercy? Would it not be safer for you to worship our gods, our images and crosses, and we would form one people, which would be united together? Then you would be free and allowed to live without harm; we would return your possessions to you and you would become rich and esteemed men." But the holy and faithful people, who so often allowed themselves to be murdered for the sake of the Lord, despised life on earth, and all of them, young men and maidens, old men and minors, adults and children who were without stain raised their voices together to the Almighty in heaven, and cried: "Hear Israel, O Lord our God, Thou who art the only one and the King of the universe, we have been murdered for Thy sake so often already, O Lord, God of Israel, let us remain faithful to Thee. We do not want to have anything in common with a lying gang and to enter into an alliance with a malicious people." Afterwards they recited the confession of sins and said: "Yes, we are guilty," and thus they recognized the divine judgement. . . . Now the villains turned upon them, and there was not one among them who did not fall a victim.

. . . Then the villains, divided into several gangs which spread over our country, destroyed all communities and demolished all our synagogues.

In Czernigow they killed about two thousand and in Chartardov nearly twelve hundred of the holy Jewish people, besides the numerous Jews who died from hunger and thirst, on the devastated roads, or who were drowned in rivers and brooks reddened by the blood of the murdered people. They ravished hundreds of women and maidens before our own eyes and dragged them captive into their land, so that our eyes were darkened. They also tore into pieces our holy books and scrolls, so that our hearts fainted and all our courage vanished. Wilt Thou, our Lord God, Thou who sittest on the throne above the clouds, remain silent in the face of all this? . . .

The number of all the Jews killed in the two said years amounted to more than a hundred thousand, all honest and excellent people. Various afflictions and troubles besides came upon us in those places to which the Jews had fled within the hostile country. Many of them died in near and distant towns; there was not one house where they had settled in which at least one refugee did not pass away. People were, therefore, not able to count the bodies, and to provide shrouds and coffins that they might rest in peace in their tombs, and thus twenty to thirty were thrown together into one pit. . . .

I have, therefore, fixed the 20th of the month of Sivan as a solemn day of fast, as a day of mourning and lamentation for myself and my contemporaries, for our children and grandchildren. . . . I have composed penitential prayers and lamentations to be sung every year on that day, and every pious man who is filled with fear of God and bears the name of an Israelite may keep that day like the one on which both Temples were destroyed. . . .

IV MISCELLANEOUS HISTORICAL WRITINGS

The Wonder-Working Wisdom of Abu Aaron
(From *The Chronicle of Ahimaaz*)

When Abu Aaron reached Beneventum the entire community came out as one man to welcome him. On the Sabbath, an esteemed young man arose to read the prayer before Him that dwelleth on high. He chanted with pleasing voice. When he reached the words "*Barechu et adonai hammevoroch*," his voice lingered on the sound, but he did not pronounce God's name. The master at once realized that the reader was actually a dead man, and (it is known that) the dead do not praise God. "Stop," he at once commanded in a loud voice, "Do not give praise, for thou art not permitted to recite prayer before God." Then he began to question the youth, to plead with him in the name of his Maker, saying, "Tell me and do not fear, do not conceal from me what thou hast done, confess the truth before the Creator." . . . Immediately he answered, "I have indeed sinned, and trespassed against God; I have rebelled and transgressed and done wrong. If you are willing to bear the burden of the sin which your servant has committed (I will confess)." And all of them were willing to bear all that he imposed upon them. Thereupon he confessed, giving thanks to God; and thus told what he had done and what had happened to him. He said:

"Hear me, oh people of God, my teachers and masters, leaders and elders, sages and scholars, princes and nobles, old and young, I will tell you plainly all that happened.

"In my time there was a Jew named R. Ahimaaz who went to Jerusalem, the glorious city, three times, to fulfil his vow. On each pilgrimage he took 100 pieces of gold with him, as he had vowed to the Rock of his salvation, to give aid to those who were engaged in the study of His law, and to those who mourned the ruined house of His glory. As he set out on his third pilgrimage, he asked my mother for me, saying, 'Let him go with me, to keep me company and help me on the way. I will bring him back to thee; at my hands thou mayest require him; if I do not bring him back to thee, I shall have sinned before God, I and my children.' Then we set out on our journey rejoicing, without a thought of sadness. As we were sitting at the table of the scholars in study with the head of the academy, the teachers of the Law exclaimed, 'Let us give praise, in pleasant and fervent song, with love and devotion to Him that is adored by myriads.' They looked at their disciples seated before them; and the head of their school turned to them and said, 'Let the young man in our midst, who has come with our Colleague R. Ahimaaz, cheer us and delight our heart with the flow of his knowledge and the utterance of his thoughts.' Then I began reverently to give praise in psalm and song to Him that putteth on light as a garment.

"There sat one of the elders in meditation, intently listening to my chanting. He began to weep bitterly. R. Ahimaaz, looking at him, noticed his actions, and arising from the company went over to him and begged him to tell why he wept. The elder simply told him that God had decreed that, in a little while, the young man would surely die. When the good man heard this his eyes filled with tears, he rent his clothes and tore out his hair, and exclaimed before them all, 'I have no place among the living; I have sworn to his mother that I would bring him back to her, without mishap or harm; how can I return to my house, if the lad is not with me? The oath which I have taken will be the means of blighting my hope and ardent expectation.' Seeing his affliction and his bitter weeping, they wrote the Holy Name that was written in the Sanctuary; they made an incision in the flesh of my right arm, and inserted the Name where the flesh had been cut. So I came away in peace and returned home to my mother. While R. Ahimaaz was alive I wandered from land to land. Living since that time, I can live forever if I so desire, for no man can know the place of the Name unless I reveal it. But I will show it to you; I am in your hands; deal with me as seems right in your eyes."

So they brought the grave clothes; he approached and put them on; he then showed where the master had made the incision, and took the Name out of it. His body became lifeless; the corpse crumbled in decay as from the dissolution of many years, the flesh returned to the dust.

Rabbi Shephatiah Foretells the Death of the Tyrant Basil

(From *The Chronicle of Ahimaaz*)

On New Year's day R. Shephatiah alone was thought worthy of the honor of sounding the *Shofar*, for the glory of God through His people. On that day he was weak, prostrated by sickness. But the whole congregation urged him insistently, saying: "Our master, arrayed in light, the radiance of our glory, the light of our eyes, blow the *Shofar* for us; as long as God spares you, no one else shall blow the *Shofar* for us." They continued to urge him and he arose to blow it. But he did not have sufficient strength and could not produce the proper sounds. The good man calmly accepting the judgment against him said to them, "My children, may this be a sign for good unto you; because of my transgression, time has turned against me." He left the house of worship and went to his home and lay upon his bed. The entire congregation followed him and entered his bedchamber. Turning his face to them, he said "I am going to my eternal rest, to my portion among the fathers of old, and I tell you dear children, my three beloved sons, that Basil the oppressor and persecutor is dead. He passes on before me, bound in chains of fire, delivered to the demons of destruction. My God, whose name is the Lord of Hosts, has sent me to go forth to meet Basil and to stand in judgment against him, for all the evil that he has committed against His people, to blot out his name and the name of his posterity, to destroy him root and branch." So they noted the day and hour. Soon afterward the report reached them, announcing that Basil the oppressor had died; the letter came just as the good man had foretold. It was the custom of the emperors of Constantinople, whenever an emperor died, to make proclamation by letter, in Bari, giving the day and the time when he had passed away. "Praised be He who alone doeth wonders, who destroyed him in this world and shut him out of the world to come. Praised be His name and the name of His glory. I shall be gathered to my people and shall go to my place and as for you my children, my devoted ones, the assembly of my people, may God be with you,—He that dispenseth death and life, I am that I am, reviving the faithful children of Benjamin and the lion's welp (Judah)."

Excerpt From the Letter of Hasdai Ibn Shaprut to the King of the Khazars

I, Hasdai,[1] son of Isaac, son of Ezra, belonging to the exiled Jews of Jerusalem, in Spain, a servant of my Lord the King, bow to the earth before him and prostrate myself towards the abode of your Majesty, from a distant land. I rejoice in your tranquillity and magnificence, and stretch forth my hands to God in Heaven that He may prolong your reign in Israel. But who am I? and what is my life that I should dare to indite a letter to my lord the King and to address your Majesty? I rely, however, on the integrity and uprightness of my object. . .

Praise be to the beneficent God for his mercy towards me! Kings of the earth, to whom His magnificence and power are known, bring gifts to him,[2] conciliating his favor by costly presents, such as the King of the Germans, the King of the Gebalim, who are as-Saglab,[3] the King of Constantineh,[4] and others. All their gifts pass through my hands and I am charged with making gifts in return. (Let my lips express praise to the God in Heaven who so far extends his loving-kindness towards me without any merit of my own, but in the fullness of his mercies.) I always ask the ambassadors of these monarchs about our brethren the Israelites, the remnant of the captivity, whether they have heard anything concerning the deliverance of those who have pined in bondage and had found no rest. At length mercantile emissaries of Khorasân told me that there is a kingdom of Jews who are called Khozars (and between Constantineh and that country is a sea

1 The name is transliterated by Elkan H. Adler as "Chisdai."

2 Abd al-Rahman, King of Spain in Hasdai's time.

3 The slavonians.

4 Constantinople.

voyage of 15 days, by land many nations dwell between us and them.) But I did not believe these words, for I thought that they told me such things to procure my goodwill and favour. I was, therefore, hesitating and doubtful till the ambassadors of Constantineh came with presents and a letter from their king to our king, whom I interrogated concerning this matter. They answered me, "It is quite true; there is in that place a kingdom Alcusari distant from Constantineh a fifteen days' journey by sea, but many peoples are scattered through the land; the name of the king now reigning is Joseph; ships sometimes come from their country to ours bringing fish, skins, and wares of every kind; the men are our brethren and are honoured by us; there is frequent communication between us by embassies and mutual gifts; they are very powerful; they maintain numerous armies, which they occasionally engage in expeditions." This account inspired me with hope, wherefore I bowed down and adored the God of Heaven.

I now looked about for a faithful messenger whom I might send into your country in order that I might know the truth of this matter and ascertain the welfare of my Lord and his servants our brethren. The thing seemed impossible to me, owing to the very great distance of the locality, but at length by the will and favour of God, a man presented himself to me named Mar Isaac, the son of Nathan. He put his life into his hand and willingly offered to take my letter to my Lord the King. I gave him a large reward, supplying him with gold and silver for his own expenses and those of his servants, and with everything necessary. Moreover, I sent out of my own resources a magnificent present to the King of Constantineh, requesting him to aid this my messenger in every possible way, till he should arrive at that place where my Lord resides. Accordingly this messenger set out, went to the

King and showed him my letter and presents. The King, on his part, treated him honourably, and detained him there for six months, with the ambassadors of my Lord the King, of Cordova. One day he told them and my messenger to return, giving the latter a letter in which he wrote that the way was dangerous, that the peoples through whom he must pass were engaged in warfare, that the sea was stormy and could not be navigated except at a certain time. When I heard this I was grieved even to death, and took it very ill that he had not acted according to my orders and fulfilled my wishes.

Afterwards I wished to send my letter by way of Jerusalem, because persons there guaranteed that my letter should be dispatched from thence to Nisibis, thence to Armenia, from Armenia to Berdaa, and thence to your country. While in this state of suspense, behold ambassadors of the King of Gebalim arrived, and with them two Israelites; the name of one was Mar Saul, of the other Mar Joseph. These persons understood my perplexity and comforted me, saying, "Give us your letter, and we will take care that it be carried to the King of the Gebalim, who for your sake will send it to the Israelites dwelling in the land of the Hungarians, they will send it to Russ, thence to Bulgar, till at last it will arrive, according to your wish, at its destination."

He who tries the heart and searches the reins knows that I did none of these things for the sake of mine own honour, but only to know the truth, whether the Israelitish exiles, anywhere form one independent kingdom and are not subject to any foreign ruler. If, indeed, I could learn that this was the case, then, despising all my glory, abandoning my high estate, leaving my family, I would go over mountains and hills, through seas and lands, till I should arrive at the place where my Lord the King resides, that I might see not only his glory and magnificence, and that of his servants and ministers, but also the tranquillity of the Israelites. On beholding this my eyes would brighten, my reins would exult, my lips would pour forth praises to God, who has not withdrawn his favour from his afflicted ones.

Now, therefore, let it please your Majesty, I beseech you, to have regard to the desires of your servant, and to command your scribes who are at hand to send back a reply from your distant land to your servant and to inform me fully concerning the condition of the Israelites, and how they came to dwell there. . .

One thing more I ask of my Lord, that he would tell me whether there is among you any computation concerning the final redemption which we have been awaiting so many years, whilst we went from one captivity to another, from one exile to another. How strong is the hope of him who awaits the realization of these events. And oh! how can I hold my peace and be restful in the face of the desolation of the house of our glory and remembering those who, escaping the sword, have passed through fire and water, so that the remnant is but small. We have been cast down from our glory, so that we have nothing to reply when they say daily unto us, "Every other people has its kingdom, but of yours there is no memorial on the earth." Hearing, therefore, the fame of my Lord the King, as well as the power of his dominions, and the multitude of his forces, we were amazed, we lifted up our head, our spirit revived, and our hands were strengthened, and the kingdom of my Lord furnished us with an argument in answer to this taunt. May this report be substantiated; for that would add to our greatness. Blessed be the Lord of Israel who has not left us without a kinsman as defender nor suffered the tribes of Israel to be without an independent kingdom. May my Lord the King prosper for ever. . .

Excerpt From the Reply of King Joseph to Hasdai Ibn Shaprut

We are of the posterity of Japhet and the descendants of his son Togarma. We read in the genealogic books of our forefathers that Togarma had ten sons; we are the issue of Khozar, the seventh. It is set down in our chronicles that from his days onward our ancestors had to fight against peoples more numerous and more powerful than they. . . Some centuries later there came a descendant of Khozar, King Bulan, a wise man and God-fearing, who drove away the soothsayers, and purified the country of idolatry. . . The Kings of Edom (Christians) and of Ishmael (Mohammedans) sent their ambassadors to him with great treasures, and also sent their learned men to convert them to their religions. But the King, in his wisdom, also sent for a learned Israelite, well versed in all matters; and he then had them as it were compete, so that each one expounded with fire the principles of his own religion and sought to refute the arguments of his antagonists. . . Then the King said to the monk: "Of the two religions, that of the Israelite and that of the Ishmaelite, which is to be preferred?" The priest replied: "That of the Israelite." Then he asked the Cadi: "Between the faith of the Israelite and the faith of the Edomite, which is to be preferred?" The Cadi replied: "The religion of the Israelite is much to be preferred to the religion of the Nazarenes." To this the Prince answered: "You both acknowledge that the faith of the Israelites is the wiser and the better; I therefore choose that religion, the religion of Abraham." From that time on God always helped him and strengthened him, and he and his people were all circumcized. He then sent for the wise men of Israel, who expounded before him the law and the precepts. From that time on we have followed this religion: God be praised for it eternally. . .

With reference[1] to your question concerning the marvelous end,[2] our eyes are turned to the Lord our God, and to the wise men of Israel who dwell in Jerusalem and Babylon. Though we are far from Zion, we have heard that because of our iniquities the computations are erroneous; nor do we know aught concerning this. But if it please the Lord, He will do it for the sake of His great name; nor will the desolation of His house, the abolition of His service, and all the troubles which have come upon us, be lightly esteemed in His sight. He will fulfil His promise, and "the Lord whom ye seek shall suddenly come to His temple, the messenger of the Covenant whom ye delight in: behold he shall come, saith the Lord of Hosts" (Mal. III, 1). Besides this we only have the prophecy of Daniel. May God hasten the redemption of Israel, gather together the captives and dispersed, you and I, and all Israel that love His name, in the lifetime of us all.

Finally, you mention that you desire to see my face. I also long and desire to see your honoured face, to behold your wisdom and magnificence. Would that it were according to your word, and that it were granted me to be united with you, so that you might be my father and I your son. All my people would pay homage to you: according to your word and righteous counsel we should go out and come in. Farewell.

[1] The rest of this section is reprinted from the *Miscellany of Hebrew Literature*, Vol. I, pp. 111-112, Translated from the Hebrew by A. I. K. D., H. Trübner and Co., London, 1872.

[2] Concerning the restoration of the Jews to their former glory by the Messiah

Chapter VIII

TRAVELERS' ACCOUNTS

No nation has wandered as extensively and as constantly as the Jews. Exiles, expulsions, commercial ventures, and religious pilgrimages caused the Jew to cross continents and oceans in search of home, bread, and the satisfaction of religious yearnings. These travels, often the result of severe persecutions, were greatly facilitated by the world-wide dispersion of the Jewish people. In every country and in every town the Jewish traveller found among his co-religionists both a friendly asylum and a sympathetic audience. This bond of friendship among the Jews of all countries and this keen interest in the welfare of their scattered co-religionists was due not only to their common culture, history, and aspirations, but also to their precarious situation and the ever-changing misfortunes that were their common lot. The mediaeval Jewish traveller was therefore not only assisted in his travels but was constantly encouraged to unburden himself and to relate his observations in the communities he traversed. This constant interest in travel eventually led some of the travellers to record their experiences, thus giving rise to the several travellers' accounts that have enriched mediaeval Jewish literature.

The nature of these records varies widely. Eldad the Danite, whose travels took place in the ninth century, left a romantic though fictitious account. He knew that the Jews longed for encouraging news of their brothers in far-off lands, and he was not too scrupulous to invent a story which he knew would satisfy their cravings. Others, such as Benjamin of Tudela and Petachiah of Ratisbon, who travelled extensively in the twelfth century, left accounts sufficiently authentic to have been recognized and accepted by the modern student of mediaeval history. The same may be said of the itineraries of Meshullam ben Menahem of Volterra and Obadiah Jaré Da Bertinoro, whose pilgrimages to the Holy Land occurred in the fifteenth century, and whose accounts are both vivid and accurate.

What is noteworthy concerning these records of the mediaeval Jewish travellers is that they have retained their original freshness and romantic flavor even for the modern student. Their very naiveté and inaccuracies have endowed them with life beyond their own day, and have given them a unique interest which the attentive reader cannot fail to discover.

I. FICTITIOUS TRAVEL ACCOUNTS

Excerpts From the Letter of Eldad the Danite

Eldad's Adventures

And this was my going forth from the other side of the rivers of Ethiopia.

I and a Jew of the tribe of Asher entered a small ship to trade with the shipmen and behold, at mid-night, the Lord caused a great and strong wind to arise and the ship was wrecked. Now the Lord had prepared a box and I took hold of it and my companion seeing this also took hold of that box, and we went up and down with it, until the sea cast us among a people called Romranos who are black Ethiopians, tall, without garment or clothing upon them, cannibals, like unto the beasts of the field.

And when we came to their country they took hold of us and, seeing that my companion was fat and healthy and pleasing, slaughtered and ate him, and he cried, "Alas for me that I have been brought to this people and the Ethiopians will eat my flesh," but me they took, for I was sick on board ship, and they put me in chains until I should get fat and well, and they brought before me all kinds of good but forbidden food, but I ate nothing and I hid the food, and when they asked me if I had eaten I answered, yes I had eaten.

And I was with them a long time until the Lord, blessed be He, perfomed a miracle with me, for a great army came upon them from another place, who took me captive, but they spoiled and killed them and took me along with the captives.

And those wicked men were fire worshippers, and I dwelt with them four years, and, behold, every morning they made a great fire and bowed down and worshipped it. And they brought me to the province of Azania.

And a Jew, a merchant of the tribe of Issachar, found me and bought me for 32 gold pieces and brought me back with him to his country. . .

Life in Eldad's Country

And these tribes, being Dan, Naphtali, Gad, and Asher, dwell in the ancient Havilah, . . and every year they make war with the seven kingdoms and seven countries. The names of these kingdoms are Tussina, Kamti, Kuba, Tariogi, Takula, Karma, and Kalom, and they are on the other side of the rivers of Ethiopia. . .

And their King's name is Uzziel and the name of their great prince Elizaphan, of the children of Aholiab, of the tribe of Dan, and their banner is white and written thereon in black is, "Hear, O Israel, the Lord our God is one God," and when they seek to go out to war the crier calls with the sound of the trumpet, and the lord of the hosts comes and the armies go forth one hundred and twenty thousand with small white bannerettes. Every three months, a different tribe goes out to war, and the tribe remains three months away, and all that they bring from the spoil of their enemies they divide among their own tribe. But the descendants of Samson, of the tribe of Dan, are superior to all. They never run away, for that were a great shame to them. They are numerous as the sands of the sea, and have no employment but war and, whensoever they fight, they say it is not good for mighty men to flee, let them die young, but let them not flee, let them strengthen their heart unto God, and several times they say and cry all of them together, "Hear, O Israel, our God is one God," and then they all take heed.

And thus they do till their three months are over and then they return and they bring all their spoil to King Uzziel, and he divides it with all Israel, and this is their statute from King David until this day, and King Uzziel takes his share and the King gives a share to all the wise men, sages of the law, dwellers in tents, and afterwards all take their portion, and the lord of the host his share. Thus they do in the three months when Naphtali goes out, and in the three months when Gad goes out, and so all of them until twelve months are completed, and then they repeat in succession.

Beyond the River Sambatyon

As to the tribe of Moses our teacher, on whom be peace, the righteous servant of God . . . the sea surrounds them, three months' journey by three months. They dwell in glorious houses and fine buildings and castles, and train elephants for themselves in their times of joy. No unclean thing is to be found with them, no unclean fowl, no unclean beast, no unclean cattle, no flies, no fleas, no lice, no foxes, no scorpions, no serpents, and no dogs. All these were in the idolatrous land, where they had been in servitude. They have only sheep, oxen, and fowls, and their sheep bring forth twice a year. They sow seed twice a year; they sow and they reap and they have gardens and olives and pomegranates and figs and all kinds of beans and cucumbers and melons and onions and garlic and barley and wheat, and from one comes forth a hundred.

They are of perfect faith and their Talmud is all in Hebrew, and thus they learn, "Thus taught us our Rabbis, from the mouth of Joshua the son of Nun, from the mouth of our father Moses, from the mouth of Almighty." But they know not the Rabbis, for these were of the Second Temple and they did not reach them.

And they can speak only the Holy tongue and they all take ritual baths and never swear. They cry out against him that takes the name of God in vain, and say that by the sin of cursing your sons would die young. But they are long lived and live a hundred or 120 years and no son dies in his father's lifetime, and they reach three or four generations, and they sow and reap themselves, for they have no manservants or maidservants, and they are all equal, and do not shut their houses at night for that would be shame to them, and a young man goes with the flocks ten days' journey and fears neither robbers nor ghosts. They are all Levites and have not among them either Priest or Israelite, and they abide in the sanctity of Moses our teacher, the servant of the Lord.

Moreover, they see no man and no men see them except these four tribes, who dwell on the other side of the rivers of Ethiopia. There is a place where these can see each other and speak if they cry out, but the River Sambatyon is between them, and they tell, "Thus it happened to us in war time," and they tell all Israel what happened to them. When they want anything important, they have a kind of pigeon known among them and they write their letters and fasten them to the wings or to the feet of the pigeon, and these cross the River Sambatyon and the pigeons come to their Kings and their Princes. They also have very many precious stones and silver and gold, and they sow flax and they rear cochineal and make pleasant gaments without end and are five times as numerous as those that came out of Egypt, for they are innumerable. The breadth of that river is 200 cubits bowshot, and the river is full of large and small stones, and the sound of them rumbles like a great storm, like a tempest at sea and, in the night, the sound of it is heard a day's journey, and they have with them six wells and they all unite into one lake and therefrom they irrigate their land, and therein are clean edible fish. The river runs and the stones and sand rumble during the six working days, but on the seventh day it rests and is tranquil until the end of Sabbath. And on the other side of the river, on the side where the four tribes dwell, is a fire which flames on Sabbath and no man can approach within a mile.

II. TRAVELS THROUGH MANY LANDS

Excerpts From the Accounts of Benjamin of Tudela.

The Inhabitants of Constantinople

The Greek inhabitants are very rich in gold and precious stones, and they go clothed in garments of silk with gold embroidery, and they ride horses, and look like princes. Indeed, the land is very rich in all cloth stuffs, and in bread, meat, and wine.

Wealth like that of Constantinople is not to be found in the whole world. Here also are men learned in all the books of the Greeks, and they eat and drink, every man under his vine and his fig-tree.

They hire from amongst all nations warriors called Loazim (Barbarians) to fight with the Sultan Mas'ud, King of the Togarmim (Seljuks) who are called Turks; for the natives are not warlike, but are as women who have no strength to fight.

No Jews live in the city, for they have been placed behind an inlet of the sea. An arm of the sea of Marmora shuts them in on the one side, and they are unable to go out except by way of the sea, when they want to do business with the inhabitants. In the Jewish quarter are about 2,000 Rabbanite Jews and about 500 Karaites, and a fence divides them. Amongst the scholars are several wise men, at their head being the chief rabbi, R. Abtalion, R. Obadiah, R. Aaron Bechor Shoro, R. Joseph Shir-Guru and R. Eliakim, the warden. And amongst them are artificers in silk and many rich merchants. No Jew there is allowed to ride on horseback. The one exception is R. Solomon Hamitsri, who is the king's physician, and through whom the Jews enjoy considerable alleviation of their oppression. For their condition is very low, and there is much hatred against them which is fostered by the tanners, who throw out their dirty water in the streets before the doors of the Jewish houses and defile the Jews' quarter (the Ghetto) So the Greeks hate the Jews, good and bad alike, and subject them to great oppression, and beat them in the streets, and in every way treat them with rigour. Yet the Jews are rich and good, kindly and charitable, and bear their lot with cheerfulness.

The Jewish Community of Baghdad

In Baghdad there are about 40,000 Jews and they dwell in security, prosperity and honour under the great Caliph, and amongst them are great sages, the heads of Academies engaged in the study of the law. In this city there are ten Academies. At the head of the great Academy is the chief rabbi, R. Samuel, the son of Eli. He is the head of the Academy Gaon Jacob. He is a Levite, and traces his pedigree back to Moses our teacher. . . And at the head of all is Daniel the son of Hisdai, who is styled "Our Lord the Head of the Captivity of all Israel." He possesses a book of pedigrees going back as far as David, King of Israel. The Jews call him "Our Lord, Head of the Captivity," and the Mohammedans call him "Saidna ben Daud" and he has been invested with authority over all the congregations of Israel at the hands of the Emir al Muminin, the Lord of Islam. For thus Mohammed commanded concerning him and his descendants; and he granted him a seal of office over all the congregations that dwell under his rule, and ordered that every one, whether Mohammedan or Jew, or belonging to any other nation in his dominion, should rise up before him (the Exilarch) and salute him, and that any one who should refuse to rise up should receive one hundred stripes.

And every fifth day, when he goes to pay a visit to the great Caliph, horsemen, Gentiles as well as Jews, escort him, and heralds proclaim in advance, "Make way before our Lord, the son of David, as is due unto him," the Arabic words being *Amilu Tarik li Saidna ben Daud.* He is mounted on a horse, and is attired in robes of silk and embroidery with a large turban on his head, and from the turban is suspended a long white cloth adorned with a chain upon which the cipher of Mohammed is engraved. Then he appears before the Caliph and kisses his hand and the Caliph rises and places him on a throne which Mohammed had ordered to be made for him, and all the Mohammedan princes who attend the court of the Caliph rise up before him. And the Head of the Captivity is seated on his throne opposite to the Caliph, in compliance with the command of Mohammed to give effect to what is written in the law, "The sceptre shall not depart from Judah nor a law-giver from between his feet until he come to Shiloh: and to him shall the gathering of the people be". . He owns hospices, gardens and plantations in Babylon, and much land inherited from his fathers, and no one can take his possessions from him by force. He has a fixed weekly revenue arising from the hospices of the Jews, the markets and the merchants, apart from that which is brought to him from far-off lands. The man is very rich and wise in the Scriptures as well as in the Talmud, and many Israelites dine at his table every day. . .

Description of Jerusalem and Its Surroundings

From there it is three parasangs to Jerusalem, which is a small city, fortified by three walls. There are many people in it, and the Ishmaelites call them Jacobites, Arameans, Greeks, Georgians, Franks, and peoples of all other tongues. There is a dyeing-house there, which the Jews rent annually from the king on condition that nobody besides the Jews should be engaged in dyeing in Jerusalem. There are about two hundred Jews dwelling under the tower of David, in one corner of the city. The first structure of the foundation of the wall of the tower of David, to the extent of ten cubits, is part of the ancient structure which our ancestors set up, but the remaining portion was built by the Ishmaelites. There is no structure in the whole city stronger than the tower of David.

The city contains also two buildings, one being a hospital, from which four hundred knights issue forth, and where all the sick that come thither are lodged and receive all their needs in life and in death. The second building is called the Temple of Solomon; it is the palace which was built by Solomon king of Israel, peace be upon him. Knights are quartered there, three hundred of whom issue forth every day for military exercises, besides the knights that come from the land of the Franks and from the land of Edom, having taken a vow upon themselves to serve there a year or two until their vow is fulfilled. In that city is the great place of worship called the Sepulchre; there is the burial-place of that man,[1] to which all the misguided repair.

There are four gates in Jerusalem; the gate of Abram, the gate of David, the gate of Zion, and the gate of Goshafat, which is the gate of Jehoshaphat, in front of the sanctuary which stood there in ancient times. There is also the Templum Domini, which is on the site of the temple, upon which 'Omar the son of al-Khattab erected a very large and magnificent cupola. The Gentiles are not allowed to introduce there any image or effigy; they only come there to pray. In front of that place is the Western Wall which is one of the walls of the holy of holies. This is called the Gate of Mercy, and thither all the Jews repair to pray in front of the wall of the temple court.

There, in Jerusalem, attached to the house which belonged to Solomon, are horse-stalls which he built; it is a very strong structure, built of immense stones; the like of this building was not seen in all the world. There is still to be seen today the pool where the priests used to slaughter their sacrifices, and the people coming thither from Judah used to inscribe their names upon the wall. A man going out through the gate of Jehoshaphat would arrive at the valley of Jehoshaphat, which is the wilderness of the nations. There is the pillar of Absalom's Monument, and the grave of king Uzziah. There is likewise a great fountain, and the waters of Shiloah flowing into the brook of Kidron. Over the spring there is a large structure, dating back from the days of our ancestors. Little water is found there, and most of the people of Jerusalem drink rain-water, for they have cisterns in their houses.

[1] Jesus

From the valley of Jehoshaphat one ascends the Mount of Olives, as only this valley intervenes between Jerusalem and the Mount of Olives. From the Mount of Olives one can see the Sea of Sodom (it is two parasangs from the Sea of Sodom to the Pillar of Salt into which Lot's wife turned; the sheep lick it, but it afterwards regains its original shape), and the whole land of the plain and the valley of Shittim as far as Mount Nebo.

In front of Jerusalem is Mount Zion; but there is no building on Mount Zion, except a place of worship belonging to the uncircumcised.

About three miles before Jerusalem are the sepulchres of the Israelites, for they used to bury their dead in caves in those days. Each sepulchre bears a date: but the children of Edom demolish the sepulchres, and of the stones thereof they build their houses. These sepulchres reach as far as the border of Benjamin at Zelzah.

Around Jerusalem there are great mountains, and on Mount Zion are the sepulchres of the house of David, and the sepulchres of the kings who arose after him. The place, however, is no longer known, on account of the following incident. Fifteen years ago part of the place of worship, which is on Mount Zion, fell in, and the patriarch said to his overseer: "Take the stones from the old walls, and restore the place of worship with them." The latter did so, and hired workmen; twenty men, at fixed wages, were pulling out the stones from the foundation of the wall of Zion. Among these men were two very intimate friends. One day one of them made a banquet for his friend. After the meal they returned to their work, and their overseer said to them: "Wherefore have ye come late to-day?" They answered and said: "Wherefore dost thou chide us? When our fellow-workmen go to their meal, we will do our work." When meal-time came, and the other workmen went to their meal, these two continued to pull out stones. They raised a certain stone, and found the mouth of a cave beneath it. Thereupon one said to his friend: "Let us go in and see whether there is any money in there." Having passed through the entrance of the cave, they reached a large hall supported by pillars of marble over-laid with silver and gold. In front was a table of gold and a sceptre and crown. This was the sepulchre of King David. At the left thereof was the sepulchre of king Solomon in like fashion, and so were the sepulchres of the kings of Judah that were buried there. Closed coffers were also there, and no man knows what they contain. When these two men wanted to enter the hall, a stormy wind came forth from the entrance of the cave, and smote them, so that they fell like dead to the ground. They lay there until evening, when another wind came forth, crying out as if with a man's voice: "Arise and go forth from this place!" The men went out from there in haste and terror, and came to the patriarch, and related these things to him. The patriarch then sent for Rabbi Abraham al-Constantini, the pious ascetic, who was one of the mourners for Jerusalem, and he related all these things to him according to the narrative of the two men who had come out from there. And Rabbi Abraham answered, and said to him: "These are the sepulchres of the house of David, that is, of the Kings of Judah; and to-morrow I and thou and these men shall go in and see what is there." On the following day they sent for the two men and found them lying in their beds. Filled with terror, the men said: "We will not enter there, for God desires not to show it to any man." The patriarch then commanded them to close up that place and to keep it concealed from men unto this day. The afore-mentioned Rabbi Abraham related these things to me.

Excerpts From the Itinerary of Petachiah of Ratisbon

The Land of Kedar (*Ukrainia*)

These are the travels undertaken by Rabbi Petachiah who travelled through many lands. He set out from Prague, which is in Bohemia, going to Poland, and from Poland to Kiev in Russia. From Russia he went for six days on the River Dnieper. On the other side of the river he commenced his travels in the land of Kedar. There they have no ships, but sew together ten extended horse hides, with a thong round the border; they then seat themselves on the hides, placing thereon also the wagons and all the luggage. They then tie the thong which is on the border of the hides to the tails of the horses, who start swimming, and thus they pass over the water. They eat no bread in the land of Kedar, but rice and millet boiled in milk, as well as milk and cheese. They also put pieces of flesh under the saddle of a horse, which they ride and, urging on the animal, cause it to sweat. The flesh getting warm, they eat it. They only travel in the land of Kedar under escort. This is the manner in which the sons of Kedar pledge their faith to each other. One man thrusts a needle into his finger and invites the intended companion of his journey to swallow the blood of the wounded finger. He and that other person become, as it were, the same blood and flesh. They have another fashion of entering into this bond. They fill a vessel of cast copper of the shape of a human face and the traveller and his escort drink thereout, after which they never prove faithless. They have no king, but only princes and nobles.

Rabbi Petachiah passed through the whole length of the land of Kedar in sixteen days. The inhabitants live in tents, they are far-sighted and have beautiful eyes, because they eat no salt and live among fragrant plants. They are good archers, bringing down birds whilst on the wing. They perceive and recognize (objects) at more than a day's distance. There are no mountains in their country, but all is level. And a day's journey behind the land of Kedar extends a gulf, intervening between the land of Kedar and the land of Khozaria. There it is customary for women the whole day and night to bemoan and lament their deceased fathers and mothers. This they continue until any of their sons or daughters or other members of the family die, and the last (survivors) lament those that preceded them in death. They teach their daughters lamentation. In the night they groan and howl. The dogs also whine and bark at their voice.

The rabbi then travelled about eight days, and came where, at the extremity of the land of Khozaria, seventeen rivers surrounding it unite, and whoever wishes to undertake a distant journey repairs hither. There is a sea there on one side, from which there arises a great stench, whilst on the other side there is a sea which does not emit any offensive smell. There is about a day's journey between the two seas. If any individual passed the stinking sea[1] he would die immediately. When the wind blows from the stinking sea to that not emitting any offensive smell many die. People only go there when the wind does not blow from it. . .

In the land of Kedar there are no Jews but only Karaites. And Rabbi Petachiah asked them: "Why do you not believe in the words of the sages?" They replied: "Because our fathers did not teach them to us." On the eve of the Sabbath

[1] The Putrid Sea.

they cut all the bread to be eaten on the Sabbath. They eat in the dark and sit the whole day on one spot. Their prayers consist only of psalms. And when Rabbi Petachiah imparted to them our ritual and prayer after meals they were pleased. They also said: "We have never heard of the Talmud." . . .

The Wonders of Nineveh

At Nineveh there was an elephant. Its head is not at all protruding. It is big, eats about two wagon loads of straw at one time; its mouth is in its breast, and when it wants to eat it protrudes its lip (trunk) about two cubits, takes up with it the straw, and puts it into its mouth. When the sultan condemns anybody to death they say to the elephant: this person is guilty. It then seizes him with its lip, casts him aloft, and kills him. Whatever a human being does with his hand it does with its lip; this is exceedingly strange and marvelous. Upon the elephant's back is set a structure like a citadel (howdah), within which there are twelve armed warriors; when the beast stretches forth its lip they climb up, using it as a bridge.

At Nineveh there was an astrologer whose name was R. Solomon. There is among all the sages in Nineveh, and the land of Assur, none as expert in the planets as he. R. Petachiah asked him when Messiah would come. He replied, I have seen this often distinctly in the planets. But Rabbi Judah the Pious would not write it down lest he should be suspected of being a believer in the words of Rabbi Solomon. . .

III. PILGRIMAGES TO THE HOLY LAND

A. The Pilgrimage of Rabbi Meshullam ben Menahem of Volterra

Alexandria

I inquired about the usages of Alexandria and their mode of life and found that they are very extraordinary in all their ways. The women see but are not seen, for they wear a black veil on their faces which has small holes, and they wear on their heads a turban of muslin folded many times, embroidered and ornamented, and upon it a white veil which reaches to their ankles and covers their bodies. The Ishmaelites also wear cotton garments and constantly sit on straw mats or rugs, and they go with bare feet and legs and wear only a cotton garment with a girdle, and the garment reaches up to the middle of the thigh, and the women wear breeches, and the wives of the Turks go to the barber once a week. But on the contrary the men wear no breeches and do not have their hair cut, but they shave their head with a razor without washing the head except with a little water.

When a man marries a wife he gives her a dowry and from thenceforward he is only obliged to feed her, eating and drinking alone, but not clothing, for she must dress herself from her own money and also, when she has children, she is bound to feed them, and when she is expecting a child he must not touch her, therefore they marry twenty-three wives and there are Ishmaelites who have twenty sons and daughters born in a single year. Everybody rides upon donkeys and mules, for nobody, not even a Moslem, may ride a horse except only the mamelukes. Their donkeys are very fine indeed and fat and they carry valuable "bardili" and "soli" as ornaments. I saw one donkey's bardili, which were worth more than 2,000 ducats, made of precious stones and diamonds with golden fringe which they put upon it and especially the front of the bardili in front of the donkey. The Ishmaelites are like camels and oxen; just as the camel is never shod, so they go without shoes. The camel crouches and eats on the ground, so they crouch and eat on the ground without a cloth but only red leather. The camel sleeps in its harness, so they sleep and crouch on their legs and on their cloths and never undress at night. The Jews do like the Ishmaelites in all the lands and provinces of the Sultan. They have neither bed nor table nor chair nor lamp, but they eat, drink and sleep on the ground always, and all their work is on the ground.

Alexandria is as big as Florence. It is well built and the city walls are high and fine, but all the city is very dry and it has more ruins than buildings. The houses are beautiful, and in each house you will find a courtyard paved with white stones and with a tree and in the middle a cistern. Each house has two cisterns, one for new water and one for old water, for the Nile comes up every year in the month of August and waters all Alexandria, and the ponds get filled up when the water comes in and replenishes the cisterns, for Alexandria is hollow in consequence of the said cisterns. The fruit of Alexandria is very good and cheap, bread and meat and all kinds of fowls are cheap, but timber is very dear, and oil, honey and wine are very dear because they have to pay a heavy tax, about 24 per cent. The flax of Alexandria is very good and their linen garments fine and cheap. Rain never falls in Alexandria, except a very little in the winter. Their fruits ripen and increase very much in consequence of the quantity of dew. I never saw so much dew in my life. It looks like rain, but when the sun comes out it evaporates. The cause of the cheapness of poultry is that they hatch them in ovens. They warm the ovens and put therein cattle and horse dung and they put in 1,000 or 2,000 eggs and consequently in about three weeks they have live chickens and get no end of fowls. . .

Last, but not least, there are in Alexandria about sixty Jewish householders with no Karaites or Samaritans among them but only Rabbanites. Their habit of clothing is like that of the Ishmaelites. They wear no shoes but sit on the ground and enter the Synagogues without shoes and without trousers. Some Jews there are who remember that in their time there were about 4,000 householders, but they have become less and less, like the sacrificial bullocks of Tabernacles. They have two Synagogues, one big and the other small, and all the Jews testify that the small one was built by Elijah the Prophet and he used to pray there; and therein there is an ark and near it a chair, and there is always a light burning inside . . .

Advice to the Traveller

And in order, my friends, that you may know the things we had to do and everyone has to do who takes this route, I will briefly relate them. From the balsam garden (Egypt) to Gaza and also close up to Jerusalem it is all desert, and every man must carry on his beast two sacks, one of biscuits and the other of straw and fodder, also water skins, for there you cannot find sweet water, but only salt. You must also take with you lemons because of the insects which I wrote about above, and you must go in a big caravan because of the robbers who frequent the desert, and you must go slowly for two reasons; the one because in the desert there is much dust and sand and the horses sink in it up to their knees and go with difficulty, and secondly because the dust rises and gets into a man's mouth and makes his throat dry and kills him with thirst, and if he drinks of the hot brackish water he is troubled worse than before. Moreover, a man who does not know Arabic must dress like a Turk in order that he may not be taken for a Jew or Frank,[1] else even a Jubilee would not set him free from paying much money to the coffre, that is, taxes; but you must wear a white cover on your head like the Turks and Moslems do, and there is great danger, lest, God forbid, anyone of the caravan should tell that you are a Jew or Frank; and if you have escaped all these you will always find people lying in wait on the road who are hidden in sand up to their necks, two or three days without food or drink, who put a stone in front of them, and they can see other people but the others cannot see them, and when they see a caravan rather smaller and weaker than their own they go out and call their fellows and ride on their horses swift as leopards, with bamboo lances topped with iron in their hands, which are very hard. They also carry a pirate's mace in their hands and bucklers made of parchment and pitch, and they ride naked with only a shirt upon them, without trousers or shoes or spurs, and they come upon the caravans suddenly and take everything, even the clothes and horses, and sometimes they kill them; but generally they rob but do not kill them, therefore it is good to be in a caravan of Turks who are all good bowmen, and the robbers fear them

[1] Christian.

because they are naked and cannot shoot, and two Turks could put ten Ishmaelites to flight. And if you escape them there is another great danger from corsairs. These are all foreigners who come in "Schioppette" (sloops) and are armed, and they are good fighters and wear Turkish clothes. When you come to the custom houses if you do a single thing not according to their usage they will at once understand that you are not a Turk or an Ishmaelite, and they are always on the watch, and if you ask me what their manner is and what to do, it is necessary that when you reach those places you must immediately take your shoes off and sit on the ground and bend your legs under you and never let your legs appear or stand upon them at all, but you must eat on the ground, and if crumbs fall from the bread pick them up, but do not eat the bread until you have put it on your head, and you must give to the people around you a little of all you eat, even if they are not eating with you; and you must never take any of your clothes off, but you must sleep in them at night, and if they pass you anything to eat you must stretch forth your hand to take it with a bow, and when you go to relieve yourself, take care not to lift up any of your clothes and keep close to the ground. You must never go to the house of anybody with shoes and never speak to anybody except seated with your legs bent beneath you, and even if you have only one loaf of bread and one cup of wine and a man comes and takes it and eats and drinks you must let him do so, for even if they take from Kings there is no redress and nothing to do, and it is their custom when they go to eat to sit in a circle, and they all eat out of one vessel, slaves and masters are all alike, and they place their hands into the dish and take a handful out and do not place before them either a napkin or a knife or salt; and they never wash their hands except after eating, when they wash their arms up to the elbow.

Some people clean their hands in fine white dust somewhat scented, which in Arabic they call "raihān." It is also their custom to give no fodder to donkeys and nothing to drink, only all the caravan together, for it is by their law a great sin that the other horses or small donkeys should see one of them eat, because that would hurt those that are not eating, and that is cruelty to animals; and, therefore, every man must be careful not to transgress their customs lest, God forbid, they find out that he is a Jew or Frank, and unlucky is he that falls into this trap. . .

An Excerpt from the Letter of Obadiah Jaré Da Bertinoro

Customs of the Arabian Jews

The following is the arrangement of the Sabbath meal customary to Jews in all Arabian countries. They sit in a circle on a carpet, the cup-bearer standing near them near a small cloth which is spread on this carpet; all kinds of fruit which are in season are then brought and laid on the cloth. The host now takes a glass of wine, pronounces the blessing of sanctification (*Kiddush*), and empties the cup completely. The cup-bearer then takes it from the host, and hands it successively to the whole company, always refilled, and each one empties it, then the host takes two or three pieces of fruit, eats some, and drinks a second glass, while the company say, "Health and life!" Whoever sits next also takes some fruit, and the cup bearer fills a second glass for him saying, "To your pleasure," and the company join in with the words "Health and life," and so it goes round. Then a second kind of fruit is partaken of, another glass is filled, and this is continued until each one has emptied at least six or seven glasses. Sometimes they even drink when they smell the flowers which are provided for the occasion; these flowers are the *dudaim*, which Rashi translates into Arabic by jasmine; it is a plant bearing only blossoms which have a delightful and invigorating fragrance. The wine is unusually strong, and this is especially the case in Jerusalem, where it is drunk unmixed. After all have drunk to their heart's content, a large dish of meat is brought, each one stretches forth his hand, takes what he wants, and eats quickly, for they are not very big eaters. R. Moses brought us confectionery, fresh ginger, dates, raisins, almonds, and confectionery of coriander seeds; a glass of wine is drunk with each kind. Then followed raisin wine, which was very good, then malmsey wine from Candia, and again native wine. I drank with them and was exhilarated.

There is yet another custom in the country of the Arabs: on Friday all go to bathe, and on their return the women bring them wine, of which they drink copiously; word is then brought that the supper is ready, and it is eaten in the day-time, before evening. Then they all come to the synagogue, cleanly and neatly dressed. They begin with psalms and thanksgiving and evening prayer is read until two hours after dusk. On their return home they repeat the *Kiddush*, eat only a piece of bread of the size of an olive, and recite the grace after meals. . .

Chapter IX

FOLK-TALES

STORY telling is an art which has been cultivated and prized by people of all nationalities and all times. At the family hearth, the popular tavern, in the market place the story teller found interested audiences who eagerly welcomed his tales because they provided both pleasant entertainment and ethical instruction. The gallant prince, the enchanting beauty, the haunting ghost, the speaking animal were, as a rule, the subjects of these breath-taking adventures in which goodness, courage, and wisdom always triumphed over wickedness, cowardice, and folly. But the chief characters of these folk-tales were not always supernatural and grotesque figures, such as dwarfs, giants, hobgoblins, and flying horses. Very often they were real, historic characters such as national and religious heroes. But in time these heroes too were endowed with supernatural powers and quite often became indistinguishable from the purely mythical figures of the average folk-tale.

An outstanding feature of folk-tales is their tendency to migrate from their original home and to spread in ever widening circles. They are usually passed on from father to son and from neighbor to neighbor, and in the process not only gather new elements like a rolling snow ball, but often assume the status of the unwritten lore of a whole nation. Eventually the folk-tales cross national boundaries and continue to migrate until they become the property of practically all mankind. Thus, some of our best known tales have travelled from distant countries and crossed continents and oceans before they reached us to become part of our folk-lore.

In this process of spreading folk-tales, the mediaeval Jew played a most vital role. Dispersed everywhere and, as a rule, the master of several languages, he automatically became a convenient vehicle for the spreading and exchanging of tales, legends, and fables. But it was not in the oral dissemination of the tales that he took part, for the Jew was seldom afforded the opportunity of joining his neighbors at their intimate gatherings where tales were told and exchanged. It was only through the medium of translation that the Jew aided in the diffusion of these tales. No sooner were the folk-tales of a given locality collected and reduced to writing than the opportunity for translation presented itself and the Jews were quick to avail themselves of it. Thus the famous book, *The Fables of Bidpai* (known in Hebrew as *Kalila we-Dimna*), whose popularity and importance may be seen from the fact that it has been translated into thirty-eight languages in 112 different versions,[1] came from its original home, India, first to the Mohammedans and then to the Christians, chiefly through the medium of Jewish translators.

In addition to being a vital factor in the diffusion of folk-tales, the Jews have developed a substantial folk-tale literature of their own. Like all other peoples they assimilated many of their neighbors' tales and adapted them to their own tastes. These tales were Hebraized and altered so that they assumed a thoroughly Jewish character. Thus the animals in the fables not only speak but invariably quote the Bible and the Talmud; and the ethical implications of the stories are usually summed up in quotations culled from the Bible, Talmud, Midrash, and other standard works of the Rabbis. The finest collection of such fully Hebraized folk-tales is *The Book of Delight* by Joseph

[1] Jacobs, Joseph, Introduction to *The Fables of Bidpai*, p. XII, London, 1888.

Ibn Zabara, a portion of which is quoted in this chapter. The stories are connected by a frame or central plot which unites the various parts of the book and helps to sustain the reader's interest to the very end. The author tells us how he was once awakened from his sleep by a stranger who urged him to migrate with him to his native country, where everything was a thing of delight. Joseph Ibn Zabara is reluctant but finally sets out on the journey. On the way they keep up a lengthy conversation in which they exchange tales, proverbs, scientific knowledge, humorous remarks, etc. They finally reach their destination, but instead of experiencing delight, the author meets with one disappointment after another. To cap it all, he discovers that his companion is a demon. He manages to make his escape and finally arrives safely among his own people. This *Book of Delight* is in truth a most delightful book, a worthy classic, as may be judged even from the inadequate selections quoted in this chapter.

In addition to translating and assimilating many non-Jewish folk-tales, the Jews also collected the numerous tales, parables, and legends which clustered around the names and exploits of their Biblical and post-Biblical heroes. To these ancient tales were added many new legends which were evolved after the completion of the Talmud and the Midrashim. These latter tales usually glorified the saints and martyrs of the Middle Ages, whose piety, meekness, and fortitude always proved a source of strength and encouragement to the whole community. The tales were collected and published chiefly for the edification and entertainment of the Jewish young women in Germany, who found in them a storehouse of romance and adventure. Since the mediaeval Jewish young women were not given the intensive Hebrew education that was provided for boys, these *Ma'asebücher* (story books) necessarily had to be written in the current Judaeo-German jargon, transcribed into Hebrew characters. They were exceptionally popular and enjoyed a very wide circulation. The three stories quoted in this chapter are all mediaeval in origin and therefore not altogether representative of the *Ma'asebücher*, where most of the tales are culled from the Talmud and Midrash. But since this is an anthology of mediaeval literature, it was thought advisable to leave the more ancient tales for an anthology of the literature of the Talmudic period. It is hoped, however, that the selections quoted, though few and not altogether adequate, will prove as much a source of delight to the modern reader as they did to the readers of a bygone century. After all, that is the test of a true classic—its endurance from generation to generation.

I. THE BOOK OF DELIGHT
by Joseph Ibn Zabara

The Framework of The Book of Delight

There lived a man in the city of Barcelona whose name was Joseph ben Zabara. From his youth up had he dwelt at ease, in amity with his friends and comrades. All that knew him became his friends, and they that were his friends loved him; among them was he respected and esteemed, bound to all by ties of affection. He for his part honored and exalted them, served them and healed them. For those of them that were sick he compounded suitable remedies, in accordance with his knowledge and his skill. In his love and charity he busied himself with his patients whether old or young, and served them, and ministered to them. Everyone, then, loved Joseph and sought his company eagerly; but as Scripture hath it (Psalms CVII, 5), "Joseph was sold for a servant."

Came then a night when I, Joseph, was sleeping upon my bed. My sleep was sweet upon me, for that alone was my portion of all my labor. . . And it came to pass as I slumbered that I saw an appearance before me in my dream, in the likeness of a man exceeding tall, who did then rouse me as is the wont of a man who arouseth another from his sleep. "Arise, thou son of man," quoth he. "Wherefore slumberest? Awake thee, and look upon the wine as it floweth red. Arise, and recline at my side and eat whereof I have brought thee, as my means did avail."

So I arose in haste, just as dawn brake, and I beheld wine and bread and viands before me, and a lamp burning in the man's hand, whereof the light shone into every corner. Then I spake and said, "What may these be, good sir?" "My wine," he replied, "and my bread and my viands. Sit thee down, and eat and drink with me, for I love thee as thou wert of my mother's sons."

But after that I had thanked him for the kindness of the honor he did me, for his love and for the generosity of his hand, I said, "Sir, I may neither eat nor drink until that I have prayed to Him that discerneth my way and maketh my footsteps firm and vouchsafeth unto me all my needs. For indeed the choicest of the prophets and the chief of them that were called, our teacher Moses, may he rest in peace, hath said (Leviticus XIX, 26): "Ye shall not eat anything with the blood: neither shall ye use enchantment nor observe times." Thereby did he admonish the children of Israel that they should not eat until that they had prayed for their souls, for in truth *the blood* signifieth *the soul*. . .

Then said the stranger, "Pray, if such be thy desire; do as is good in thy sight." So I bathed my hands and face, and prayed before the Lord. Then I ate of all that was before me, for his soul was become dear in my sight. . .

And it came to pass after that I had eaten and drunk with him that I asked concerning his place and his name, saying, "Prithee, good sir, now that thou hast honored me and given me to eat of thy bread and victuals and mine heart hath drunk of thy dear love, tell me pray, what is thy purpose and whence comest thou, what is thy country and of what people art thou?" And he answered and said to me, "I come from a distant land, from pleasant and fruitful hills; my wisdom is as thy wisdom, my people as thy people and my laws as thy laws. My name is Enan Hanatas, son of Arnan Hadesh."[1] I said to myself, "Surely this is a wonderful and awful name. Never before have I heard its like.'

He said to me, "Thou mayst not know the secret of my name until that thou hast become my guest and comrade. Come with me from this land and I will tell thee all my secret lore; leave this spot, for here they appreciate neither thy worth nor thy skillful wisdom. I will take thee to another place, in which thou wilt find great delight; a place choice and good, like a fruitful garden, and they that people it are lovable and pleasant and exceeding wise."

And I said to him, "But, good sir, how may I forsake my house and abandon my heritage and depart from my native land wherein my abode is fixed, where dwell gentle folk, noble and princely, and wise sages who possess understanding of all matters? The greater among them graciously do me honor, and the lesser attend me for their own honor. As long as I shall live they will bear me on the pinions of their love and when I am dead their physicians will embalm me. . . "

But he mocked and said, "The sage hath said, 'He that doth lean on his own knowledge and wisdom will stumble by his speech and perish by his counsel.' What will it profit thee after thy death whether they embalm thee skillfully or tear thee in pieces? Why dost thou speak without counsel and without wisdom, being a man of understanding and

[1] By inverting the second and the last words of this name, one discovers the stranger's identity, which did not become known to Ibn Zabara till the last stage of his adventure. The stranger's name properly read is Enan the Satan, son of Arnan the Shed (Demon).

discernment? . . . Rouse thyself to words of spirit, come with me to security and tranquillity. If thou hast found honor in thine own place and art favored of the many among thine own people, wherefore shouldst thou withhold from coming with me, to show thy pleasantness and to cause thy name to be remembered? They say that the man who dwelleth in his own city, even if it should please the king to do him honor, he will not perceive his glory nor recall his name or fame until that he have removed to another land, and there become honorable and glorious, above the exalted ones of the city. . . Furthermore the Arab hath said, 'Every journey and every change doth cause blessing and salvation.' " . . .

He persuaded me by the strength of his speech and prevailed over me with the smoothness of his lips, for his tongue was as the oil of Aaron that went down to the skirts of his garments. He drew me on with the bonds of his love and with the chains of his kindness and his generosity. So I said to him, "I will but kiss my brethren and my friends, whose love burns in my body, and thereafter will I journey forth with thee."

I kissed all my comrades and wept over them. My heart was moved within me and mine eyes ran streams. After that he had taken me from my native land, I went with him in the way that he led me and we journeyed and went upon the king's highway.

The Fox and the Leopard

A leopard once lived in content and plenty: ever he found easy sustenance for his wife and children. Hard by there dwelt his neighbor and friend, the fox. The fox felt in his heart that his life was safe only so long as the leopard could catch other prey. "If other prey should be wanting for a single day he will seize me in his might and slay me in the strength of his wrath, for he is in truth but shameless and he will apportion me unto himself and his sons as viands. Surely I mūst bespeak him cunningly and beguile him with words of deceit; mayhap I shall prevail by wile and cast from my neck the yoke of his burden. 'Before the evil cometh,' the sage hath said, 'counsel is good, but after trouble hath arrived it is but vain.' Therefore will I remove him from my dwelling place and cause him to depart from my habitation. I will banish him from his place ere he swallow me, and cast him from his station ere he cast me down and devour me. Perhaps I can lead him in the path of death, for have not our sages of blessed memory declared, 'If one come to slay thee, arise thou betimes and slay him?' "

On the morrow then it came about that the fox came to the dwelling of the leopard in order to fulfill his purpose. The leopard addressed him, "Whence comest thou?" Reynard replied, "From a place of amazing beauty and goodness, a place of gardens and orchards, of lilies and myrtles, of turtle doves and pigeons, of hinds and does, of conies and wild goats and asses. They bray amongst the bushes and the fatted oxen lie in the grass. And I have come to give thee the tidings and to lead thee unto that place, for this place is despised and rejected and not fat but lean."

The leopard spake, "Show me this place, for I am indeed eager to see it." And he led him to that place, but the leopard knew not it was to be at the cost of his life. When he saw the comeliness of the place and its delights, the pleasantness of its situation, its approaches and its avenues, its woods, its shrubs, its herbage, its orchards and myrtles, its hinds and does, he rejoiced exceedingly and was filled with gladness and delight. The fox said in his heart, "How many joys have been turned to sorrows! This, God willing, shall be added to that number." The leopard said, "Now do I know that thy soul is bound fast unto mine, and that love of me is cherished in thy heart, for by reason of the love thou hast for me hast thou chosen a place whose like mine eye hath never beheld nor hath mine ear heard report thereof. Be thou richly blessed, good and beloved sir. I will but go and take counsel with my wife and reveal unto her my secrets, for she is my comrade and the wife of my youth."

But the fox feared her, for that she was clever, and of sound sense, and subtle. So he said, "Take heed of a woman's counsel, for woman is evil and bitter in spirit and hard. Her heart is of flint, an accursed plague is she in the house. Wise and understanding men heed not their wives, for they are of light mind. The sage hath said, 'Guard against their love; ask their counsel and do the opposite.' Whoso heeds them and follows after them brings it about that both he and they are consumed in flames."

The leopard replied and said, "Nevertheless it is incumbent upon a man and by statute ordained, that he take counsel of the wife of his bosom. Furthermore the sage hath said, 'Take counsel with thy brother or with thy friend, and thy paths will be made firm.'"

The fox then said, "How much have I counseled thee and taught thee and instructed thee and commanded thee, yet have I not found thee one who hearkens! Surely the prophet hath said (Micah VII, 5), 'Keep the doors of thy mouth from her that lieth in thy bosom.'"

The leopard then replied, "Truth is with thee in all that thou hast spoken, for at times woman makes of sweet bitter and of bitter sweet. But I will go and ask her, and if she forbid me I will not hearken to her counsel." The fox said, "So be it then, go in peace and I will wait until thou return hither."

Then the leopard went to his house, rejoicing and glad of heart. His wife addressed him, "What is this joy wherewith thou art rejoiced and this gladness which shines forth in thy countenance?" To her he replied, "My friend the fox, whose love for me is without let or deceit, has shown me a place spacious and secure for my dwelling. All that see it covet it and all that hear of it speak its praises; it is my purpose to remove hence and to dwell yonder." "Why and wherefore?" said his wife. He replied, "Because our place is strait and our abode scant, and day by day our prey minishes and here bread nor meat suffices us. But there we shall find all our wants; we shall eat according to the pleasure of our hearts."

But his wife replied, "Beware of the fox, of his gifts and his offerings, for he counsels for his own advantage. . . And hast thou not heard how the fox bound the lion by his cunning and slew him by his guile?"

Then said the leopard to his wife, "And how was the fox so confident as to approach a lion? Did not dread restrain him?" She replied, "The lion loved the fox with all his heart, and advantaged him and befriended him, but the fox had small faith in him and plotted to slay him, for in truth he feared him greatly. Once on a day then, the fox came to the dwelling of the lion and was in great pain and cried out. The lion addressed him, 'What ails thee, beloved of my soul?' And the fox replied, 'A great pain hath seized my head.' The lion asked, 'And what may be done for thee, to assuage thy pain?' And the fox replied, 'I have heard it said of the physicians of Araby that they prescribe that they who suffer from aches of the head be bound hand and foot, which doth then relieve them of their pain.' Then said the lion, 'I will bind thee, as thou sayest; mayhap thy pain will be eased by thy bonds.' The lion took a forged chain and bound the fox hand and foot. The fox then said that his pain was departed, and the lion loosed him; nor did the pain return. Then it came to pass after a number of days that the lion found a great ache in his head, for so is his custom and wont, and he went to the fox and said to him, 'Dear brother, my head is seized of a great pain, so that I am like to pray for death. Do thou quickly bind me with thy chain, both hand and foot. Mayhap my ache will be assuaged, even as befell thee.' So the fox took fresh withes and bound him well and went from him and forsook him. Then he brought great stones and smote him upon the head and slew him.

"Perhaps that which befell the lion will befall thee also—forfend it Heaven—for his heart is but for guile, for wherefore chose he not that place for himself, to be his abode and his delight and his pleasure? Therefore do I tremble before him lest he take us in his snare and cause us to wander from this place to our hurt."

But the leopard spoke to her: "Silence! for thou speakest as one of the shameful women! Be not bold to answer my words, for full oft have I tried him, yet never have I found dross in the pure silver of his love." But she said, "Hearken to my voice and abide in thy home, and destroy not thy seat and thy heritage." But he would not hearken to her counsel, to her hurt and to his own. . .

Thereupon they removed thence, they and their children, and the fox went before them to show them the way and to bring them to that place of infinite goodness. They came to the place and lo, it was a region of great rivers and broad streams, and they encamped there upon the water. The fox gave them his blessing and returned to his house rejoicing from tail to snout, for he saw that his plan had been accomplished. "The Lord hath now made me at ease," said he, "for the leopard is far from my boundaries."

After seven days there descended great rains, and all the pits and cisterns and pools were filled, and all the streams were flooded. And it came to pass at midnight, as he and his wife and children were sleeping upon their beds, that the waters prevailed over them and the river overwhelmed them. The leopard sank into the water crying, 'Woe, Woe to him who puts his faith in a fox and his counsel, and doth not hearken to the voice of his wife." So he perished, dying before his time.

Jacob of Cordova and the Nobleman

There was a certain Jew in Cordova who was called Jacob, the Factor, and he was good and faithful, ready and obedient to the bidding of the judge. One day there was intrusted to him a chain of choice stones and precious pearls to be sold for five hundred pieces of gold. He was walking by the way, carrying the chain in his hand, when he was met by a certain noble of the king's favorites, who thus addressed him: "Jacob, what manner of chain is that?" He replied to him, "My lord, it is intrusted to my hand to be sold." "And for how much wilt sell it?" "The price is five hundred pieces of gold," he replied. Said the noble, "Wilt sell it for four?" Jacob replied, "I cannot, for its owner hath laid it upon me not to accept less than five hundred pieces of gold." The noble said, "Take it then to my house, and if it please my lady I will buy it." So he went with him until they reached the gate of his house, where the noble said, "Stand thou here until I bring out to thee either the money or the chain." Thereupon he entered into his house but shut the door behind him; the Jew waited until even, but no man came forth from the door of the house.

And it came to pass when the sun set, that Jacob went to his house full of wrath; death had been pleasant to him. Sorrow oppressed his heart and wounded it. He came then and lay him upon the ground, nor partook of bread, neither he, nor his sons, nor his wife, nor did his tunic from off him, nor did he close his weary eyes, but tossed all the night, like clay turned to the seal. In the morning he arose and went to the house of the noble, but lo, he had gone forth from his house. He saw him, and ran to meet him, and said to him, "My lord, buy the chain if thou wilt, or else return it, and I will sell it to another." The noble replied, "Of what chain dost thou speak? Hast thou perchance dreamt of a chain?" But he said, "The chain of pearls which thou didst take from mine hand but yesterday." "Thou art lunatic, afflicted with some evil spirit," said the noble. "By my life and the life of the king, did I not respect the position I bear, I would take thy head from upon thee, and thyself would I trample in thy heart's blood." When Jacob perceived his wrath and the hardness of his words, dread of death fell upon him, and he turned his back and fled from before him, for he saw that the noble glared upon him sore.

He went to the house of his master, the judge, and when the judge looked upon him he perceived that sorrow had bitten into him with its fangs, until that his appearance and the cast of his countenance were altered. The judge addressed him, "What ails thee that thou hast altered; hast thou then been sorely afflicted?" He replied, "My lord, I am in sore straits, nor may I tell thee of it, lest thou shouldst discredit my words and distrust my speech." But the judge said, "Do thou but relate the matter, for all thy words are faithful in my sight and thou art righteous in all thy speech."

So he related all that had befallen in the matter of the chain and petitioned that his life be spared. Said the judge,

"Remove anger from thy heart and put away sorrow from thine inward parts; tremble not nor groan in thy pain, for I will restore the chain to thee."

And it came to pass on the morrow that he summoned all the great men of the city, its elders, and wise men, and sages, to come to the place of judgment, for so was it his wont upon occasion, to send and fetch the wise men and to speak with them of justice. So they all came to his house, to hearken to the words of his understanding and his wisdom. But ere they came the judge said to his servant: "When that certain noble doth come, take thou his shoe and go to his house and say to his wife, 'My lord, thy husband, hath sent me to thee, that thou shouldst give him the chain which he bought yesterday or the day before, for he would display its worth and its beauty, and as a sign and testimony, lo, he hath given me his shoe.' "

When the woman saw her husband's shoe she delivered over the chain, and the servant of the judge brought it to his master and hid it in his bosom until that the men should depart from the seat of judgment. When they had so departed, his master spake to him, "Hast brought the chain?" "I have brought it," he replied, and drew it forth from his bosom, and gave it to him. Then the judge sent and summoned Jacob, the Factor, and said to him, "Be silent, nor sigh longer, for I have returned thee the chain; I have abstracted from the noble's house that which he hath stolen." When the Jew saw the chain he kissed the judge's hand and blessed him and carried it to his house joyful and glad at heart.

II. THE MA'ASEH BOOK

A Jewish Pope

There was once a Rabbi, Simeon the Great, who lived in Mayence on the Rhine. In his house he had three mirrors, in which he saw everything that had happened in the past and all that would happen in the future. He also had a spring at the head of his bed, whose waters came from his grave in the cemetery. He was a great man, you see. This Rabbi Simeon had a little son whose name was Elhanan. One day, on a Sabbath, the *Sabbath goya* [2] came as usual to light the stove fire, and upon going away took the little boy with her. The Jewish maid who was in the house paid no attention to the matter. She thought the *goya* would soon bring back the child. The rest of the family was in the synagogue. The *goya* took the child and had him baptized. She thought that she had brought a sacrifice to God, for in those days they attached great importance to the baptism of Jews. When Rabbi Simeon the Great came home, there was no one in the house. The maid had run after the *goya* but could not find her. Suddenly the maid rushed in, crying bitterly. Rabbi Simeon asked her why she was crying so,

[2] Gentile woman who does the chores for a Jewish household on the Sabbath

and she said to him, "Dear Rabbi, God save us, the *Sabbath Goya* has taken away the child and I don't know where she has disappeared." They searched for the child everywhere, but could not find him. Father and mother bitterly lamented their beloved child, as one can well imagine. Rabbi Simeon fasted days and nights, but the Holy One, blessed be He, concealed from him the child's whereabouts.

Well, the child passed from one to another until he fell into the hands of the priests, who brought him up. And he became a great scholar, for he had the intellect of Rabbi Simeon the Great. And the lad passed from one academy to another, until he came to Rome. There he earnestly studied many languages and finally became a cardinal in Rome. His fame spread far and wide, and men could not praise him enough. He was respected by all and he was handsome besides. Then it happened that the Pope died, and the young man, because of his subtle mind and his mastery of many languages, was made Pope. He well knew, however, that he had been a Jew and the son of Rabbi Simeon the Great of Mayence. But things went so well with him, as one can well imagine, and he was so highly esteemed that he remained among the Christians.

One day he said to himself, "I must see if I can bring my father from Mayence to Rome." He then wrote a letter to the Bishop of Mayence (for he was now Pope and all the bishops were his subordinates), commanding that he forbid the Jews to keep their Sabbath or to circumcize their sons, and that he forbid the Jewish women to take their ritual baths. The Pope thought that his father would be sent to him to plead for the annulment of the decree. And so it was. As soon as the Papal letter reached the Bishop, he immediately informed the Jews of the evil decree. And when the Jews pleaded with the Bishop, he showed them the Pope's letter and said that he could not help them. If they wished to plead their case, they would have to go to Rome to the Pope himself.

Was anyone ever more disheartened than those poor Jews? They did penance and prayed and gave charity. Then they decided to send Rabbi Simeon the Great with two more Rabbis to Rome, to intercede with the Pope, hoping that the Holy One, blessed be He, would perform a miracle for them. In the meantime they secretly circumcized their children, for they had obtained permission from the Bishop to do so in great secret.

When the Rabbis came to Rome, they informed the Jews of their arrival and told them of the situation. When the Jews of Rome heard the story, they wondered greatly, for they said that in the memory of man there had been no kinder Pope to Jews. He could not live without Jews. He always had Jews about him in secret and they often played chess with him. Also they had heard nothing of the evil decree. They could not believe that it had come from the the Pope. The Bishop himself must have issued it. Whereupon Rabbi Simeon the Great showed them the Papal letter and seal, so that the Jews were convinced. And they said, "A great sin must have been committed among you Jews in Germany." And the Jews of Rome too did penance and prayed and gave charity. And the *Parnassim* (Jewish notables) of Rome went to the cardinal with whom they were on friendly terms and pleaded with him to intercede. But the cardinal said, "The Pope with his own hand wrote that letter to the Bishop of Mayence, and we can do little for you." Neverthless, he promised to do all he could and told them to prepare a petition and he would see that it got into the hands of the Pope.

The Jews therefore prepared a petition and gave it to the Pope. As soon as the Pope read it, he at once knew how matters stood and ordered the Jews to appear before him.

Then Rabbi Simeon the Great and his colleagues appeared before the chief cardinal, who presented the Rabbis to the Pope as the Jews of Mayence who wished to see and speak to him in person. And the Pope gave permission that the oldest among them should appear before him. Now Rabbi Simeon the Great was the oldest among them, and his appearance was like that of an angel of the Lord. As soon as he entered, he fell upon his knees. The Pope was sitting playing chess with one of his cardinals. When he saw Rabbi Simeon, the Pope became very much frightened and asked him to rise and take a seat until he finished the game. For he at once knew his father, although the father did not recognize him. When the game was over, the Pope asked Rabbi Simeon what he wished. The Rabbi answered amid tears and lamentations, and again was about to fall on his knees, but the Pope would not permit it, saying: "I have now heard your plea, but many strange reports came to me from Mayence, which forced me to issue the decree." The Pope then began a Talmudic disputation with Rabbi Simeon and, God forbid, almost vanquished the Rabbi in the dispute. Rabbi Simeon was greatly astonished to find such an intellect among the Gentiles. They spent almost a half day together, when the Pope said, "My learned man, I see well that you are a great scholar, else the Jews would not have sent you. Now I have Jews here every day playing chess with me. I should like you too to play a game with me. Your mission will not suffer for it."

Now Rabbi Simeon was a master chess player, whose like was not to be found throughout the whole world, and yet the Pope check-mated him. The Rabbi was greatly astonished. And again they began to talk about religion, so that Rabbi Simeon was astounded at the keen, subtle mind of the Pope. Finally, after further pleading and entreaty by the Rabbi, the Pope asked all the cardinals to withdraw, and with tears in his eyes fell upon Rabbi Simeon's neck and said, "Dear old father, do you not know me?" And the father replied,"How am I to know your royal grace?" And the Pope said, "Dear old father, did you not lose a son once?" When the Rabbi heard that, he was greatly frightened and said, "Yes." Then said the Pope, "I am your son Elhanan, whom you lost through the *Sabbath goya*. What sin was responsible for it or how it came about, I do not know. He, Whose Name be praised, must have willed it so. I therefore issued the decree, hoping that you would come to me, as has actually happened. For I wish to return to my faith. I will therefore annul the decree." And he gave him letters to the Bishop of Mayence revoking the evil decree. Then the son asked, "Dear father, tell me how I can expiate my sin." And Rabbi Simeon said, "My dear son, do not be troubled. You are still one of us, for you were only a child when you were taken from me." Then the Pope said: "Dear father, all this time that I have been living among the Gentiles I knew that I was a Jew, but my happy existence kept me from returning to my faith. Can I be forgiven for that?" The son again spoke to the father: "Return home, in the name of the God of Israel, and give these letters to your bishop, but say nothing more about me. I shall soon be with you in Mayence. But before I go I wish to leave a memorial behind me, one that will be a boon to the Jews".

Rabbi Simeon went back to the Jews of Rome and showed them the letter by which the decree, with God's help, had been revoked, and there was great rejoicing. Whereupon Rabbi Simeon and his companions returned to Germany and brought the letter to the Bishop, and all rejoiced. And Rabbi Simeon told his wife the whole story, how things had gone with him, and that the Pope was her own son. When she heard that, she wept bitterly, but Rabbi Simeon said to her: "Do not grieve. Our son will soon be with us." Then the Pope wrote a book against the dominant faith and locked it in a vault and ordered that every candidate for the papacy should read it. There is much to tell as to what is written in that book.

Soon after this he gathered much wealth and left for Mayence and again became a faithful Jew. In Rome no one knew what had become of him. Rabbi Simeon the Great commemorated this incident in a poem recited on the second day of the New Year. Now you must not think that this is merely a story, for it really happened as it is told here. Some say that Rabbi Simeon recognized his son through a chess move which he had taught Elhanan when still a child. And the son made that same move when he played with his father in Rome. Then Rabbi Simeon realized that the Pope was his son. May the Holy One, blessed be He, forgive us our sins through the merits of Rabbi Simeon. Amen. Selah.

The Blooming Staff

There was once an apostate who was a very wicked man and through his wickedness caused the destruction of many in Israel. This wickedness he continued for many years. One day he came to Rabbi Judah He-Hasid and asked him to impose penance upon him, for he bitterly rued all the sins he had committed. And he related to the Rabbi the many grave sins he had committed in the years he had been an apostate. When the Rabbi heard the terrible things he had done, he refused to give him penance and said: "Your sins are too grave." Rabbi Judah He-Hasid was whittling a staff at the moment and he said to the apostate:

"You have as much chance of atonement as this staff has of becoming green and sprouting green leaves. Therefore, what kind of penance can I set for you?" The apostate left Rabbi Judah He-Hasid and said: "Since the Rabbi will impose no penance, I will become even more wicked than I have been."

Soon after the apostate had gone, Rabbi Judah He-Hasid saw that the staff had turned green and that it had sprouted green leaves. The Rabbi was greatly astonished. He recalled the words he had said to the renegade and thought: "The apostate may still find atonement, for the staff has become green again." He immediately sent for the renegade and said to him: "I would impose no penance upon you, for I said that you had as much chance of atonement as this staff had of becoming green and sprouting green leaves. Now tell me, What good deed have you done? A miracle has happened. Therefore I will set a heavy penance, and if you perform it faithfully, you will gain forgiveness." Then said the apostate: "I must confess my sins. Dear Rabbi, I will tell you all. As long as I was an apostate I never did a Jew a kindness. On the contrary, I perpetrated all manner of wickedness against them. Once, however, I came to a city in which there lived many Jews. The Gentiles hated them bitterly and wished to be rid of them, but did not know how. So they invented a lie. They threw a dead child into a Jewish house and said that the Jews had killed him. Whereupon all the citizens of the town gathered together to make an attack upon the Jews and put them all to death. Now there was a man of high rank among them who was very friendly toward the Jews. And he spoke to the citizens who had gathered together, counselling them not to be hasty in shedding innocent blood. 'For we will get to the root of the matter and find out if they really need our blood. And how can we find that out?

I will tell you. We have a baptized Jew among us. We will ask him. He must surely know. If he says that they must have our blood, then they surely must have killed the child. If the baptized Jew says no, that they need no blood, then they have certainly not done it. Why then should you shed innocent blood?' Then the citizens sent for me and placed me under heavy oath that I should tell them the truth whether or not the Jews had to have blood, for such and such a thing had happened to the child. Then I said to them under oath that an injustice was being done the Jews with such an accusation. And I gave them many proofs showing that it must be a lie. In the first place Jews are not allowed to eat meat unless they first slaughter the animal in order to remove the blood entirely. Then they must keep the meat in salt for an hour. Then they must wash the meat so that no trace of blood is left. For it is written in their Torah that they must eat no blood. How then could they use the blood of a human being? Then said the citizens: 'If that is so, then no harm shall come to the Jews.' And so the evil was averted. But had I said 'Yes,' then, God forbid, all of them would have lost their lives. This is the best deed I have ever done in my whole life." Then said the Rabbi: "That was truly a good deed." Then the Rabbi gave him penance, which he diligently carried out, and he became a pious Jew.

The Martyrdom of Rabbi Amnon

There was once a great Rabbi whose name was Rabbi Amnon. He was held in high esteem at the court of the Bishop of Mayence, for he was a distinguished man in all things. He had learning, wisdom, wealth, and was of good family. He had all the virtues which a good Jew should possess and was therefore highly respected by all, princes, counts and lords. They loved him very much and highly prized his company. And yet there was none like him for piety.

Once, at the Bishop's court, the princes said to him: "Master Amnon, why do you not accept our faith? Then our gracious prince would make you chief counselor, for he dearly loves you. We have often discussed the matter with him, asking him to confer some high honor upon you. But his answer has always been, if you were to accept his faith, he would raise you to a place of high honor. Therefore, we entreat you, do accept Christianity." But Rabbi Amnon whould not listen to them. Once the Bishop himself asked him to consent to baptism, but he would not listen to him either. And so it continued day after day, but he refused to listen to them. One day, however, the Bishop became so insistent that Rabbi Amnon said to him: "I will think about it and give your grace an answer within three days." He did so only to put off the Bishop and to gain a little time. But when he had left the Bishop, he realized what he had done. He had told the Bishop that he would consider the matter. As if baptism could be a matter for consideration with him! It meant, Heaven forbid, a denial of the Holy One, blessed be He. The thought lay heavy upon his heart. He went home sad and dejected and would not be comforted. His wife asked him what he had done or what had happened to him, for it was not in his nature to be so sad. But he would say nothing to his family. To himself he said: "I will never rest in peace until I expiate this sin or I will go down in grief to the grave."

When the third day came, the Bishop sent for Rabbi Amnon to hear his decision, but Rabbi Amnon refused to go and sent word that he would have nothing to do with the Bishop. Then the Bishop sent for him twice, but he would not go. Whereupon the Bishop ordered that the Rabbi be brought by force. And when he came the Bishop said to him: "What do you mean by refusing to come after I have sent for you three times? And you promised to give me an answer within three days. Therefore I now demand an answer to that which we have asked of you." The pious man said: "I can give you no answer to that which you have asked of me or are still asking. And for the sin of having thoughtlessly said that I would 'think of it in three days,' an utterance which is equivalent to a denial of the Holy One, blessed be He, I will set my own punishment. For having said 'I will think of it' my tongue shall be cut out." For Rabbi Amnon sought to do penance and to glorify the Holy Name. Then said the wicked Bishop: "I cannot accept the penalty which you have set for yourself. It is by far too light. For the tongue which uttered those words spoke nothing but the truth. But the feet which refused to come to me, they shall be cut off. And the other parts of your body we shall also torture." And he ordered his hands and feet cut off. And each time a limb was cut off, Rabbi Amnon was asked whether he still refused to be converted, and each time he said "Yes." And he added: "Torture me still more, for I have deserved it for the words that I have spoken." When the wicked Bishop had accomplished his will and had inflicted the most cruel torture, he ordered Rabbi Amnon placed on a bed, his limbs alongside him, and carried to his home. And so it was done. When his wife and children saw him, they raised a great cry. Then Rabbi Amnon said to them: "I have well deserved all that has happened to me, for, God forbid, I was on the verge of denying the Holy One, blessed be He. I hope to God, whose name be praised, that this will atone for my sins in this world, so that I may have a share in the world to come."

Shortly after this event came Rosh Hashanah (New Year), and Rabbi Amnon asked to be taken in his bed to the holy synagogue and to be placed near the cantor. And just as the cantor was about to begin the *Kedushah* [1] of the *Musaf* [2] service, the Rabbi said to him: "Wait, I want to sanctify God's name before I die." And he began to recite the "*Unethaneh Tokef Kedushath Hayom,*" [3] which we still repeat every year on Rosh Hashanah and Yom Kippur (Day of Atonement). As soon as he had finished, he disappeared from amidst the throng and no man ever saw him again. For the Holy One, blessed be He, had taken him to the other pious souls in Paradise.

On the third night after this event he appeared in a dream to Rabbi Kalonymus ben Meshullam and begged him to send the *Unethaneh Tokef*, which he had composed, to all communities where Jews were to be found. And Rabbi Kalonymus did so. And it is still recited everywhere on Rosh Hashanah and Yom Kippur in his memory. May the Holy One, whose name be praised, permit us to enjoy the merits of this saint.

[1] A prayer based on the visions of Isaiah VI and Ezekiel III, in which the Holiness, Glory, and Kingdom of God are proclaimed.

[2] The second half of the morning service on Sabbaths and holidays.

[3] This is the first line of a mediaeval Jewish hymn recited on New Year's Day and the Day of Atonement. It is a sombre hymn describing the day of Judgment and forms a most solemn part of the Holy Days' services.

BIOGRAPHICAL NOTES

Abraham Ibn Daud (*1110-1180*), *the author of the* Book of Tradition, *is known for his many-sided interests and activities. Like many other Spanish Jewish scholars of his day, he earned his livelihood from the practice of medicine, at the same time applying his active and penetrating mind to several fields of knowledge. He distinguished himself particularly in philosophy and in history, in which fields he made contributions of lasting value. In his philosophical work,* The Sublime Faith, *Abraham Ibn Daud staunchly defends scientific investigation against those who mistrust it and fear its consequences. "There are many in our time," he says, "who have dabbled a little in science, and who are not able to hold both lights, the light of belief in their right hand and the light of knowledge in their left. Since in such men the light of investigation has extinguished the light of belief, the multitude think it dangerous and shrink from it. In Judaism, however, knowledge is a duty, and it is wrong to reject it." To Abraham Ibn Daud philosophy really strengthens religion, and to oppose it is to oppose God's plan, for God has endowed man with reason so that he may use it. Abraham Ibn Daud may therefore be said to have the distinction of being the first medieval Jewish rationalist who attempted to reconcile Judaism with Aristotelian philosophy, an attempt in which Maimonides later proved more successful.*

Abraham Ibn Daud's most important work is his Book of Tradition. *In it he establishes the continuity of Jewish life from Biblical times to his own day. It is definitely a polemical work in which he tries to ward off the attacks and to expose the contradictions and errors of the Karaite sect, which challenged the authority of Rabbinic Judaism. In spite of its polemical nature, the* Book of Tradition *is one of the finest and most accurate medieval Jewish histories.*

We know little about the non-literary activities of Abraham Ibn Daud. Tradition asserts that he not only labored in behalf of Judaism and defended it against philosophic and sectarian attacks, but that he died a martyr's death. In the year 1180, when the Jews of Toledo were attacked, the famous philosopher and historian was among the victims.

Abraham Ibn Ezra *was born in the year 1092 in Toledo, the birthplace of his contemporary, Judah Halevi. He was a genius whose restlessness caused him to wander from land to land, and whose versatility caused him to scatter his intellectual powers in many fields.*

Travelling in the Middle Ages was extremely dangerous and no one dared to indulge in it as a luxury. Usually it was hunger or persecution, and only occasionally love of adventure that caused the mediaeval Jew to leave his home on distant journeys. Yet Abraham Ibn Ezra visited North Africa, Egypt, Palestine, Babylonia, Italy, France, and England, whence he returned in his old age to his native land, Spain. These travels were of great literary significance because through them Ibn Ezra brought Spanish Jewish culture to the Jewish communities beyond the Spanish Peninsula and thus stimulated a revival of Jewish learning, particularly in Italy, France, and England.

In the intellectual field, too, Abraham Ibn Ezra proved himself a restless and wandering genius. He was a poet, a grammarian, a philosopher, a mathematician, an astronomer, a Biblical scholar, and a wit. In only two fields, however, did Abraham Ibn Ezra excel—in poetry and in Biblical scholarship.

Throughout his life he composed poems, mostly religious and epigrammatical. His serious poems lacked genuine warmth, but his witty epigrams showed a remarkably keen intellect and an extraordinary agility in the handling of the Hebrew language.

His fame, however, rests mainly on his Biblical commentaries. He has been called the father of commentators and for a long time had no rival in this field. His comments are brief and keen. His deep penetration led him to such revolutionary discoveries as that the book of Isaiah was the work of more than one prophet and that some verses in the Pentateuch were not of Mosaic origin.

As rich as he was in knowledge and understanding, so was he poor in worldly possessions. His poverty has become proverbial. But his keen sense of humor enabled him to laugh at those things which most people would bewail, and even such a tragedy as the apostasy of his son did not rob him of his wit. Even on his death bed (1167) he wittily applied to himself the Biblical verse, "and Abraham was seventy-five years when he left Haran."

Ahimaaz Ben Paltiel (*1017-1060*) *was the descendant of a prominent family of poets, scholars, and statesmen. His pride in ancestry led him to write a family history, known as the* Chronicle of Ahimaaz, *which has become one of the most important source-books of mediaeval Jewish history. In this chronicle the author describes the lives and accomplishments of his family from about 850 to his own day (1050). The chronicle is full of legends and miracles as well as reliable accounts which shed much light on the history of the Jews of Byzantium, South Italy, and Egypt.*

The story of the author's own life, paradoxically enough, is shrouded in obscurity. The only fact we know is that he was true to the tradition of the family in that he wrote liturgic poems, some of which were incorporated in the prayer book. Ahimaaz died at Oria in 1060 and was survived by two sons, neither of whom achieved any great prominence.

The life of Joseph Albo, *the author of* The Book of Principles, *is veiled in obscurity. Neither the place nor the date of his birth is known. Historians merely surmise that he must have been born not later than 1380. His occupation, too, is unknown, although there are some vague conjectures about it. His frequent use of medical analogies and illustrations has encouraged people to believe that he was, like Judah Halevi and Moses Maimonides, a physician by profession. His homiletic style also suggests preaching as his avocation. But there is one event in his life that is known, an incident that must have deeply affected him and must have considerably influenced his philosophy. This incident was his participation in the famous disputation of Tortosa.*

Of all religious disputations that the Church forced upon the Jews, none was so imposing and so far-reaching in its effects as the disputation which took place at Tortosa in 1413-1414. It was a most remarkable disputation not only in that it lasted fully a year and nine months, but also in that it was presided over by a pope anxious for his own temporal advancement. The official participants consisted of a baptized Jew, Jeronimo de Santa Fé, who sought to prove his loyalty to the Church by persecuting his former co-religionists, and twenty-two representatives of the various Jewish communities of Aragon. Among these defenders of Judaism was Joseph Albo, the author of The Book of Principles. *This experience of being forced to defend his faith for a year and nine months in the presence of a most imposing assemblage of church officials and lay nobility undoubtedly convinced Albo of the necessity of writing a book dealing with the basic principles of Judaism. He felt it necessary not only to define Judaism but to defend it against its detractors, and to point out its superiority to Christianity. It is thus that Albo's work is the most apologetic of all important Jewish philosophical writings.*

Joseph Albo died in the year 1444, leaving to posterity no record of his life except The Book of Principles. *But this legacy made his life sufficiently significant to render its obscurity a matter of deep regret.*

Solomon Alkabiz, *author of the "Hymn of Welcome to the Sabbath" (p. 103), was a famous Kabbalist of the sixteenth century. His mystic bent induced him to leave his home in Salonica, Turkey, and to migrate to the city of Safed in upper Galilee, where a large number of Kabbalists had made their home and from where Kabbalistic teachings were disseminated to all parts of the world. He was greatly esteemed by his contemporaries and by posterity, as may be seen from the many legends which cluster about his personality. The most interesting of these relates that an Arab poet, envious of Solomon Alkabiz's superior knowledge and popularity, assassinated his Jewish rival and buried him under a fig tree. The tree miraculously began to blossom before its season and thus attracted attention which in turn led to an investigation and to the disclosure of the assassin. The latter confessed his guilt and was hanged on the same fig tree.*

Solomon Alkabiz's literary activity was limited to Kabbalistic commentaries on several Biblical books and to liturgic poems, the most famous of which is his "Hymn of Welcome to the Sabbath."

The exact dates of his birth and death are uncertain, but it is known that he lived to a ripe old age, fostering and disseminating the mystic teachings of the Kabbalah.

Amittai ben Shephatiah:—*Prior to the discovery of the famous* Chronicle of Ahimaaz (*See Chapter* VII), *the life of Amittai ben Shephatiah was shrouded in total obscurity. Although the Chronicle gives little information regarding Amittai's life, it furnishes us with his family history and thus renders him a real historical personality.*

From the Chronicle of Ahimaaz *we learn that Amitta lived in the late ninth and early tenth centuries and that he was a resident of Oria, Southern Italy. His family was famous for its scholars, poets, and statesmen, and Amittai, true to the family tradition, cultivated the art of versification. He must have been a prolific writer. Not only did he write numerous* piyutim, *many of which are still extant, but, according to the* Chronicle of Ahimaaz, *he also wrote many occasional poems for his family and for the community.*

The poem, "Lord, I remember" (p. 71), is a worthy specimen of Amittai ben Shephatiah's liturgic writings.

Bachya Ibn Pakuda *belongs to that large class of famous men of the Middle Ages whose lives are veiled in almost complete obscurity. The few known details concerning his life may be summed up in one sentence. He lived in Saragossa in the first half of the eleventh century and occupied the position of "Dayan" (Judge) in the Rabbinical Court of that city.*

To know more about the life of Bachya Ibn Pakuda, one must turn to his masterpiece, the Duties of the Heart, *and from its exalted teachings reconstruct the author's personality.*

Judging from this ethical treatise, we may conclude that Bachya was master of the Rabbinic learning as well as the philosophic literature of his day. This thorough knowledge of Jewish religious teachings and of secular systematic philosophy enabled him to produce in his Duties of the Heart *the first systematic work on Jewish ethics, a work distinguished for its logical exposition and deep piety.*

In addition to his scholarship Bachya Ibn Pakuda must have possessed a sensitive soul and a discriminating sense of moral values. He tells us that he was induced to write his ethical treatise because of the unethical conduct he observed about him, and because no one seemed to consider ethics a subject worthy of scholarly attention. There were some who devoted themselves to philosophy, there were many who devoted themselves to Rabbinic law, but hardly any one realized that noble living was above logical thinking and legal exactness. This realization caused Bachya Ibn Pakuda to write the Duties of the Heart, *a book which has proved to be one of the classics of Hebrew literature. If one is to reconstruct the character of Bachya Ibn Pakuda from his great work, one must surely conclude that he "was one of those natures whose energy of spirit and powerful moral force, if favored by the circumstances of the time, effect reformations."*

Benjamin of Tudela *was the most celebrated Jewish traveller of the Middle Ages. He journeyed from Spain in the year 1160 and visited France, Italy, Greece, the islands of the Levant, Syria, Palestine, and Mesopotamia. From the city of Baghdad he started his homeward journey and traversed the Indian Ocean, Yemen, Egypt, Sicily, and finally reached Castile in the year 1173. Throughout these years of travel Benjamin of Tudela noted his observations and* also collected information concerning places and events which he could not personally witness. His interests were wide in scope and the record he left covers the life not only of the Jewish communities he visited but of the non-Jewish as well. Invariably he showed a deep understanding of affairs and more than a superficial acquaintance with the history of the places which he described. In his accounts of the Jewish communities he records the size of the community, its leading scholars, the occupations of its residents, and the peculiar customs of the Jews. He gives similar accounts of the Samaritan and Karaite sects.

The itinerary was not written by Benjamin himself. Some unknown author compiled, condensed, and edited Benjamin's original notes and thus preserved in an easy, fluent Hebrew style the observations of the famous traveller.

Beyond his travels nothing is known of Benjamin of Tudela's life. Most probably there was nothing else in his life that was of any special significance. What has earned him the gratitude of modern historians is his great contribution to our knowledge of conditions in many communities in the twelfth century.

Obadiah Jaré da Bertinoro (died about 1500) is known to every Talmudic student as the author of the famous Mishnaic commentary which bears his name. His fame, however, rests on many other accomplishments of equal importance, particularly his reorganization and revitalization of the Jewish community in Jerusalem.

Obadiah left Italy in October, 1486, and arrived in Jerusalem in March, 1488. The Jewish community of Jerusalem was at that time depopulated, impoverished, and generally *demoralized mainly because of the heartless oppression by a few individuals. With Obadiah's arrival began a new era for those Jews. As rabbi he devoted himself primarily to the intensification of Jewish learning. He surrounded himself with a select group who devoted themselves to a thorough study of rabbinic literature, and he regularly delivered lectures for the edification of the masses. When, in 1492, the Jewish community of Jerusalem was greatly increased through the arrival of Jewish exiles from Spain, Obadiah thought the community large enough to become a center of learning. He thereupon founded an academy, which was supported through funds received from many Jewish communities willing to tax themselves because of their respect for the head of this new academy.*

Obadiah also exerted a wholesome influence on the political and social life of the community. He succeeded in freeing the people from their oppressive leaders and in establishing model philanthropic agencies for the relief of the poor and the sick. His court of justice became so popular that even Mohammedans often brought to him their judicial cases.

In addition to his famous commentary on the Mishnah and his splendid achievements in Jerusalm, Obadiah Jaré Da Bertinoro is known for his travel observations, which he recorded during his journey to Palestine. Unlike other itineraries, his information was transmitted in letters written during his travels. These letters are of great importance to modern historians because they are a source of unprejudiced information regarding the Jewish, Samaritan, and Karaite communities of Greece, Egypt, and Palestine.

Eldad the Danite: *In the ninth century the scattered Jewish communities were thrilled by the romantic tales of a traveller by the name of Eldad. He personally communicated his tale to the Jews of Babylonia, North Africa, and Spain, and ultimately it reached every important Jewish community.*

Eldad claimed to be a descendant of the tribe of Dan and asserted that his own tribe, along with the tribes of Asher, Gad, and Naphtali, lived an independent life somewhere in Eastern Africa. So skillfully and attractively did he describe the civil, religious, and military organization of his so-called native land that the Jews were filled with joy and hope, joy at the prosperity of their distant brothers and hope for their own ultimate redemption.

Eldad also described the life of the other so-called lost tribes of Israel. The tribe of Issachar, he said, lived a peaceful life in the mountains of Media and Persia. The tribes of Zebulun and Reuben lived in a province extending from Armenia to the Euphrates River. They were always allies in war and regularly divided their spoils. In the mountains of Southern Arabia dwelt the warlike tribes of Ephraim and half of Menasseh. The tribes of Simeon and the other half of Menasseh dwelt in the land of the Khazars, and they too were very warlike and exacted tribute from many nations. Finally, the sons of Moses lived in peace and prosperity "on the other side of the river Kush," protected by the miraculous river. Sambation, which encircled their land.

Eldad also asserted that the language of all these Israelites was Hebrew, and he supported his claim by pretending to know no other language than Hebrew. Eldad also described their religious laws, which he claimed were contained in a Talmud originally taught by Joshua, who received his instructions from Moses.

Eldad's story regarding his own life is limited to the fictitious account of his adventures, which began with his departure from his native land. Nothing else is known of the man. However, his obscurity is more than compensated for by the fame of his account. His contemporaries believed every detail of his story, and for more than a thousand years this fictitious account continued to be a source of renewed hope for the oppressed Jewish communities throughout the world.

Of the many disciples reared by Judah He-Hasid, Eleazar Ben Judah *of Worms undoubtedly attained the greatest fame. He was a descendant of a prominent family of scholars and poets, and he proved himself a credit even to his distinguished ancestor, Rashi.*

Eleazar ben Judah was born in Mayence in 1176, but his active life he spent in Worms. His wife was a pious and energetic woman who supported her family by conducting a business in parchment scrolls. She thus freed her scholarly husband from all economic worries and enabled him to devote himself exclusively to his studies. Eleazar of Worms was thus able to develop into a many-sided scholar and a prolific writer. He was a keen student of the Talmud and a commentator on it, a worthy composer of hymns and prayers, an author of many mystic (Kabbalistic) works, a scientist of note, and, above all, a writer of several ethical works, at least one of which has achieved fame.

His private life, however, was not a happy one. Eleazar ben Judah tells us of the following tragic experience. On the twenty-second of Kislev (December) 1196, while he was engaged in writing his commentary on Genesis, two Crusaders entered his house, cruelly maltreated and killed his wife, killed his two daughters and his only son. He alone escaped with his bare life. In the light of this tragic experience, it is all the more remarkable that Eleazar ben Judah should have written his

Rokeach, *which does not betray any bitterness or any vengefulness. On the contrary, it teaches cheerfulness, patience, and love of mankind. In his old age his sufferings began to show their effects. He became subject to many hallucinations and began to see angels and demons. When he died in 1238 he was mourned because of his great scholarship, his deep piety, and his boundless love of humanity.*

Eleazar of Mayence *died in the year 1357. His will is entitled by Israel Abrahams* The Ideals of an Average Jew *because he "was not a Rabbi, he is merely described with the conventional honorary title of* Haber." *His testament, representing the ideals of the average Jew, is one of the finest tributes to the ethical standards of mediaeval Jewry.*

Elijah De Veali *was rabbi in Alessandria, North Italy, from 1738 to 1792. He was known for his versatility, being not only a scholar of note but also a poet and Kabbalist. His will is long, elaborate, and most valuable as an ethical treatise.*

Ephraim of Bonn (*1133-1200*) *was peculiarly fit to write of the life and sufferings of the Mediaeval Jew, not merely because he was a contemporary but because he had the misfortune to live through one of the most tragic episodes in Jewish history. At thirteen Ephraim was an eyewitness of the inhuman massacres perpetrated by the Crusaders on the peaceful Jewish communities of the Rhine Country. His life was saved in the tower of Wolkenburg, which the Cardinal Bishop, Arnold of Cologne, had set aside as a refuge for the Jews of that district. The frightful terror which filled the hearts of the Jews within the castle of Wolkenburg and the unspeakable calamities which befell the Jews outside this retreat left their stamp on practically all the writings of Ephraim.*

In his chronicle Ephraim of Bonn gives a striking picture of the sufferings of the Jews during the Second Crusade. He also describes the many persecutions that followed this crusade, both in his own district and elsewhere. His accounts, though written with enthusiasm, are sufficiently accurate to be of historical value.

Ephraim of Bonn's other literary activities consist mainly of poetic writings of a liturgical character. His poems prove the author's extraordinary linguistic ability and betray his constant consciousness of the martyrdom of his people. He invariably reverts to the theme of this suffering, often devoting entire poems to lamenting the bitter fate of his co-religionists.

Although Ephraim of Bonn was not a rabbi, the Jews of the twelfth century recognized his scholarship and often referred to him complex Talmudic problems. Several of his answers to such questions are quoted in the various contemporary collections of responsa.

Joseph Ezobi *who lived in Perpignon, Provence, in the 13th century, was the author of several religious poems, the best known of which is the elegy on "The Ten Martyrs"* *(p. 78)**. He is also the author of a wedding song, "The Silver Dish," written on the occasion of his son's marriage. In this wedding song, Joseph Ezobi attempts to teach his son how to live ideally, and he urges him to devote himself exclusively to the study of the Talmud and to avoid all secular learning which only misleads a man. In spite of this narrow outlook the poem was considered important enough to merit translation into Latin by so great and broad-minded a scholar as Reuchlin.*

As a poet Joseph Ezobi does not rank high. His poetry lacks depth of feeling and beauty of expression.

Saadya Gaon (*892-942*) *performed a permanent service for Judaism by creating not only a philosophical but also a scientific foundation for the Talmudic idea of the Jewish religion. His greatest literary contribution,* The Book of Doctrines and Beliefs, *was the first organized presentation and philosophical basis of Judaism. Saadya Gaon's talents were not confined to literary accomplishments. In disputes with authorities of Palestine and Babylonia concerning the calendar, he showed that he had a vigorous mind, robust courage and a thorough education. Revealing the force of his energy, Saadya destroyed the dominating influence of the Karaites, fighting them with their own defense: reason. Before Saadya, the Academies had been satisfied with the exposition of the Talmud, ignoring the changing world. By harmonizing Jewish philosophy with trends of the Medieval Age, Saadya made Jewish dogmas applicable to contemporary life.*

Hasdai Ibn Shaprut (*c. 915-c. 970*) *is undoubtedly one of the most interesting characters in Jewish history. He was a prominent physician, a keen and successful diplomat, and a great patron of Jewish learning. In his youth he mastered Hebrew, Arabic, and Latin, all of which helped him in his future career. The opportunity for his advancement came to him through his profession. The enlightened Caliph, Abd al-Rahman, appointed Hasdai court physician and soon discovered in his Jewish medical adviser a useful diplomat. Before long Hasdai Ibn Shaprut became the unofficial secretary of state, minister of finance, and vizier of Arabic Spain. He controlled the customs and duties of the port of Cordova, received foreign ambassadors, formed alliances with foreign powers, and acted as confidential adviser in all important matters of state. It was in the course of his diplomatic duties that he learned the encouraging news concerning the existence of an inde-*

pendent Jewish state called the Land of the Khazars. In order to ascertain the truth of this rumor and to get accurate details concerning this Jewish state, Haṣdai wrote a letter to the King of the Khazars in which he described his own position and begged for information about the land, the people, the political and military organizations. etc.

Hasdai Ibn Shaprut is of even greater importance as a patron of Hebrew learning. When Moses ben Enoch was stranded in Cordova (see "The Four Captives," 239), *Hasdai helped him to establish his school, which in time made Spanish Jewry self-sufficient intellectually, and eventually made Spain the cultural center of world Jewry. Hasdai Ibn Shaprut, by surrounding himself with Hebrew poets and grammarians, caused Hebrew poetry and the scientific study of the Hebrew language to flourish not only in his day but for several centuries to come. It is thus that Hasdai was instrumental in initiating on the Spanish Peninsula what is commonly called the Golden Era of Jewish learning.*

Israel Abrahams tells us that Joel, Son of Abraham Shemariah, *who died in 1799, "wrote his will a quarter of a century before his death. He tells how on Iyar (May) 21 of the year 1773 he was seized with faintness in his bath. After his escape he felt it incumbent on him to set his house in order, lest he be taken unawares by death. The document was edited by his pupil, Avigdor ben Meir Ha-Cohen, who thus exhorts the public: 'My friends despise silver, despise gold, and buy this little book, small in quantity, great in quality.'"* (Hebrew Ethical Wills, *Vol.* II, *p. 343, The Jewish Publication Society of America, Philadelphia, 1926*).

Jose ben Jose, *author of the hymn, "Supplication" (p. 70), was one of the earliest Jewish religious poets of the Middle Ages. He probably lived in Palestine in the sixth century, and since his name is exactly like his father's, it has been inferred that he was an orphan from infancy. Except for a few of his religious poems which are still to be found in our High Holy Day prayer books and which bear witness to his poetic ability, we have practically no material that sheds light on his life.*

As a religious poet he is distinguished for his clarity of expression and his genuine tenderness. The few hymns that have been preserved reveal both simplicity of form and depth of thought. Except for the use of the acrostic (beginning the verses with consecutive letters of the alphabet) his poetry possesses none of the external characteristics of poetry. However, the absence of rhyme and rhythm is more than redeemed by the poet's fertile imagination.

His themes are all taken from the High Holy Day services. They deal with God's majesty, justice, and mercy; the insignificance of man; and Israel's glorious past and promised future. Particularly praiseworthy are his poetic descriptions of the Temple Service for the Day of Atonement. These are still recited in synagogues throughout the world.

Joseph Ha-Cohen's *(1496-1575) parents were among those unfortunate Jews who were forced to leave their native land, Spain, during the expulsion of 1492. Joseph was born at Avignon shortly after this tragic event and from his early childhood seems to have been destined for a life of wandering. When Joseph was five, his father migrated to Genoa, where the family lived for fifteen years. Driven from Genoa, Joseph Ha-Cohen settled at Navi, living there for about twenty-two years. Then he again returned to Genoa. There he practiced medicine for about twelve years, at the end of which time he was again forced to leave. This time the expulsion of the Jewish community was due to the unsuccessful rivalry of the non-Jewish physicians. Joseph Ha-Cohen settled in the small town of Voltaggio, to which he was welcomed because of his medical reputation. When the Jews were finally expelled from all the territories of Genoa, Joseph Ha-Cohen once more had to take up the wanderer's staff. He settled at Costeletto (Montferrat), where he dwelt until the Jews were re-admitted to Genoa. He returned in 1571, and died there in 1575.*

Despite his many wanderings and his wide medical practice, Joseph Ha-Cohen found time for literary activities. He was a prolific writer in many fields, but he excelled as a historian. His two most famous historical writings are the History of the Kings of France and Turkey *and the* Vale of Tears. *The former is a world history in the form of annals, dealing mainly with the constant struggles between Europe and Asia or between Christianity and Islam. Since France and Turkey represent the champions of the two contending historic forces, he devotes most of his annals to their wars. The history begins with the fall of Rome and ends with his own day.*

The Vale of Tears *is the story of the sorrows and sufferings of his own people. Persecutions, expulsions, and massacres constitute the main elements of this history. This martyrology is brought up to the last year of the author's life (1575).*

Joseph Ha-Cohen's importance as a historian is due to his method and style. He was both industrious and careful in the collection and the choice of his material. He gathered his information from all possible sources, corresponded with eye-witnesses, and carefully sifted his material. He wrote in a flowing Biblical narrative style which lends charm and interest even to the driest accounts of his annals.

Joseph Ibn Zabara (*born c. 1140*) *was one of those fortunate individuals who immortalize themselves through a single achievement. Were it not for his* Book of Delight, *posterity would have known the name of Joseph Ibn Zabara only because his teacher, Rabbi Joseph Kimhi, mentions it twice in his commentary on* Proverbs. *However, through the* Book of Delight, *which is ostensibly autobiographical, we learn that Joseph Ibn Zabara was a highly cultured person worthy of the intellectual traditions of Spanish Jewry. He seems to have mastered the knowledge of his day, particularly medicine, which appears to have furnished him with his profession. Judging from the numerous scientific discussions recorded in the* Book of Delight, *Joseph Ibn Zabara must also have been well versed in the other sciences of his day, such as physics and astronomy. Similarly, his frequent quotations from the Bible, Talmud, and Greek philosophers prove his acquaintance with religious and philosophical literature.*

Some scholars have claimed that even the "framework" of his book is biographical, and they have therefore deduced the fact that at one time Joseph Ibn Zabara must have been lured away from his birth-place, Barcelona, by one who subsequently proved to be both unfriendly and dangerous. Ibn Zabara, however, managed to free himself from the snare of his companion and returned to his family and friends, among whom he was proud to number the famous physician, Rabbi Sheshet Benveniste, to whom the Book of Delight *is dedicated.*

Joseph, King of the Khazars (*10th century*). *Life in the kingdom of the Khazars offered a most striking contrast to the darkness of the Middle Ages. At a time when Europe was sunk in gross ignorance, fanaticism, and barbarism, we find the Khazars boasting of their religious freedom, and of their sympathetic attitude toward all forms of life; at the very time when Western Europe used all possible means to degrade and torment the Jews, we find the Khazars adopting Judaism and becoming its zealous defenders. This kingdom, which was situated in what is now South Russia, was powerful and warlike, exacting tribute from the Russians and striking terror into the hearts of the Persians and the Byzantians. In the eighth century its ruling class and many of its other inhabitants were converted to Judaism, and the state continued to be Jewish until it was conquered by the Russians in the latter part of the tenth century.*

King Joseph, with whom Hasdai Ibn Shaprut corresponded, boasted of the peaceful state of his kingdom. Little did he expect that the end of Khazaria was at hand, for only a few years after he had answered Hasdai's letter, the Russians began their formidable attack which not only freed them from the degradation of a tributary state, but subdued their masters, the Khazars, and eventually wiped this kingdom from the face of the earth. King Joseph was the last important ruler of this mediaeval Jewish Kingdom and with him it practically ceased to exist.

In the year 1293 the famous Rabbi Meir of Rothenberg died in prison, where he was being held for ransom. The fate of this famous scholar served as a warning to all prominent Jews in Germany. We, therefore, hear of the great scholar, Rabbi Asher ben Yehiel, leaving Germany for Toledo, Spain, where he was immediately chosen rabbi of the community.

His son, Judah (Asheri), *the author of this will, was thirteen years of age at the time of the family's emigration (1305), and in 1328 succeeded his father as rabbi. He was beloved and greatly honored for his piety, to which the will bears adequate witness. He died in the year 1349.*

Judah Halevi, *the greatest of mediaeval Hebrew poets, was born in Toledo about 1085. He received his Jewish education in the school of the famous Talmudist, Isaac Alfasi. In addition he mastered Greek and Arabic philosophy as well as the medical science of his day. Like Ibn Gabirol, he achieved fame at an early age, as the prominent poet, Moses Ibn Ezra, testifies:*

"How can a boy so young in years
Bear such a weight of wisdom sage?"

It was during these early years that he wrote his many love poems, riddles, and epigrams. But unlike Ibn Gabirol, who was morose and vitriolic, Judah Halevi distinguished himself by his captivating charm and winning manner. His numerous wedding odes and songs of friendship bear witness to the host of friends he possessed and cherished.

As he grew older his writings became more serious. His people's suffering, particularly during the period of the Crusades, when entire Jewish communities were massacred, and the weakening of the Jewish faith among the more learned because of the influence of Greek philosophy caused him to devote all his talents to the service of his people. To check the encroachments of philosophy he wrote a philosophical defense of Judaism called The Cusari. *This work still occupies a prominent place among Jewish philosophical writings and stands out as the most characteristically Jewish contibution to this literature. Unlike Ibn Gabirol's* Fountain of Life, *which was studied for many centuries without any intimation of its Jewish origin,* The Cusari *can be singled out as a Jewish work by the mere reading of a single paragraph* [1]

His poetry too ceased to be light and personal. It was devoted almost exclusively to the exalted themes of God and Zion. In his religious poems he sings God's praises with love and unbounded zeal. In his national poems he sings of Israel's past glory, of its present degradation, and of its hopes of redemption. He sings of his great love of Zion and of his deep sorrow for Zion's desolation. So intimately did his poetry touch the heart of the Jew that to this day he has remained the greatest and most beloved religious and national poet of post-Biblical times.

But Judah Halevi was not content with merely singing about his love of Zion. He decided to leave his only daughter and his beloved grandchild, his host of friends, and all his worldly possessions in order to make a pilgrimage to the City he loved. When he was warned of the dangers of the pilgrimage, his characteristic reply was, "Shall a body of clay stop a soul urged on by eagle's wings?"

After a stormy passage he arrived at Alexandria, where the Jews received him with great honor. They tried to dissuade him from continuing his journey, but their pleas were of no avail. No argument and no inducement could alter his resolution to visit the Holy Land. He continued his journey toward his

[1] Several selections from *The Cusari* will be found in Chapter III.

beloved city, Jerusalem. Here history loses sight of the great poet. One legend claims that Judah Halevi succeeded in coming within sight of Jerusalem. He saw it in the distance and went toward it, singing his famous "Ode to Zion." But he never entered the City proper. An Arab, legend claims, pierced him with a lance just as he was about to enter the Holy City. Like Moses he saw Jerusalem from afar but was not privileged to enter it.

The life story of Judah He-Hasid *of Regensburg is largely a mixture of fact and fiction. Legend asserts that Judah was so ignorant at the age of eighteen that he was still unable to read his prayers. But, miraculously, enlightenment suddenly came to him and thenceforth he showed intellectual brilliance. Among the numerous other miraculous incidents which legend ascribes to the life of Judah the Saint is that on a Passover night the prophet Elijah actually appeared at his home and partook of his Seder meal. He was also reputed to have known the exact date when the Messiah would appear.*

Factually we know that Judah the Saint was a descendant of an old family of scholars and mystics who migrated from the East and settled in Germany. Judah was born in Speyer in the latter part of the twelfth century and received his early education from his father.[1] *About 1195, because of the intolerable persecutions in Speyer, Judah He-Hasid left the city and settled in Regensburg (Ratisbon). Here he opened a school where he taught many famous disciples who, throughout their lives, strove to emulate their teacher in scholarship and piety.*

When Judah the Saint died in 1217, he left to Jewry a

[1] See *Biographical Note* on Samuel ben Kalonymus.

threefold legacy. He introduced Jewish mysticism, known as the Kabbalah, to the Jews of Germany; he wrote many liturgical poems which have since been incorporated in the prayer books;[1] *and he wrote the famous* Book of the Pious, *a considerable part of which, as we now have it, consists of later additions by his many disciples. Like Resh-Lakish, the famous rabbi of the Talmud, who began his career as a gladiator and ended as a scholar and teacher, so, legend has it, did Judah He-Hasid begin his career as an excellent bowman and ended as an inspiring scholar, teacher, and saint.*

Judah Ibn Tibbon (*1120-1190*) *was born in Granada and migrated thence to Lunel, Southern France, in the year 1150. He and his son Samuel were physicians and prominent men of letters. It was Judah Ibn Tibbon and his son who translated into Hebrew several of the Jewish classics which in their original Arabic would have been lost. Among the most important translations by Judah Ibn Tibbon are* Duties of the Heart *by Bachya Ibn Pakuda, and* The Cusari *by Judah Halevi. The outstanding contribution of Samuel Ibn Tibbon is the translation into Hebrew of* The Guide for the Perplexed *by Maimonides.*

Eleazar Kalir *was a Palestinian of the seventh century. Tradition has woven many legends about his name, a fact which indicates the high esteem in which he was held by posterity. His very name has been explained in a most unusual manner. It is told that in his early childhood, when Eleazar was brought to Hebrew school for*

[1] See *The Hymn of Glory*,

the first time, he was given a little cake with some Biblical verses inscribed upon it. It is from this little cake that Eleazar is said to have derived his name "Kalir" which comes from a Greek word meaning "little cake," and it is to the magic power of the verses upon it that legend attributes his intellectual prominence. Legend also asserts that Kalir ascended to heaven and there received instruction in the art of versification.

Despite his popularity throughout the Middle Ages and the inclusion of more than two hundred of his poems in the various prayer books, Kalir's poetry is now generally being eliminated from the liturgy, for his poems are usually clumsy and lacking in poetic beauty. They are full of allusions to the Talmud and Midrash and are therefore obscure and meaningless to the average reader. However, he possessed unusual skill and was able to weave into his poetry acrostics of consecutive letters of the alphabet as well as of his own name. It was due to this skill that he eventually became a model for most Jewish mediaeval liturgic poets.

His death is shrouded in the same legendary obscurity as the rest of his life. It is maintained that his teacher, Jannai, became so jealous of his pupil's superiority that he placed a scorpion in Eleazar's shoe and thus caused his famous pupil's death.

Kalonymus ben Judah (*12th century*) *belonged to the famous Kalonymus family which for many generations furnished the German Jewish communities with prominent scholars, poets, and mystics. Of the many religious poems that Kalonymus ben Judah wrote, at least thirty have been preserved in the various prayer books. Many of these poems are devoted to a description of the inhuman massacres that the Crusaders perpetrated on the defenseless Jewish communities, and of the heroic sacrifices made by the thousands of Jewish martyrs who died "for the sanctification of God's name." "The First Crusade" (p.242) is characteristic of the many dirges written by Kalonymus ben Judah as well as by the other liturgic poets of the Crusading period.*

Joseph Karo *(1488-1575), author of the* Shulhan Aruch *(Prepared Table), was one of the most remarkable personalities of his day. At the age of four he was exiled from Spain during the great expulsion of 1492. After many wanderings his parents settled at Nicopolis, European Turkey. Young Joseph was taught by his learned father, and early in life began to attract attention because of his brilliance. Before long he was recognized, at least locally, as a thorough Talmudist. In 1522, Joseph Karo, then residing at Adrianople, began his gigantic literary masterpiece, known as the* Beth-Joseph *(House of Joseph), a commentary on Jacob Asheri's code.*[1] *Twenty years he labored on this monumental work, and then spent twelve additional years in revising it. This commentary definitely established the author's reputation as an international authority in the field of Jewish law, for he did not merely comment on the text of Jacob Asheri's code, but quoted all sources, both Talmudic and post-Talmudic, a task which required an exhaustive knowledge of this vast field of learning.*

While Joseph Karo was engaged in his painstaking task of writing the Beth Joseph, *he happened to meet that colorful, romantic and enthusiastic Kabbalist and Messianic pretender, Solomon Molko. The latter exerted a powerful influence over him, until, like Molko, he sincerely longed for a martyr's death in order to sanctify God's name. He was also convinced of the imminence of the Messianic era and of the important*

[1] Jacob Asheri was a famous codifier of the early fourteenth century. His code, *The Four Turim* (Rows), was the basis of all future codes, including Karo's *Shulhan Aruch.*

role which he was to play in it. Like Molko, he too became addicted to visions and strange dreams in which a heavenly mentor whispered to him revelations regarding the future and directed almost every phase of his life. His diary, in which he jotted down these conversations with his heavenly mentor, tells us how for almost half a century this mentor-power guided Karo's life, rebuking him for the neglect of the minutest religious duty and imposing on him strict ascetic rules such as abstinence from meat or sleep. These mystic inclinations finally led him to migrate to Palestine. He settled in the city of Safed, where he spent the rest of his life among many kindred spirits.

In his old age, Joseph Karo compiled what proved to be not only his masterpiece, but one of the epoch-making works of Rabbinic Judaism, the Shulhan Aruch. *This code, the last and most authoritative Rabbinic code, was published for the first time in 1567 and within a short time found its way to almost every Jewish community and became the accepted guide for the mass of Jewry in all religious matters. Despite many contemptuous criticisms of contemporary scholars and despite the author's assertion that his code was meant "for young students" who could not study his* Beth Joseph, *it later became the unquestioned authority in the regulation of Jewish life. With Rabbi Moses Isserles' supplementary notes, which added the religious customs of the German and Polish Jews, this code has served the Jews everywhere to our own day as the final authority in problems of Jewish law.*

Joseph Karo died at the ripe old age of eighty-eight, revered by Jews everywhere for his scholarship and for his classic code which "blends the multitudinous fragments of Jewish conduct into a harmonious unit of devotion to God's revealed will and to the hallowed traditions of a long past."[1]

[1] Margolis, M. and Marx, Alexander, *History of the Jewish People*, p. 521, Jewish Publication Society of America, Philadelphia, 1929.

Shabbatai Kohen (1621–1662) was one of the survivors of the devastating massacres of 1648–49 when the Cossacks, under their cunning leader Chmielnitzki, rebelled against the Poles and vented their bitterness and savagery against the peaceful Jewish population. Many Jewish communities were laid waste; hundreds of thousands of Jews were slaughtered; and the remnants ran for safety, only to find the anguish of homelessness and poverty. In 1649 Rabbi Shabbatai Kohen proclaimed a fast day, to be observed annually on the anniversary of the first of the Cossack massacres, which took place in the city of Nemirov on the 20th day of Sivan. Rabbi Shabbatai Kohen, who was then only 28 years of age, was already firmly established as a leading Talmudic scholar. The fast day which he proclaimed was therefore widely accepted and annually observed for many years.

To this day Rabbi Shabbatai Kohen, known by the initials of his name as the SHaKH, is recognized as one of the keenest Talmudic scholars of all time. He published his great legal work, Siftey Kohen, *a commentary on one of the books of the* Shulhan Arukh, *when he was only 26 years of age. He was thereafter recognized, even by many of his contemporaries, as the outstanding legal authority of his generation.*

The destruction of the Jewish communities of Poland, the martyred death of over a quarter of a million Jews, and the spiritual glory achieved by whole communities who chose death to apostasy, touched the young scholarly rabbi. In his Epistle to the Jewish communities, he describes the heroic struggles against the Cossack hordes, the agonizing death of whole communities, and the sanctification of God's Name by thousands of men, women and children who were given a choice of apostasy or death. The young rabbi not only called for the observance of the annual fast, but he also composed a number of penitential prayers to be recited on that day. The excerpt from his Epistle included in this anthology reflects depth of feeling and scholarly restraint in relating the tragic facts of the catastrophe.

Moses Maimonides'[1] *greatness is summed up in the traditional phrase, "from Moses (the Lawgiver) till Moses (Maimonides) there was none like Moses (Maimonides)." That he deserved this distinction has seldom been challenged, for he was the greatest genius of mediaeval Jewry. He has been characterized as the greatest Jewish thinker and scholar of all time, and to this day is admired by all who are acquainted with his intellectual achievements.*

Moses Maimonides was born in Cordova on the eve of Passover (March 30), 1135. His father was a prominent scholar who traced his ancestry to the House of David. Little did Moses' father suspect in the year 1135 that his fame was to rest on his progeny rather than his ancestry. He introduced his brilliant son, Moses, to both Jewish and secular learning and thus prepared him for his future scholarly tasks.

At the age of thirteen, Moses Maimonides tasted the bitterness of persecution and exile. The fanatical Mohammedan sect known as Almohades (Unitarians) overran Cordova and offered unbelievers the choice of Islam or exile. Maimonides' family chose the latter and wandered about for more than a decade. It was in the midst of these wanderings, to use Maimonides' own words, "working aboard ship or sojourning at an inn," that he composed his first great work, the commentary on the Mishnah. In it he revealed his unprecedented ability to systematize, elucidate, and simplify all knowledge, for this commentary not only clarified the meaning of the text but gave a clear exposition of religious practice, religious beliefs, and secular learning. It was in this, his first great work, completed at the age of thirty-three, that he developed his famous thirteen articles of faith which have since been incorporated in the Orthodox prayer books.

[1] Maimonides is also known by the name of RaMBaM—Rabbi Moses Ben Maimon.

After wandering for more than a decade, he settled near Cairo, where he began to devote himself to medicine. He achieved great fame as a physician, and in a short time became the court physician to Saladin. His indefatigable industry becomes even more evident at this period of his life. It is most remarkable that he was able to discharge his duties as court physician and to minister to the countless patients who sought his aid, and at the same time to be the rabbi of the Jewish community and to answer the continuous stream of questions that poured in from Jewish communities and from Jewish scholars the world over. At the same time he succeeded in writing his two monumental works, his gigantic Rabbinic code, known as the Mishneh Torah (*Repetition of the Law*), *and his rationalistic philosophic treatise,* The Guide for the Perplexed, *two achievements which prove him to have been a great genius in assimilating and systematizing all the knowledge of his day. In the Rabbinic code, Maimonides sifted and logically arranged that mass of Rabbinic learning which had accumulated in the preceding thousand years. This Rabbinic learning was almost limitless in extent and hopeless in its confusion. Maimonides not only mastered the Talmud, but in his code he succeeded in organizing all this material into one coherent system, thus making it accessible to the average student.*

In his Guide for the Perplexed *Maimonides attempted to reconcile Judaism with philosophy, the Bible with Aristotle, faith with reason. The book, written in the form of letters to one of his disciples, clearly stated that his aim was to help those who could not harmonize the convictions of the mind with the dictates of religion. In this treatise he produced the greatest philosophic exposition of Judaism. It is even now a stimulating work and will continue to be admired as one of the greatest Jewish classics of the Middle Ages.*

Moses Maimonides died in the year 1204, mourned by Jews and Mohammedans. In Jerusalem a general fast was observed, and his death was likened to the departure of the Torah from Israel. He was buried in Tiberias, and to this day his grave attracts numerous pilgrims who come from all parts of the world to pay homage to the great mediaeval Jewish sage.

Meir of Rothenberg (*1215-1293*) *was considered in his day the greatest Talmudic scholar, and so highly esteemed was he that he was crowned with the distinguished title,* Me'or Ha-Golah, *the "Light of the Exile."*

His scholarship and personality were in truth a source of enlightenment to the Jewish people throughout the world. His instruction was sought by numerous disciples who flocked to him from everywhere, and his religious guidance was sought by the Jewish communities both far and near. Weary of the numerous persecutions, Rabbi Meir decided to migrate to the Holy Land in the hope of finding peace and rest. But before he could leave Germany, it was his misfortune to be imprisoned for the crime of being a distinguished Jew. Emperor Rudolph hoped to secure a large ransom from the Jewish communities, who idolized their famous Rabbi. And the emperor was not mistaken, for no ransom would have been too large for Rabbi Meir. But the great scholar, realizing that his costly release would serve as a precedent for similar outrageous demands, refused to be ransomed. For seven years Meir of Rothenberg remained in prison, teaching his disciples and guiding Jewish life in the various communities through correspondence. When he died the authorities continued to hold his body for ransom, and tradition has it that he received no burial for fourteen years.

Rabbi Meir of Rothenberg was not only a Talmudic scholar of note and a prolific writer of Rabbinic commentaries, codes, and responsa, but also a poet of distinction. The excerpt from his poem, "The Burning of the Law" *(p. 76)**, reveals depth of feeling and a fine command of the Hebrew language, characteristics common to all his poetry. It is not surprising, therefore, to find his religious poems even in so important a ritual as that of the Day of Atonement.*

Meshullam Ben Menahem of Volterra *was one of the most successful merchants of the 15th century. His expert knowledge of jewelry and precious stones not only brought him great profits but also enabled him to write a book on these subjects.*

In the year 1481 Meshullam started out on a journey which he ably described in his itinerary. He passed through Rhodes, Alexandria, Cairo, and finally reached the city of Jerusalem. After recuperating from a serious illness, he continued his journey, visiting Jaffa, Damascus, and Crete. Before he had reached Italy, however, it was his misfortune to be shipwrecked. All the precious stones which he had purchased in the course of his travels were thus lost. He also contracted a most dangerous sickness, and it was only through the devoted care of a Jewish physician who happened to be on board ship that he was saved. He reached Venice in October of that year and from there journeyed to his home in Florence.

Although in his own day Meshullam was famous for his great wealth, posterity gratefully remembers him for his accurate and dependable account of the life of many 15th century Jewish communities.

Moses de Leon *was born at Leon about 1250 and, true to the Spanish tradition, mastered not only the Bible, the Talmud, and other Rabbinic works, but also the philosophy of Solomon Ibn Gabirol, Judah Halevi, and Moses Maimonides. But he became especially adept in the Jewish mystic literature of his day and eventually became a prolific author of mystic works, none of which brought him either fame or royalties. Toward the end of his life, however, he published a work which was destined to immortalize him and to influence Jewish life and history. As has already been mentioned, this work, commonly known as* The Zohar, *was attributed by Moses de Leon to the famous Rabbi Simeon ben Yohai of the second century. Scholars, however, have conclusively disproved this claim and have definitely established that Moses de Leon's relationship to this work was more than that of a mere publisher. C. D. Ginsburg in his book,* The Kabbalah *(London 1865), claims that Moses de Leon was the real author of* The Zohar, *and among other proofs he gives the following abridged paraphrase of a significant excerpt from the* Sefer Ha-Yuhasin:[1] "*When Isaac of Akko, who escaped the massacre after the capture of this city (1291), came to Spain and there saw* The Zohar, *he was anxious to ascertain whether it was genuine, since it pretended to be a Palestine production, and he, though born and brought up in the Holy Land, in constant intercourse with the disciples of the celebrated Kabbalist,*

[1] *Sefer Ha-Yuhasin* by Abraham Zacuto is a chronological history of the Jews from creation to the year 1500.

Nachmanides, had never heard a syllable about this marvelous work. Now, Moses de Leon, whom he met in Valladolid, declared to him on a most solemn oath that he had at Avila an ancient exemplar, which was the very autograph of Rabbi Simeon ben Yohai, and offered to submit it to him to be tested. In the meantime, however, Moses de Leon was taken ill on his journey home, and died at Arevelo, in 1305. But two distinguished men of Avila, David Rafen and Joseph de Avila, who were determined to sift the matter, ascertained the falsehood of this story from the widow and daughter of Moses de Leon. Being a rich man and knowing that Moses de Leon left his family without means, Joseph de Avila promised that if she would give him the original manuscript of The Zohar *from which her husband made the copies, his son should marry her daughter, and that he would give them a handsome dowry. Whereupon the widow and daughter declared that they did not possess any such manuscript, that Moses de Leon never had it, but that he composed* The Zohar *from his own head, and wrote it with his own hand. Moreover, the widow candidly confessed that she had frequently asked her husband why he published the production of his own intellect under another man's name, and that he told her that if he were to publish it under his own name nobody would buy it, whereas under the name of Rabbi Simeon ben Yohai it yielded him a large revenue."* [1]

Whether Moses de Leon was the mere publisher of an old manuscript, or the redactor of a great mystic work, or the actual author of The Zohar, *posterity remembers him as the person who brought into being what later became the "bible of Jewish mysticism."*

[1] Ginsburg, C. D., *The Kabbalah*, pp. 90-91, London, 1865.

Moses Ibn Ezra (*c. 1070-1139*) *was the most talented of four distinguished brothers, all of whom were worthy members of a cultured, aristocratic, and wealthy family. His early training was both thorough and many-sided, befitting the noble traditions of the distinguished Ibn Ezra family. He mastered the Bible, the Talmud, and Rabbinic learning as well as the Hebrew and Arabic languages. In addition, he possessed a thorough knowledge of the Greek and Arabic philosophies of his day.*

But despite his ideal education and despite the wealth, luxury, and prestige into which he was born, he was not destined to be a happy man. His life and writings were deeply influenced by an unfortunate love affair. In his early years he fell in love with his niece, who, though she loved him, could not get her father's consent to the marriage. Broken-hearted, Moses Ibn Ezra left Granada and wandered about for several years till he learned of the tragic death of his beloved. Deeply affected by her premature and sudden death, he wrote a touching elegy to her memory and sent it to her father. This elegy, in addition to easing his emotions, helped to reconcile him to the family. He thereupon returned to his native city of Granada, where he spent the rest of his life. The general effect of this unfortunate love affair was to lend a melancholy tone to all his poems. Even in his songs of wine and joy one detects a note of sadness and resignation.

Moses Ibn Ezra was a prolific writer. More than five hundred of his poems are extant. Of these about two hundred are penitential and other religious hymns, many of which have found their way into the liturgy of the New Year and the Day of Atonement.

He was greatly esteemed for his mastery of the Hebrew language and for his poetic skill, which he retained till his old age. When he died, about 1139, he was mourned by his many admirers, among them Judah Halevi, who referred to him as

"The fount of wisdom, in whose mouth I find
The place of gold, the mine of purest ore."

Nathan Ha-Babli's *life is veiled in almost complete obscurity. The one thing we definitely know is that he was a Babylonian and a contemporary of the famous Saadiah Gaon (10th century). We also gather from a few stray remarks in his* Order of the Academies *that he was, at least for a while, a resident of Kairawan, where he wrote his account to satisfy the curiosity of the North African Jews concerning the intellectual and social life of the Babylonian Jews. It is also evident that he was a keen observer of the life about him, a fact which has rendered his book a most illuminating source of knowledge concerning Jewish life in Babylonia in the tenth century.*

Petachiah of Ratisbon (*12th century) was a member of a famous family of Talmudic scholars. His own fame, however, rests upon his celebrated travels. He journeyed through Poland, South Russia, Armenia, Persia, Babylonia, and Palestine. Throughout these travels Petachiah kept a detailed itinerary wherein he recorded such facts as he thought would be of interest to a 12th century Jew. He noted the political and economic status of each Jewish community, its customs, its population, and even its climatic and geographical peculiarities.*

Historians who have studied Petachiah's reports have invariably found him a keen observer and an accurate transmitter of his observations. These traits are particularly noteworthy when we realize that he is not the author of his itinerary, for his notes were compiled and edited by the great scholar and

saint, Judah He-Hasid of Ratisbon. It is this faithfulness of observation and report that makes Petachiah's itinerary a thing of interest and value to historian and reader of today.
Samuel ben Kalonymus (*12th century*), *author of the poem, "Hymn of Unity for the Seven Days of the Week"* (*p. 58*), *was a descendant of one of the most celebrated Jewish families in Germany. Samuel was true to the tradition of the famous Kalonymus family and devoted himself to the acquisition of knowledge and the cultivation of piety. That he succeeded in the field of scholarship is evident from his commentary on the Talmudic treatise* Tamid. *His poem, "The Hymn of Unity for the Seven Days of the Week," bears witness to his command of the Hebrew language and his philosophical acumen. That he succeeded in the cultivation of piety is evident from the titles given him by posterity, such as "the saint," "the holy," and "the prophet."*

Samuel ben Kalonymus did not belong to that class of scholarly and saintly men who lead the life of a recluse. He participated in the life of the community by being president of a Beth Ha-Midrash (*house of study*), *and, in accordance with the Biblical commandment, "thou shalt teach them diligently to thy children," he personally taught his children the precepts of Judaism. Unfortunately, he did not live long enough to complete their education. When Samuel ben Kalonymus died, his children were still young, but his labor was not in vain, for they, too, particularly Judah* (*He-Hasid*), *became famous for their scholarship and piety.*

Simeon ben Isaac ben Abun *of Mayence (10th and 11th centuries) whose hymn, "Belovéd, Hasten to Thy Hallowed Dwelling," is included in this chapter (p. 64) was one of the most prominent liturgical poets of his day. Later generations usually refer to him as Rabbi Simeon the Great, and often speak of his powers as a miracle-worker. Three mirrors, we are told, used to hang in Rabbi Simeon's home, and in these mirrors he could see everything that had happened in the past and everything that was to happen in the future. It is also related that after Rabbi Simeon died a spring of pure water appeared at the head of his grave, a symbol that his influence for good endured even after his death. An even more interesting legend states that Rabbi Simeon had a son, Alhanan, who was in his infancy taken away from his parents and brought up as a Christian. This child inherited some of his father's brilliance and rose to the highest position in Christendom, the papacy.*[1]

In addition to his scholarly and literary activities, Rabbi Simeon ben Issac ben Abun devoted himself to the safeguarding of his co-religionists against the unfavorable legislation of the government and the malicious attacks of the mob. He was a man of influence and power and he spared no effort, even to the point of self-sacrifice, in behalf of his people. He gave them both his genius as a religious poet and his power as a man of influence. His people, in return, gratefully remembered him and crowned him with the distinguished title, "Rabbi Simeon the Great."

Solomon Ibn Adret *(1235-1310), commonly known as the* Rashba,[2] *was the foremost Rabbinic authority of his day. He was a man of remarkable erudition,*

[1] See *A Jewish Pope*, Chapter IX.

[2] *RaShBA* is an abbreviation of the name *R*abbi *S*olomon *B*en *A*dret.

a master of the Talmud, and a devoted follower of its teachings. His unwavering attachment to Judaism and his ever-ready, earnest, and energetic labors in its behalf made his authority paramount everywhere. Officially he was the Rabbi of the Jewish community of Barcelona, but his influence extended far beyond the Iberian Peninsula. His opinions were sought after by Jewish communities throughout the world. Congregations in Spain, Portugal, France, Italy, Germany, North Africa, and even Asia Minor sent their questions to the famous Rabbi of Barcelona, and his Responsa, seven volumes of which are extant, became authoritative religious guides not only in his own day but for many generations after him. These responsa show Solomon Ibn Adret to have possessed a keen, intelligent, and systematic mind. What they are especially valued for today is the accuracy with which they mirror the life of the Jewish communities of the thirteenth century.

In addition to his Responsa Solomon Ibn Adret was the author of many scholarly works, the most important being a code entitled The Law of the House. *This code was lengthy and argumentative, yet its popularity was sufficiently great to be re-issued in an abridged form.*

His influence upon his own generation was also exerted through the personal contacts of teacher and pupils. His academy attracted students from distant places and his lectures were at all times attended by a throng of disciples. Among them were some who came even from Germany, where the Rabbis and academies boasted of their superiority and seldom recognized the possible equality of academies elsewhere.

As a leader of Jewry we find Solomon Ibn Adret continually called upon for assistance and guidance. When the famous Rabbi Asher Ben Yehiel came to Spain as an exile from Germany, it was the Rashba *who induced the community of Toledo to accept him as their rabbi. When Maimonides' grandson, David, was in serious difficulties and needed financial assistance, he turned to the* Rashba *and the latter secured the necessary funds. When the Jews of Rome wanted a complete copy of Maimonides' famous commentary on the Mishnah, they likewise turned to the* Rashba, *who arranged for the completion of the partially translated commentary and thus not only satisfied the request of the Jewish community of Rome but also saved this classic from oblivion. When Judaism was attacked by Christians and Mohammedans, particularly by the Dominican monk, Raymond Martini, the* Rashba *wrote polemical works to repel these attacks and to defend Judaism against its detractors. When the Jews of Sicily were perplexed by claims of Messianic pretenders, such as Abraham Abulafia and his successors, they too turned to the Rabbi of Barcelona for guidance and, in spite of his leanings toward mysticism, the* Rashba *was able to see clearly the dangers of Messianic movements and to unmask properly the Messianic pretenders.*

The last few years of Solomon Ibn Adret's life were embittered by a serious controversy into which he was drawn against his will and in which he became the central figure. A certain Jew, Abba Mari, a pious and energetic fanatic of Lunel, France, discovered that the French Jewish liberals were taking many liberties with the Bible, and that in their desire to effect a conciliation between philosophy and religion, they were interpreting the Bible and the Talmud in quite unorthodox ways. He was shocked at their laxity and felt that Judaism was in danger of being displaced by science and philosophy. In order to scotch this new monster of liberalism, he set out to gain the support of the foremost scholar and leader of the time, Solomon Ibn Adret. The extravagance of these French liberals, exaggerated by Abba Mari, also shocked the Rashba. *Heir to the liberal traditions of Spanish Jewry and yet a loyal follower of the strict orthodox teachings of the German school, Solomon Ibn Adret attempted to steer a middle course. He was averse to proscribing scientific studies, yet he desired to assure the supremacy of the Talmud. On the Sabbath before the Fast of Ab (July 31), 1305, a ban of excommunication was issued in the city of Barcelona, proscribing the study of all science and philosophy except medicine on the part of anyone who had not reached the mature age of thirty. This ban was issued in the name of Solomon Ibn Adret and thirty other scholars of the City. The liberals answered with counter-excommunications and the Jewish communities were threatened with a serious rift. The crushing tragedy of the expulsion from France in the year 1306 sobered the minds of all who were bent on widening and perpetuating the schism. Nevertheless, the* Rashba's *last years were embittered by his half-hearted leadership of the anti-liberal forces.*

Solomon Ibn Adret died at the age of seventy-five, but his leadership did not pass with his death. His influence over his numerous disciples, and his opinions recorded largely in his many responsa continued to guide Jewry for many centuries after his death. Even today the name Rashba *evokes feelings of deep reverence in the hearts of all learned Jews.*

Solomon Ibn Gabirol *was born in Malaga about 1021. His childhood was a most unhappy one in that he was orphaned and poverty-stricken early in life. He speaks of himself as a child "grieved, without mother or father, inexperienced, lonely and poor, . . . alone without a brother and without friends, save my own thoughts."*[1] *These early experiences were probably the seeds out of which grew the poet's somber, melancholy, and often bitter feelings which later found expression in his poems.*

[1]Davidson, Israel, *Selected Religious Poems of Solomon Ibn Gabirol*, p. XVIII, Jewish Publication Society of America, Philadelphia, 1923.

In his early adolescence he already showed a natural aptitude for poetry. Some of his poems written at the age of sixteen are the work of an accomplished poet. These early poems show a remarkable command of the Hebrew language, an extraordinary maturity of thought, and a profound depth of feeling.

In his loneliness and poverty he wandered about till he found, in the city of Saragossa, a generous patron in the person of Yekutiel Ibn Hassan, who befriended him and relieved him of all want. But before he could achieve peace of mind, his patron died, and, at the age of seventeen, he was again forced to become a wanderer. Once more he fell prey to a deep melancholy which is reflected in the poetry written at that time.[1] *Fortunately he found in Granada a new Maecenas in the person of the famous Rabbi and Vizier, Samuel Ibn Nagdela. It was during the few peaceful years that followed that he wrote some of his best poems as well as his famous philosophical work, the* Fountain of Life. *When his patron died, Ibn Gabirol once more became despondent. He left the city and spent the rest of his life as a wanderer. He died prematurely in the year 1069 at the age of forty-eight.*[2]

Though Gabirol the poet has been known and honored, Gabirol the philosopher was rediscovered only in recent times. Throughout the Middle Ages and in the centuries that followed, Christian philosophers and theologians studied a philosophical work known as Fons Vitae, *by a certain Avicebron, or Avencebrol. The author of this work was believed to have been one of the Christian scholastic philosophers. No one questioned the Non-Jewish authorship of the* Fons Vitae *because it in no way betrays its Jewish origin. It was not until the middle of the last century that Solomon Munk, examining the Hebrew*

[1] See *A Song of Redemption*,

[2] Some scholars claim that Solomon Ibn Gabirol died in the year 1058, that is, before he reached his thirtieth birthday.

manuscripts of the Bibliothèque Nationale in Paris, discovered a Hebrew Manuscript by Shem-Tob Palquera entitled Likkutim min Sefer Mekor Hayyim (*Excerpts from the Book Fountain of Life*). *A careful study of these excerpts established that they were identical with the corresponding sections of the* Fons Vitae, *that both the Hebrew manuscript and the* Fons Vitae *were translations from a common Arabic original, and that Avicebron or Avencebrol was a corruption of Ibn Gabirol.*

Any account of Ibn Gabirol's life is incomplete without the well-known legend which ascribes his death to the envy of a contemporary Moslem poet. The latter is said to have murdered Ibn Gabirol and buried him under a fig tree. The tree immediately began to blossom and to yield the most luscious fruit. This extraordinary phenomenon led to an investigation which resulted in the discovery of the crime and the punishment of the criminal. This legend is significant because it reflects the popular estimate of Ibn Gabirol's poetic gifts, an evaluation which coincides with that of all students and scholars who regard Ibn Gabirol's poetry and philosophy with deepest admiration.

Solomon Ibn Verga's *life is so typical of his generation that the few biographical details which we possess enable us to reconstruct it with reasonable accuracy. He was born in Spain in the second half of the fifteenth century and was a physician by profession. In 1492, when the Jews were expelled from Spain, he left for Portugal, which was the nearest place of security. But this haven of refuge proved but a trap, and Solomon Ibn Verga, along with thousands of his unfortunate co-religionists, was forced outwardly to accept Christianity. At the first opportunity, however, he escaped from his spiritual prison and made his way to Turkey, where he joyously returned to Judaism.*

In this new land of peace and security, Solomon Ibn Verga began to record the martyrdom of his people, a martyrdom which he knew so well from personal experience. His historical work, The Scourge of Judah, *was begun as a supplement to Judah Ibn Verga's account of certain persecutions, and was finally completed by his son Joseph. This martyrology is therefore an eclectic work without order, lacking even chronological sequence. The book, as we have it now, contains an account of sixty-four persecutions; full, though not always accurate, accounts of religious disputations; and also an account of Jewish customs in different parts of the world. The style of* The Scourge of Judah *is clear and graceful, though not Biblical. Modern historians value the book particularly for its folk-lore, and for its record of Jewish customs.*

Alexander Suesskind *died in Grodno in 1794. He was blessed with both learning and piety and was anxious to instil the love of God into his fellow-men. His will was not written for his immediate family; it was meant to be an inspirational introduction to the prayer book. But his wish was never fulfilled because of the testament's excessive length. However, the fact that it was printed independently several times testifies to its popularity.*

Süsskind Von Trimberg's *poem, "Why Should I Wander Sadly"* *(p. 84)**, does not logically belong in this anthology. The author was not a Hebrew poet, but a German Jewish "minnesinger" of the thirteenth century. By profession Süsskind Von Trimberg was probably a physician, but his poetry must have been a greater source of income than his medicine. Lute in hand, he used to appear before the lords and ladies of his day and sing his verses. Six of his* *poems have come down to us and they evince profound emotion and noble thought. He sings of ideal womanhood, of true nobility, of freedom of thought, and of similar edifying themes. The poet's Jewish origin, however, was the cause of discrimination against himself and his poetry. This eventually led him to abandon the "minstrels' choir and roam a Jew again."*

The authors of Josippon *and* The Book of Jashar *intentionally concealed their identity and ascribed their books to ancient authorities. This practice of falsely ascribing one's work to famous men of old is neither exceptional nor accidental. We find many of our Biblical as well as mediaeval books falsely ascribed to prominent personalities. The books of* Proverbs, Song of Songs, *and* Ecclesiastes *were assigned to King Solomon, and the Kabbalistic* Book of Creation *and* The Zohar *were ascribed to the patriarch Abraham and to Simeon ben Yohai respectively. This practice of ancient and mediaeval writers has often been falsely interpreted as deception and plagiarism. Actually, the reverse is true. The ancients sought no glory for themselves but aimed primarily at popularizing their ideas and convictions. Since one could not, under ordinary circumstances, get a fair hearing, and since our modern attitude toward plagiarism was unknown, many of the ancient and mediaeval authors resorted to the practice of ascribing their work to ancient men of fame. The spirit of this practice is well conveyed by Judah He-Hasid, when he exhorts his contemporaries to emulate these unknown authors. "The ancients of our nation," says Judah He-Hasid, "composed works and sent them forth without their names; they disclaimed to seek recompensing delight for their labor in this lower earthly life. And if there be anyone who of pure vanity is minded to perpetuate the memory of himself in some work, very surely he will miss his aim."*

INDEX OF TITLES

INDEX OF AUTHORS

INDEX OF TRANSLATORS

ACKNOWLEDGMENTS

The editor and publishers herewith render thanks to the following publishers and individulas for permission to reprint from their publications:

To the American Jewish Publication Society (New York) for the excerpts from *Book of the Pious* and *Rokeach* from "Extracts from Jewish Moralists" in *Hebrew Characteristics* by L. Zunz.

To Behrman's Jewish Book House (New York) for Maurice Samuel's translation of Fleg's *The Jewish Anthology* from which five excerpts are herein reprinted.

To Benjamin Harz (Berlin) for "Old Jerusalem, the Focal Point of Mediaeval Jewish Travellers" from *The Holy Land* by E. M. Lilien.

To Bloch Publishing Company (New York) for J. H. Hertz's translation of "The Second Crusade," for E. H. Plumptre's translation of "The First Crusade," for D. N. Carvalho's translation of "Adon Olam," and for G. Gottheil's translation of "Adir Hu" from *A Book of Jewish Thoughts;* for Meyer Waxman's translations of "When I Hunger to Praise Thee," "I Come in the Morn," and "To Whom Shall I Cry in My Anguish," from *A History of Jewish Literature*, Vol. I; and for Hartwig Hirschfield's translation of Judah Halevi's *Kitab Al Khazari* from which six excerpts are herein reprinted.

To Columbia University Press (New York) for Moses Hadas's translation of Zabara's *The Book of Delight* from which three lengthy excerpts are reprinted; and for Marcus Salzman's translation of *The Chronicle of Ahimaaz* from which two excerpts are herein reprinted.

To Deutscher Verlag (Berlin) for "A Jewish Delegation Greeting the Pope During the Council of Constance" from *Geschichte der deutschen Juden* by Adolph Kohut.

To Dodd, Mead and Company (New York) for Israel Abrahams' translation of Ibn Gabirol's "Water Song," for Israel Cohen's translation of Judah Halevi's "The Pride of the Jew," for D. E. de L's translation of Abraham Ibn Ezra's "God Everywhere," and for the translation of Jose ben Jose's "Supplication" from Joseph Friedlander's *The Standard Book of Jewish Verse.*

To E. P. Dutton and Company (New York) for M. Friedlander's translation of Maimonides' *The Guide for the Perplexed* from which ten excerpts are reprinted, and for Edwin Collins' translations from Bachya Ibn Pakuda's *The Duties of the Heart* from which five excerpts are herein reprinted.

To Eugen Diederichs (Leipzig) for "Rellgious Disputation Between Jews and Christians" and "Torturing Jews on the Rack Because of a Ritual Murder Accusation" from *Das Judentun in der deutschen Vergangenheit* by Georg Liebe.

To East and West Library (London) for Alexander Altman's translation *The Book of Doctrines and Beliefs*, from which three excerpts are herein reprinted; and for *A Treasury of Jewish Letters* by Franz Kobler, from which three excerpts are herein reprinted.

To Eyre and Spottiswoode (London) for Israel Abrahams' translation of "Loved of My Soul" from *A Companion to the Authorized Daily Prayer Book.*

To George Routledge and Sons (London) for Alice Lucas' translations of Abraham Ibn Ezra's "Resignation" and "Prayer for Help," of Moses Ibn Ezra's "Dawn" and "Penitential Prayer," of Judah Halevi's "The Ways of God," "Servant of God," "Ode to Zion," and "The Sun and Moon Forever Shine," of Samuel Bar Kalonymus' "Hymn of Unity for the Seven Days of the Week," of Kalir's "Palms and Myrtles," of Solomon Ibn Abun's "Even as the Daily Offering" and of "Praise Ye the Almighty" from *The Jewish Year;* of I. Zangwill's translations of "The Hymn of Glory," "The Lord Is King, the Lord Was King, the Lord Shall Be King for Ever and Ever," and "All the World Shall Come to Serve Thee" from *Service of the Synagogue* (New Year); of Elsie Davis' translation of "Lo! As the Potter" from *Service of the Synagogue* (Day of Atonement); of I. Zangwill's translation of "Belovèd, Hasten to Thy Hallowed Dwelling" from *Service of the Synagogue* (Passover); and of I. Zangwill's translation of "The Angels Came A-mustering," and H. M. Adler's translation of "O Lord, Save We Beseech Thee" from *Service of the Synagogue* (Tabernacles).

ACKNOWLEDGMENTS

To Houghton, Mifflin and Company, (New York) for Emma Lazarus' translations of Ibn Gabirol's "A Degenerate Age" and of Judah Halevi's "Separation" from *The Poems of Emma Lazarus*, Vol. II.

To Isaac Meyer for the six quotations from his book *The Qabbalah*.

To Dr. I. Sossnitz for his translation of Franck's *The Kabbalah* from which five selections are herein reprinted.

To the Jewish Publication Society of America (Philadelphia) for Israel Zangwill's translations of "At the Dawn," "My Refuge," "I Have Sought Thee Daily," "Six Years Were Decreed," "God and Israel," and "Established Peace" from *Selected Religious Poems of Solomon Ibn Gabirol;* and for Nina Salaman's translations of "My Heart Is in the East," "Beautiful of Elevation," "To Mount Abarim," "On the Sea," "Vision of God," "Before Thee Is My Whole Desire," "Wonderful Is Thy Love," "The Physician's Prayer," "Unto the Stars to Reach Thee," "Dove Beside the Water Brooks," "To the Bridegroom," and "Amid the Myrtles" from *Selected Poems of Jehudah Halevi*; and for Solomon Solis-Cohen's translations of "O Thou that Graciously Attendest," "To Dwell with All-Soul Doth My Soul Desire," "The Book of Tarshish" (Stanzas 6-12; 25), "How Long at Fate's Behest," and "The Garden Dons a Coat of Many Hues" from *Selected Poems of Moses Ibn Ezra;* and for Nina Davis' translations of "The Prophet Jeremiah by the Cave of Machpelah," "A Song of Love," "The Burning of the Law," "The Lord Is My Portion," "Song of Redemption," and "Hymn of Weeping," from *Songs of Exile;* and for Gustav Karpeles' translations of "Why Should I Wander Sadly," and "With Hopeless Love My Heart Is Sick," from *Jewish Literature and Other Essays;* and for B. Halper's translations of "Pious Reflections and Admonitions to the Soul," "Mattathias Charges His Sons Before His Death," "The Installation of an Exilarch," and "Description of Jerusalem and Its Surroundings," from *Post-Biblical Hebrew Literature;* and for Israel Abrahams' translation of the *Hebrew Ethical Wills* from which seven lengthy excerpts are reprinted in this Anthology; and for Isaac Husik's translation of Joseph Albo's *The Book of Principles* from which seven excerpts are herein reprinted.

To the Jewish Theological Seminary of America (New York) for "Autograph of Moses Maimonides with His Signature" from a manuscript in the Museum of the Seminary.

To Julius H. Greenstone (Philadelphia) for Israel Abrahams' translation of Ibn Gabirol's "From Thee to Thee" from *Festival Studies*.

To the Libraries of the Jewish Theological Seminary of America (New York) and of the Dropsie College (Philadelphia) and to their librarians and staffs for the numerous books which they graciously placed at the editor's disposal.

To Liveright Publishing Corporation (New York) for "At Prayer" from *Orpheus* by Solomon Reinach, 1930.

To Luzac and Company (London) for Gollancz's translation of "The Ten Martyrs" from *Translations from Hebrew and Aramaic*.

To the Macmillan Company (New York) for Joseph Jacobs' translations of Judah Halevi's "The Storm" and "The Rogue" from *Jewish Ideals and Other Essays*.

To the New York School of Social Work for Louis Feinberg's translation of *Section on Charity from the Shulhan Arukh* from which several excerpts are reprinted.

To N. Trübner and Company (London) for M. Adolf Neubaur's translation of "Specimen of the Book Cusari" and for A. I. K. D.'s translation of "The Reply of King Joseph to Hasdai Ibn Shaprut" from *Miscellany of Hebrew Literature*, Vol. I.

To Dr. Solomon Solis-Cohen for his translations of "Sabbath, My Love," "Wake My Darling from Thy Slumbers," "The First White Hair," "God that Doest Wondrously," "Out of Luck," "The Lord Is King (*Adonai Melek*)," and "Hymn of Welcome to the Sabbath," from *When Love Passed By and Other Verses* (The Rosenbach Company, Philadelphia).

To Soncino Press (London) for the excellent translation by Harry Sperling and Maurice Simon of *The Zohar* from which most of the excerpts of the fifth chapter are reprinted.

To the United States Publishing Company (New York) for Edward B. M. Browne's translation of *The Book of Jashar* from which the selection "Jacob and His Sons Wage War with the Amorites and Conquer the City Gaash" is reprinted.